Disasters and Development

Disasters and Development

FREDERICK C. CUNY

Sponsored by Oxfam America
Edited by Susan Abrams for Oxfam America

New York   Oxford
OXFORD UNIVERSITY PRESS
1983

Library of Congress Cataloging in Publication Data
Cuny, Frederick C.
Disasters and development.
Bibliography: p.   Includes index.
    1. Disaster relief—Case studies.
I. Abrams, Susan.   II. Oxfam America.   III. Title.
[DNLM: 1. Disasters. HV 553 C973d]
HV553.C86   1983   363.3'48   83-8319
ISBN 0-19-503292-6   ISBN 0-19-503293-4 (pbk.)

Printing (last digit) 9 8 7 6 5 4 3 2

Printed in the United States of America

To my son, Craig

Foreword

For Oxfam America and all the individuals concerned with publishing this book, a steady impetus has been to disseminate the knowledge that should, but too often does not, accompany efforts to provide development and disaster assistance.

This book is encyclopedic in its ideas, recommendations, and questions yet to be answered. It should humble every voluntary and government agency that presumes to give effective disaster assistance, because it indicates the degree of expertise, organizational ingenuity, and above all, sensitivity to Third-World needs and cultures that is essential for truly constructive disaster assistance.

Throughout its thirteen-year history, Oxfam America has been attempting to understand how an agency like ours, primarily dedicated to aiding self-reliant development, should and can respond effectively to the all-too-frequent disasters in areas where we work.

Disaster *mitigation* and *preparedness* should be the main objectives, obviously, and Fred Cuny makes clear that disasters are largely preventable, even when natural catastrophes are beyond human control or even prediction. Beyond this, a major contribution of the book is to significantly advance understanding of the interactions between disasters and poverty; between disaster recovery needs and ongoing development needs; and between the relief and development assistance strategies and programs of aid organizations.

Poor people are the most frequent victims of disasters. Cuny shows why the poor are especially vulnerable to natural and political catastrophes. Similarly, disasters may further entrench or exacerbate poverty; or, seen from another perspective, interrupt or reverse the progress of poor people in achieving self-reliant development.

On the other hand, a disaster may open a society to development possibilities. Some have contended that the Managua earthquake disaster (1972) contributed to the downfall of the Nicaraguan dictator Somoza. Cuny explores several notions of how a disaster, for all its destructiveness, presages possibilities for development.

Aid agencies should read this book closely for its implications for relief and development assistance strategies and programs. One striking theme is that disaster relief ought not to be seen as an isolated intervention, unrelated to the affected society's prospects for long-term recovery and development. This implies at least two questions. Are specialized aid organizations, which provide relief exclusively, inherently unaware of or indifferent to the development processes at work in the disaster-affected community? It is well documented that food relief organizations inundated Guatemala with unneeded food aid after the earthquake in 1976. Development-minded agencies, on the other hand, heard the Guatemalan villagers say that their priorities were: shovels to recover food from collapsed household granaries; funds to build larger granaries for the oncoming harvest; and protection of local grain markets against a glut of imported food relief.

The parallel question is whether or not development agencies will have the expertise and outlook that will permit them to respond effectively to development processes that may be interrupted, temporarily blocked, or even shattered by disaster. Development agencies, in their understandable concern that relief may breed or perpetuate dependencies, can easily move to the opposite extreme of ignoring disaster situations that require relief. Worse, they may close their minds to understanding the interactions between disaster recovery and development processes.

Encouraging local self-help works at the relief stage at the same time that it is a bridge to the rehabilitation and development stages for a completely shattered society. Both relief and development assistance should be predicated upon respect for the recuperative and self-help inclinations of people affected by a disaster.

Oxfam America welcomes this book's elaboration of the reasons why respect for local cultures and realities, and for the potential of working partnerships with local people, is not only desirable but necessary for effective disaster assistance. It elucidates the forces within disaster situations and organizational dynamics that repeatedly drive aid organizations into costly errors of omission and commission. Aid organizations persistently yield to the pressures of crisis, time constraints, funding sources, and management imperatives in providing the wrong kind of assistance, in the wrong way at the wrong time. After the last Guatemalan earthquake, one respected international aid organization, by its own admission, launched an inappropriate housebuilding program for the homeless. The houses were culturally incompatible with local preferences, very susceptible to environmental ravages, and too expensive to be maintained by poor *campesinos*. Incredibly, many houses went unoccupied. Other organizations, working with *campesinos* and their organizations, developed more appropriate house repair and replacement options, featuring adaptations of traditional houses, locally affordable and available materials, and training programs for area builders. Even this advanced approach produced mixed results from which we should learn.

Yet Cuny never goes off on flights of fancy. His book moves much beyond the platitudes about the blunders or heroics of aid organizations to clarify first principles for action and to prompt us as designers and administrators of disaster assistance to be more reflective and critical of what we are doing. Indeed, one major finding is that aid organizations tend not to learn from their experience because of the lack of a reflective attitude, memory loss due to staff turnover, and a general absence of training programs to encourage learning within and between aid organizations.

Working together in the housing construction education project of Programa Kuchuba'l, a disaster response to the Guatemalan earthquake, Oxfam America and Intertect decided the experience was full of possibilities for learning by local and international aid agencies. What began as a casestudy of Programa Kuchuba'l (Chapter 10) evolved into this more ambitious and eclectic book.

Oxfam America learned much from the collaboration in Programa Kuchuba'l with Guatemala community leaders, World Neighbors and the British Oxfam, and Intertect, the Dallas consulting firm that Fred Cuny heads. We sustained and appreciated continual dialogue with Fred over several years, in which he was diverted from this publication project by consulting or operational roles in yet new disasters, as in the Caribbean, India, and Kampuchea. We thank especially the Wolohan Family and the Tinker Foundation who, seeing the promise of this book, underwrote the early stages of the project and waited so patiently for the results.

JOSEPH SHORT
Executive Director
Oxfam America

Acknowledgments

This book was made possible by a grant from the Tinker Foundation, administered by Oxfam America. The author wishes to thank both institutions for their support throughout the project.

An early advocate for the book was Nathan Gray, formerly of Oxfam America. Nathan spearheaded the effort to obtain funding and helped to develop the concept for the book.

Larry Simon served as coordinator for Oxfam America and liaison to the Tinker Foundation. Throughout the long time it took to write the book, he remained a constant supporter.

The author would like to acknowledge the many people who contributed to shaping the text. Frederick Krimgold provided not only encouragement and advice, but was always available as a sounding board for ideas. He helped enormously by suggesting technical references and other materials for the book. Large portions of chapter 12 are based on his work in pre-disaster planning.

Wolf Bulle reviewed the first draft and provided many useful comments that helped to shape the final draft.

Ian Davis read early drafts and provided many suggestions on style and content.

Paul Thompson and Charlotte Thompson critiqued many of the chapters and provided many helpful suggestions, especially in the "how to do it" sections. Parts of chapters 12 and 13 are based on unpublished materials written jointly by Paul and myself during our long association.

The artwork in the book was prepared by Juliana Marek and Jim Viets. They put in many long nights to do these and bore up well under my constant revisions.

The actual production of the various drafts was supervised by Jinx Parker. She helped out in all phases, transcribing, typing, selecting photos, and doing her best to correct my atrocious spelling.

The typing was handled by several people. Jodi Hendon did the lion(ess)'s share and Karen Tuel did the Borracho Hurricane and other sections.

When it came time to prepare the final draft, Donna Sanders listened while I read it through completely and made many helpful suggestions on what to cut and how to reorganize. She also helped on many of the final inserts.

Oxfam America selected Susan Abrams to help me edit the book. Her advice on style, sentence structure, and organization was helpful, but most important, her rewriting of many of my paragraphs to bring out what I really meant to say have enhanced the book throughout.

The work of any person is shaped by the people with whom he works and comes into contact. It has been my honor to be associated with many fine individuals who have dedicated a large part of their lives to development and disaster concerns. These people receive little recognition for their work (and usually inadequate compensation), yet year after year they continue to try to change the system. In a way each of the following made a contribution to the ideas expressed in this book and for their comradeship I would like to express my thanks.

Nick Carter	Franklyn McDonald
William Castillo	Sue Peel
Ian Davis	E. L. Quarantelli
Marc de Bruycker	Everett M. Ressler
Claude de Ville de Goyet	John Seaman
Frances D'Souza	Haresh Shah
Russell R. Dynes	Alan J. Taylor
Robert Gersony	Paul Thompson
Julius Holt	Stephen R. Tripp
Frederick Krimgold	Julio Vargas Neumann
Michel Lechat	Kenneth W. Westgate
James Lewis	Giles M. Whitcomb
Tim Lusty	Gilbert White

Many people and organizations graciously allowed me to use their materials in the book. They are too numerous to list, but three should be mentioned here. Oxfam U.K. and World Neighbors permitted me to use many materials from Progama Kuchuba'l in Guatemala, and Karl Western allowed me to use many of the charts and tables from his doctoral dissertation. To the many other authors, organizations, and publishers who allowed us to quote from their works, to use their photos, or otherwise to employ their materials—a grateful thanks.

F.C.C.
Dallas
June 1983

Contents

Disasters and Development

Introduction

Disasters hurt people. They injure and kill. They cause emotional stress and trauma. They destroy homes and businesses, cause economic hardships, and spell financial ruin for many. And the people hit worst are the poor. A natural disaster can happen anywhere, but for a combination of reasons—political as well as geographic—most large-scale disasters occur in the region between the Tropic of Cancer and the Tropic of Capricorn. This region encompasses most of the poorer developing nations, which we call the Third World.

For the survivors of a natural disaster, a second disaster may also be looming, for the very aid that is intended to help them recover may be provided in such a way that it actually impedes recovery, causes further economic hardship, and renders the society less able to cope with the next disaster.

This book is about disaster response and the way in which relief agencies and other organizations provide aid and assistance in the developing countries. The book focuses on international disaster assistance, the aid provided by the industrialized nations through myriad international organizations, both governmental and private, which the public calls the international relief system.

International aid is highly visible, yet it represents only a small part of the total recovery picture, both in terms of resources and the actions taking place within the affected society. The reader should remember that even in the most intensive international response, outside aid will probably not amount to more than 30–40 percent of the total expenditures for disaster recovery.

The international response has added importance, however, for it sets the tone and often defines the scope and methods used by the affected countries themselves in dealing with the disaster. Unfortunately, many of the techniques developed by the industrialized nations for dealing with disasters in their own societies are inappropriate for use in the Third World. Many of the fundamental assumptions are wrong, and many of the actions are counterproductive and actually delay recovery.

For years, disasters have been treated as separate events, and relief has tended to ignore the implications of disasters for the social and economic development of a society. The most basic issues in disasters are their impact on the poor and the links between poverty and vulnerability to a disaster. (Ironically, high vulnerability is often a direct result of people's desire for modernity. Those most capable of coping with disaster are those who live in the least sophisticated but most self-reliant societies, while those who have begun to seek a change in their social and economic status are least equipped to deal with calamity.)

Nevertheless, the fundamental themes of this book are that it is the poor who suffer most in disasters, that they are vulnerable in a more complete sense because they are poor, and that we must address the question of how to reduce poverty and place disaster response in the context of development if we hope to reduce suffering and to make a true contribution to recovery.

The international agencies have an opportunity to do this, for they have the interest, the technology, and valuable resources to contribute. For this reason, the developing countries look to the more developed nations for leadership. To be effective, however, we must re-examine our underlying assumptions about disasters and how people react, about aid and the role it plays in disaster recovery (and, by implication, development itself), and about the nature of the organizations that have been established to respond.

The book is divided into three parts. The first is an examination of natural disasters and what happens in a society affected by such an event. The second focuses on disaster response, especially by international agencies. The impact of response on the affected society is explored, as well as the structure and workings of the system that has evolved to respond, and the actual manner in which assistance is delivered. The final part of the book answers in practical terms the issues raised in the previous parts. It explores ways in which response can be improved through proper planning both before and after disasters.

The primary focus is on two types of events: earthquakes and hurricanes. This is because they are the most traumatic. Annually they kill the most people, thus they draw the most attention from the agencies that respond to disasters. They also provide a good platform for exploring disasters because they affect more sectors of a society and an economy than any other types of disaster.

To a lesser extent, droughts and famines are discussed. These are of rising concern, not only because of their contribution to world hunger, but also because both the scope and severity of droughts can be expected to increase, and the effects of a large-scale famine can have a major impact on food supplies and economic systems far beyond the actual borders of the shortage. The study of drought and famine has not received the same level of interest and research as the more dramatic disasters, and the focus of this book regrettably reflects this. But while the effects of drought, the needs of the victims, and the response patterns are different, it is important to remember that concerns about the vulnerability of the poor, the long-term impact of the response, and the necessity of approaching disasters from a development context remain the same.

Throughout the book, four disasters are mentioned frequently: the Managua, Nicaragua, earthquake of 1972; the Andhra Pradesh, India, cyclone of 1977; the Guatemalan earthquake of 1976; and the drought and famine of the Sahel region of Africa in the early 1970s. The Managuan earthquake demonstrates the impact of a disaster on a large capital city, and Andhra Pradesh cyclone that on a rural agricultural region. The Guatemalan earthquake shows the impact on virtually an entire country, and the Sahel drought and famine illustrate what can happen to an entire region. It should be evident after reading the book that while the areas affected are different, the lessons are the same.

In our examination of disaster response, we will explore in detail the nature of disaster assistance and consider several important questions. Is the emphasis on rapid response desirable? Is response focusing on the most important needs? Do the relief approaches used and the goods commonly supplied meet the needs of the victims or those of the donors? Are we concentrating our response during the most appropriate phase of the disaster?

Our review of the relief agencies should also stimulate some questions. Are these organizations the most appropriate vehicles for disaster assistance? If disasters are such an important part of the development equation, why does the system rely so heavily on untrained staff and volunteers? Why is it so difficult to improve the performance of the relief agencies? And, most important, what are appropriate roles for relief and for development groups?

The most common approach to providing disaster assistance is through formal programs. A program is the focal point where all the ideas, ideals, and resources are translated into action. Yet programs, the process by which they are formulated, and the techniques by which they are managed are little understood. Agencies give little training to their staff on project planning or management, and few programs are thoroughly evaluated. This book explores the usual process of program planning and some reasons why programs often fall short of their goals.

To provide the reader with a working example of how a program is developed and executed, some of the problems typically encountered, and a look at the consequences and long-term impact, we will examine Programa Kuchuba'l, conducted by OXFAM U.K., OXFAM America, and World Neighbors. Programa Kuchuba'l was established in the Guatemalan highlands following the earthquake in 1976. It was primarily a housing reconstruction program, although several other post-disaster projects and activities were conducted by the program staff. This particular program was chosen for several reasons. It was one of the largest and longest programs conducted in Guatemala. It trained people to build earthquake-resistant housing using local materials and technology, rather than providing housing outright, a unique approach at that time. The program was rather sophisticated, using ideas, training materials, and approaches that were not common at that time. Many of these were copied by other organizations in Guatemala, and many of the ideas and materials are finding their way into reconstruction programs in other parts of the world. Finally, I was consultant to the project and am familiar with most of the details in its planning and operation, as well as many of the shortcomings that developed.

Only a few of the approaches used by Programa Kuchuba'l were, in fact, new. The material subsidy schemes, for example, have been used many times in the past. But the way in which elements of the program were combined showed a good deal of sophistication. Although many of the ideas and approaches once considered unique have found expression elsewhere and have been improved upon, Programa Kuchuba'l is still by most standards a good program. For this reason, it provides a positive example for examining operational programs and illustrates how, with a little forethought, concern for the long-term impact, and the use of an essentially developmental approach, disaster response can have a substantial impact on a society.

Throughout this book, housing programs are emphasized. The damage to and destruction of housing in cataclysmic disasters are the single highest cause of death and injury and result in the greatest economic loss to the poor in terms of property. Housing also illustrates how many of the related development issues come into focus when a disaster strikes. For example, land tenure, urbanization, and job skills are all related to housing and must be taken into account in both disaster response and development. And the housing sector is complex, providing a good viewpoint from which to examine agency response to various needs.

To a large extent, this book explores disaster response without considering the political context. In reality, just as disasters and development cannot be separated, neither can disaster response be divorced from politics. Unfortunately, few governments in the Third World are democratic and many regimes perpetuate underdevelopment because it supports the needs of an oligarchy or other privileged class. Thus many of the ideas presented here are anathema to these groups. For them, control of disaster relief is another way of maintaining the status quo, and a paternalistic dole of relief goods from foreigners is the preferred method of aid, for it is in keeping with the dictatorial system.

Some disaster specialists argue that any examination of disasters in the context of development automatically becomes political, that reducing the vulnerability of the poor is a development question, and that such questions must be answered politically. I agree. But this should not deter us from examining disasters individually. For a society to develop, many obstacles must be overcome, and it is important that each be examined thoroughly in its own right. In this way, basic problems can be identified and alternatives reviewed. This is important in the field of disasters, for even if all players have the best of intentions, current practice complicates—not complements—development.

A word should be said about two terms used in this book: *victims* and *intervention*. The term victims has many negative connotations. It provokes images of helplessness, of people who must be taken care of. For this reason, many agencies have used substitutes such as beneficiaries or recipients. These do not adequately describe all the people affected, however, and may not accurately depict the actions taking place (as we shall see, not all people benefit). The term *survivors* could be used, but technically it applies only to those who have escaped a life-threatening situation. Thus, rather than create a new buzzword, the author has chosen to go with *victims*. Victims, however, are not helpless. They are capable of making intelligent choices and when special allowances are made so that victims can cope with personal losses, they can participate effectively in all post-disaster activities. It is hoped that the reader will come to understand that in disaster response, the term *victim* should be coterminous with *participant*.

Intervention is the most important term used in this book. It is used in the medical sense of acting in order to bring about a change in the course of events. The purpose of intervention is to improve the circumstances of the disaster victim. Any disaster response initiated from outside the affected community is a form of intervention, and the failure to treat it as such is one of the underlying causes of many of the problems relief agencies encounter.

As in medicine, intervention here too can have positive results, and it is our intention to show that successful intervention can play an important part in the development process.

(The term "OXFAM" as used in this book denotes both OXFAM U.K. and OXFAM America.)

I
Disasters and Their Impact

1
Disasters and Development

Until recently the connection between disasters and development was not recognized. Disasters were not seen as providing an opportunity to aid development, and development organizations often tried to avoid becoming involved. But some unsettling facts began to emerge. Countries on the road to development, experiencing a disaster, suddenly lost momentum. Resources became scarce, and development programs had to compete with reconstruction plans for available funds.

At first it was assumed that the answer was more relief aid from the industrialized countries, and annually the appropriations grew. Yet material losses and numbers of people affected continued to increase. Perhaps the answer was to speed the response, to devote more resources, or to expand the international delivery system. But these measures and others were applied, few with meaningful results. Why?

The basic problem was the conceptual failure by aid organizations to link disasters to development. The concept of a disaster as a separate event requiring a rapid response of medical and material aid was not entirely accurate and led to efforts that were not only very ineffective, but in many cases counterproductive. The relief agencies tended to view disasters solely as emergencies. This meant that the best way to respond was by providing emergency medical assistance, basic goods (especially personal articles such as clothes and blankets), and temporary emergency shelter, usually tents. Emergency aid, collectively called "relief," was distributed free, as a form of charity. Even if this were totally effective in meeting emergency needs, and could be provided at an appropriate time, such aid would still not address the roots of the problem: poverty and underdevelopment.

More than any other human event, a disaster traumatically brings into focus all the basic problems in a society. It reduces all issues to their most fundamental level and strips away all the ancillary issues that obscure or confuse the fundamental questions that must be faced. Critical decisions, previously unaddressed, can no longer be ignored, and choices must be made.

Disasters highlight the inherent weaknesses in a society and often force a reappraisal of goals. When it became evident in Guatemala that the earthquake had affected the poorer sectors (especially the Indian communities) to a far greater extent than the middle- and upper-class families, everyone recognized the portent this held for the future of the country. For the first time, people who had been unconcerned about poverty or even unaware of the extent of poverty in Guatemala were brought face-to-face with the reality. Many of the middle-class youth and students who volunteered to help in rural communities were appalled by what they saw, and new organizations sprang up to work not only in reconstruction, but also toward more fundamental changes in the society. Existing organizations also received a boost from this new awareness and many were able to expand the scope and range of their programs to serve more people directly as a result of the earthquake. There can be no doubt that the increased awareness of poverty and greater level of participation led many Guatemalans to become politically active. It is clear that the old order will be forced to change as a result.

Disaster-induced changes occur because disasters create a climate wherein changes in society are more acceptable. While not all people, least of all the governments, experience a desire for change, pressures from victims often evolve into demands for fundamental changes—demands that may cover not only changes in the society, but also changes in the form of the environment, including land and housing.

Governments usually expand their role and range of services following disasters. Once a government has entered areas, it is unlikely that it will withdraw. Once established there, it must continue to provide a high level of services or face criticism from the community.

The changes that can occur are many and varied. Researchers have noted that changes in building styles, methods, and materials can often be traced to a disaster event such as an earthquake or hurricane. Shifts or migrations of people from one area to another can result in changes in urbanization or rural living trends. Land invasions following earthquakes have affected the makeup of peripheral settlements around large cities and have, in many cases, affected the pattern of land ownership and tenure, not only in the immediate area of the invasion but also in surrounding communities. In wars or droughts, when large numbers of people are forced to migrate, the place at which they stop in order to receive relief supplies often becomes a new settlement.

The loss of economic opportunity or the need to find alternate sources of income have often caused small-scale migrations of skilled workers from rural areas into the cities. Following the Guatemalan earthquake, large numbers of skilled masons and carpenters left the rural areas to go to Guatemala City to find work in order to obtain the capital needed to repair or rebuild their homes. Once they became established in the city, however, few returned (Bates 1980).

The very face of the land may be altered by a disaster. Droughts have led to famines, famines to migrations; and when the people ceased to farm the areas they left behind, creeping deserts swallowed the arable land and made it untenable. But positive changes have also been recorded. Better cropping patterns have often followed droughts. Reforestation efforts and better use of contours for hillside agriculture have often followed rain-induced landslides. Where contour planting has been introduced, economic benefits have often followed.

For the society, disasters often bring changes in the structure of community leadership. New organizations may be born out of necessity to deal with the disaster and remain to continue the work of bringing economic change to the community. New leaders often emerge, sometimes to replace leaders felled by the disaster, but more often to replace those who have proved ineffective or unable to cope with the aftermath of a disaster.

We have the technology to prevent much of the destruction that now follows most natural hazards. But to do this requires development: stronger housing, better agriculture, a more diversified economy, and more responsive governments. To see this, one need only compare disaster response in an industrialized country with response in a developing country. An industrialized country is better able to absorb a disaster. In contrast to many developing countries, where the economy revolves around one or two major enterprises, the economies of the industrialized countries are more diversified, thus spreading any losses that occur.

THE SCOPE OF THE PROBLEM

In order to comprehend the magnitude of the potential for disaster, particularly as it relates to the Third World, it is first necessary to understand the nature of a disaster and to place it in a geographic context.

To restate a central point, a disaster should be defined on the basis of its human consequences, not on the phenomenon that caused it. An earthquake, for example, is simply an event in nature, and even a very strong one is not a disaster unless it causes injury or destroys property. Thus an earthquake occurring in an uninhabited area (as do scores of tremors each month) is only of scientific interest and is not considered a disaster. While natural phenomena such as earthquakes, hurricanes, and excessive rains can occur worldwide, their potential for widespread disaster is more a function of the ability of communities to cope with these events—in terms of their social and economic systems as well as their physical structures—than of the phenomena themselves.

When a natural event does affect a human settlement, the result may still not be a major disaster. Consider the earthquake that struck San Fernando, California, in 1971. The quake registered 6.4 on the Richter Scale. Yet San Fernando, with a population of over seven million, suffered only minor damage and fifty-eight deaths (Denevi 1977). Two years later, an earthquake of a magnitude of 6.2 struck Managua, Nicaragua, and reduced the center of the city to rubble, killing an estimated six thousand people. What was the difference between the two locations that caused such a disparity and made one an "earthquake," while the other was a "disaster"? To oversimplify, the answer is the different level of development in the two cities.

Are disasters in the Third World on the increase? The answer is both yes and no. The average number of natural events occurring each year has not changed; there are no more hurricanes and earthquakes today than there were in past years. What has changed is the magnitude (deaths, damage, costs) of each disaster and the increased attention given to developing countries.

The increase in disaster potential is one result of the cycle of poverty common to developing countries. The roots of poverty, which are also the predominant roots of vulnerability, are the increased marginalization of the population caused by the high birthrate and the lack of resources (or the failure of governments to allocate resources) to meet the basic human needs of an expanding population. At the center of the resource issue are the parallel problems of land and economic opportunity. As the population increases, land in both rural and urban areas becomes more scarce and those seeking new land for farming or housing are forced to accept marginal lands. These offer less productivity and a smaller measure of physical or economic safety. Such trends result in both rapid and unchecked urbanization and massive deforestation of mountainous and jungle regions that occurs as small farmers push into less tenable areas for farming. In addition to the political failure of governments to develop new economic systems and to reallocate resources (especially land) to benefit the nation as a whole, there is a inappropriate attempt to use high technology to instantly "modernize" the society. This has two contradictory results: higher unemployment and rising expectations.

To understand how these tendencies affect vulnerability, let us examine the case of rapid urbanization. As the cities and towns expand, the land that is serviced by utilities and that is safe for development is in high demand for both housing and industry; thus the price rises. Low-income families in search of land for housing must settle in areas of low value. These lands may be the slopes of steep hillsides or ravines, or may lie along the banks of flood-prone rivers. Worldwide, millions of families live in squalid shanty towns constantly under the threat of landslides or flooding. Nor are the houses safe. In part, this is due to the fact that the housing styles with which they are familiar are often inappropriate because of the change in soils, unavailability of materials, or the demands of an urban environment.

Consider the case of Peru. Many of the squatter settlements in the rapidly expanding coastal cities have been built by families moving down from the mountainous regions where adobe houses are popular. Adobe housing in Peru is not particularly safe in any case. Along the coast, where soils are much sandier, the adobes are much weaker. This, added to the loose, uncompacted ground the houses are built on, almost guarantees that they will fail during a strong tremor. In some instances, people attempt to build with materials such as brick or concrete block, but without adequate engineering input, these houses are not safe either.

Recognizing poverty as the primary root of vulnerability and disaster in the Third World is the first step toward developing an understanding of the need for change in current disaster response practices. *For if the magnitude of disasters is an outgrowth of underdevelopment and poverty, how can we expect to reduce the impact with food, blankets, and tents, the traditional forms of assistance?*

THE INTERNATIONAL POLITICAL CONTEXT

While actual vulnerability is on the increase, so too is Western awareness of the Third World and its problems. For the industrialized nations, Latin America, Africa, and Asia simply were not a part of geopolitical conscious-ness prior to the 1960s when the colonial period (and, in the case of Latin America, the neocolonial period) began to draw to a close. Scores of new nations joined the United Nations and received media coverage. Former colonies suddenly became both potential markets and suppliers and (from the "big powers'" point of view) potential allies or enemies in the international competition for influence. This competition took many forms, most notably in aid to help the countries "develop" into societies like those that provided the aid. A whole new corps of foreign aid organizations was born; and, to provide trained staff, the colleges, universities, and private foundations offered training and research facilities.

A new generation of leaders emerged in the Third World. Many were eloquent spokesmen for a reappraisal of the world's economic systems and of how to meet the needs of the developing countries. Others were forceful advocates of massive aid to redress the economic imbalance created by centuries of colonialism. They were, however, mistaken in thinking that aid is the only answer. As the countries and their leaders demanded more attention, the news services began to establish regional and even local bureaus. Aided by the rapid advances in communications technology, the media of the industrial world were soon filled with news of events in the Congo, Nigeria, Bangladesh, and India.

With this new awareness and the realization that these countries were votes to be vied for, disasters in these areas have taken on new interest. Governments of industrialized nations feel honor-bound to respond with a demonstration of concern as well as a show of resources. This is not to say that humanitarian concerns do not transcend the political issues, for along with the increased awareness of the plight of the developing countries has come a genuine interest in helping them with their problems. Yet political interests are always present and thus a factor in the increased outpouring of aid following disasters.

All this means that within the last twenty years, our recognition of disasters in the Third World has been heightened at the same time that the extent of the disasters has increased. If recent experience is any guide, we can expect this interest to remain high.

It is possible to protect against some natural hazards through engineering and the use of planning techniques. Stronger houses are built according to building standards and codes, and land use planning aims to keep residential areas from being situated in hazardous zones. In the developing countries, scarce funds allow few elaborate engineering projects, and widespread poverty means that most people live in weak buildings, many located on vulnerable sites, along flood plains or hazardous ravines.

In the emergency period immediately after a disaster, the response in both developed and developing countries is very much the same; it includes search and rescue, evacuation of the injured, and restoration of utilities. But in the developed countries, governmental responsibilities and the available infrastructure are very different. When Indiana was struck by major flooding in 1982, for example, the local city and county governments were the focal point of all emergency activities. They were supported by the state and later by the federal government. The larger cities, many of which had their own emergency preparedness offices, were able to call upon a wide variety of resources to meet emergency needs. After the floods subsided, more than 100 different governmental agencies set up offices to help the flood victims. Few new programs had to be established, as most of the assistance offered came through existing programs whose eligibility requirements were simply broadened to permit the victims to apply for and receive priority handling.

Since few cities or provinces in the developing countries can mount the same level of response, the national government takes operational responsibility. But neither do the national governments have a highly diversified range of social and economic programs to expand for the victims. Even if they did, few among the poor could qualify. The magnitude of the response is also different, as the example of emergency shelter shows. In the United States, the government has stockpiled large numbers of mobile homes at strategic sites near areas where disasters often occur. When a disaster strikes, these mobile homes are towed to the disaster site to provide houses until people can rebuild their homes. The trailers are often surplus or out-of-date mobile homes. But even so, the total expenditure for each shelter alone averages approximately $5,500.[1] In a developed society people rarely build their own houses, and housing reconstruction may take many months or even as long as one year, justifying a large outlay for emergency shelter.

In the developing countries, most emergency shelter needs are met by the victims themselves. The survivors quickly assemble materials from the rubble and build an interim shelter. Later, when they have more time and resources, they rebuild a permanent house using a combination of indigenous and locally available commercial materials. If emergency shelter is provided by the government or by relief agencies, it normally consists of tents or building materials. The average expenditure per family for emergency shelter is approximately sixty-five dollars.

From this example we can see that both the combined level of assistance provided internally and the ability to provide that level are internally much greater in the richer nations. We can also see that while the need is the same (shelter), the response required to meet the need is very different.

In long-term reconstruction, there are also major differences. In the developing countries, there are few governmental programs to help poor families to absorb economic losses and rebuild. Thus the part foreign reconstruction assistance plays can be very important in disaster recovery. In the developed countries, most of the reconstruction burden on individual families is handled through a "safety net" of insurance and public and private assistance programs.

In the less developed countries, there are few insurance programs available for the poor and the existing economic infrastructure can rarely take the burden of increased demand generated by a disaster. The disaster victims must work doubly hard to replace losses. In fact, for many disaster victims, the greatest loss is not in property but in opportunity, imposing a substantial handicap on a family for many years to come.

Why has disaster response in the Third World developed as it has? And why are relief agencies now reassessing the basic approaches? Most of the

---

1. Figures from the Federal Emergency Management Agency. All figures expressed in this book are in 1980 U.S. dollars unless otherwise specified.

approaches and techniques used in relief operations today were developed
to help European refugees and displaced persons after World War II. Not
only were many people homeless, but millions had been moved far from
their homes. Large camps were established to provide temporary assistance
until people could be relocated or until their homes and jobs had been re-
established. Due to the transitory nature of the refugees and because of the
disruptions in local markets, chaos in the transportation systems, and many
basic shortages, the relief efforts relied heavily on temporary measures and
goods supplied from outside the affected region. Food, blankets, tents, and
clothing were all needed and were useful to the refugees. Because the relief
agencies operated in close cooperation with military occupation authorities,
the approaches were often regimented and relied heavily on military-style
planning and logistics for implementation.

The relief agencies played a vital role. Generally they were designated to
handle the people-to-people activities and emergency and short-term
needs. Governments, in the meantime, concentrated on long-term recovery
and reconstruction. Spurred on by the Marshall Plan, the Allied governments poured millions of dollars into the reconstruction of European
businesses, jobs, and housing. With few exceptions, the relief agencies were
not involved in the long-term activities.

In the late 1940s, the relief agencies operating in Europe began to expand
their services into the trouble spots of the Third World: India, Palestine,
and Korea required the agencies' help in dealing with refugees. The
agencies continued to use the techniques that they had used in Europe and
adapt them to needs in the developing countries.

Beginning in the 1950s, the agencies began to expand into relief after
natural disasters, especially in newly independent countries. In many cases
the withdrawal of the colonial powers was so rapid that many of the new
countries did not have the government agencies, nor the infrastructure or
resources, to deal with disasters. The relief agencies helped fill this need. In
many cases they played a role that foreign governments, especially the
former colonial powers, could not undertake: direct operational support.
Thus new patterns of involvement were established as well as several new
relationships between governments and the private agencies. First, the relief
agencies began to expand their scope of activities into longer-term recovery
operations. Second, nongovernmental agencies (NGOs) became the focal
point for relief activities from outside an affected country. They could move
much more quickly than could governmental and intergovernmental
organizations and could often go where governments could not. Most
importantly, the relief agencies came to be seen as the operational experts,

and many Third World governments attempted to adopt the techniques used by the agencies as their own pattern of response.

The problem was that the response pattern used by the relief agencies for natural disasters was virtually the same as that developed for use with refugees. There are many differences between war and refugee relief, and relief and recovery needs after a natural disaster. Refugees do not have access to normal markets or economic systems, while in a natural disaster the victims do, and stimulation of the market system is an important factor in recovery. Refugees are often situated in camps located far from their homes. Survivors of a natural disaster have a need to stay on site and should be moved only if a life-threatening situation still exists. The delivery of aid to refugees can be highly centralized and relies primarily on logistics. In the aftermath of a natural disaster, delivery systems must be decentralized to take the aid directly to the victims' community. Aid for refugees emphasizes relief, while aid after natural disasters should emphasize recovery. Aid to refugees is generally considered nonrecoverable, while aid in a natural disaster can be provided in such a way that the resources are an investment not only in recovery but also in long-term development. In refugee operations, the emphasis is on logistics and material aid, while in natural disasters, a much more sophisticated operational capability is required and many sectors must be addressed.

Most of the agencies operating at that time were oriented toward relief and charity. Development concerns were emerging, but few agencies had yet seen a broader role for the voluntary agency. The favored relief approaches still relied mostly on short-term staff and volunteers. Because of high staff turnover, little accumulated wisdom was incorporated into the basic response pattern of the agencies.

As new agencies were formed to meet development needs, and new relationships between private and government agencies were established, a system of sorts began to evolve. To reduce overlap, a number of measures were taken to improve coordination among the agencies. The new "development" agencies began to become involved, and the role of NGOs in a disaster began to expand further.

The first major test of the newly emerging system was the series of events that led to the establishment of Bangladesh in 1971. In November 1970, a strong cyclone had propelled a massive storm surge many kilometers inland in East Pakistan. This precipitated not only a large relief operation, but also a series of political events that led to a civil war in the spring of 1971. Many of the agencies that had been providing relief to the storm-affected area soon found themselves trying to cope with millions of war refugees fleeing to India, as well as millions more displaced persons inside the country who were unable to flee. At the end of 1971, India entered the civil war and helped to establish the new country of Bangladesh. At the end of the war, the relief agencies were needed to help rebuild the country, devastated by both war and natural disaster.

Many of the people who worked in the Bangladesh relief activities had also worked in the Nigerian Civil War that had ended only a year earlier. Nigeria was an example of a logistics operation at its maximum and in many ways represented the zenith of the old approach. Many of the workers in Biafra had, however, come to question the effectiveness of this approach in a Third-World environment and, when they were called upon to repeat the same techniques in Bangladesh, realized that a new approach was required. Furthermore, the inadequacy of the response to meet the widespread needs in Bangladesh and the failure of voluntary agencies to perform well in many of the tasks asked of them, especially in nonmedical fields, led many relief workers to call for a reappraisal of the relief system.

In the early 1970s, a number of research projects were formulated by former relief workers in the U.S. and Europe, and an informal network of relief specialists began to evolve. The research examined the various approaches. Reports of dependencies, inappropriate aid, and counter-productive results became frequent and raised doubts about the funda-mental principles of relief. These challenges were slow to find acceptance within the relief agencies. Some agencies may have felt threatened by the studies; many could not believe that assistance motivated by humanitarian concerns could have such adverse effects. Unfortunately, the researchers and critics offered few alternatives and, for this reason, it was easier for the agencies to reject their criticism and negate their impact.

Toward the end of the 1970s, a rapprochement between critics and agencies began to take place. The Guatemalan earthquake initiated a period of change. Innovative approaches took advantage of technical advances in related fields (such as earthquake engineering), and the translation of research results into applications appropriate to developing societies brought disaster relief forward by many strides.

But although the development of appropriate technologies for disasters has improved response, there are still major problems basic to the relief system and the agencies. Few organizations have changed either their structure or their *modus operandi* as a result of disaster (or development) research. Most agencies are still focusing on emergency needs, and few fully understand the events that occur in a disaster and how their intervention affects the overall outcome of recovery.

2
Disasters: Causes and Effects

WHAT ARE DISASTERS?

Natural hazards such as earthquakes, hurricanes, floods, and droughts, spring to mind when the word *disaster* is mentioned. Yet these events are in fact natural *agents* that transform a vulnerable human condition into a disaster. The hazards themselves are not disasters but rather a factor in causing a disaster. Two other factors are essential: the event's effect on people and their environment, and human activities that increase its impact.

Disaster Hazards

Of the three factors, disaster hazards are the easiest to identify. Extensive research since World War II has increased our knowledge of the causes and working of each of these natural hazards and has done much to demystify their nature. The relevance of this information for purposes of planning mitigation, preparedness, and response actions cannot be overestimated. The figure on page 22 is a map of the world's regions where natural hazards are most frequent. In many cases, countries are vulnerable to more than one type of hazard. Jamaica, for example, suffers from earthquakes, hurricanes, floods, and droughts.

In order to provide a basic understanding of the cause-and-effect relationships, a brief explanation of the four major natural hazards follows.

EARTHQUAKES

Of all natural hazards, earthquakes seem to be the most terrifying. They can inflict tremendous damage within seconds and without warning at any time of day, on any day of the year. Ground shaking and surface faulting are

21

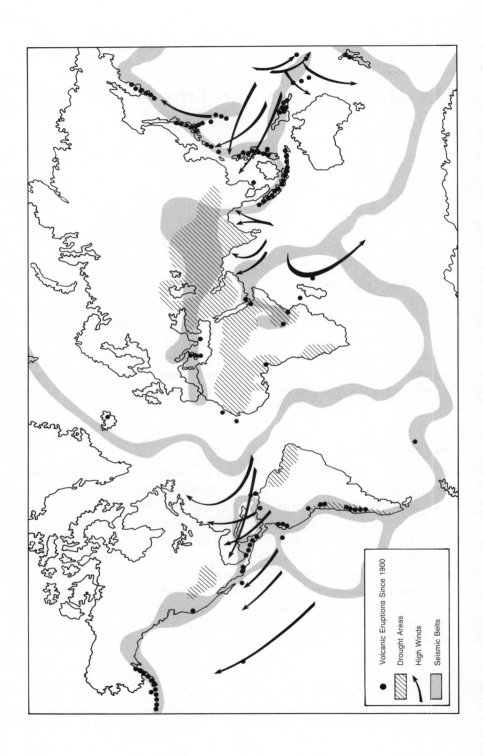

Volcanic Eruptions Since 1900

Drought Areas

High Winds

Seismic Belts

often just the forerunners of secondary damage, such as fires, floods (caused by dam failure), landslides, and tsunamis (seismic seawaves).

Earthquakes are caused by the movement of massive land areas, called plates, on the earth's crust. Often covering areas larger than continents, these plates are in a constant state of motion, acted upon by the periodic forces of the solar system and movement caused by the rotation of the earth. As the plates move relative to one another, stresses form and accumulate until a fracture or abrupt slippage occurs. This sudden release of stress is called an earthquake.

The place at which the stresses are released is known as the *focus* of an earthquake. From this point, mechanical energy is initiated in the form of waves that radiate in all directions through the earth. When this energy arrives at the earth's surface, it forms secondary surface waves. The frequency and amplitude of the vibrations produced at the surface, indicating the severity of the earthquake, depend on the amount of mechanical energy released at the focus, the distance and depth of the focus, and the structural properties of the rock or soil on or near the surface.

Primary effects. The onset of a large earthquake is signaled by a deep rumbling, followed shortly by a series of violent motions in the ground. Often the ground cracks, and there can be large permanent displacements as deep as 15 meters.

As the vibrations and waves continue to move through the earth, buildings on the earth's surface are set in motion. Each building responds differently, depending on its construction. When the waves strike, the earth begins to move backward and forward along the same line. The lower part of a building on the earth's surface immediately moves with the earth. The upper portion, however, remains at rest; thus the building is stretched out of shape. Gradually the upper portion tries to catch up with the bottom, but as it does so, the earth moves in the other direction, causing a "whiplash" effect, speeding up the top of the building, and creating a vibration known as *resonance*. The resonance can cause structural failure in itself, or adjacent buildings having different response characteristics (caused by different building materials) can vibrate out of phase and pound each other to pieces (Office of Emergency Preparedness 1972). The walls of buildings without adequate lateral bracing frequently fall outward, leaving the upper floors or roof to collapse into the inside of the structure.

Another primary effect is known as *liquefaction*. Loose sandy soils with a high moisture content separate when shaken by an earthquake. The water moves upward, giving the surface a consistency much like that of quicksand. Heavy structures resting on these soils slowly sink into the ground. Large portions of Port Royal, Jamaica, were damaged in this way during the earthquakes that struck the city in 1694 and 1907.

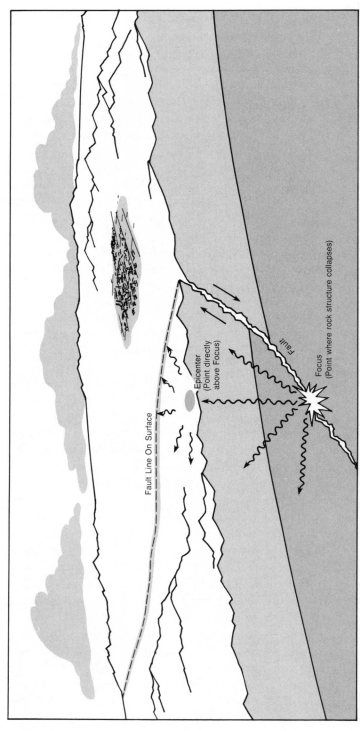

Fault Line On Surface

Epicenter
(Point directly
above Focus)

Fault

Focus
(Point where rock structure collapses)

DESCRIPTION OF AN EARTHQUAKE

Motion of the earth's plates causes increased pressure at faults where the plates meet. Eventually the rock structure collapses and movement occurs along the fault. Energy is propagated to the surface above and radiates outward. These waves of motion in the earth's crust shake landforms and buildings, causing damage.

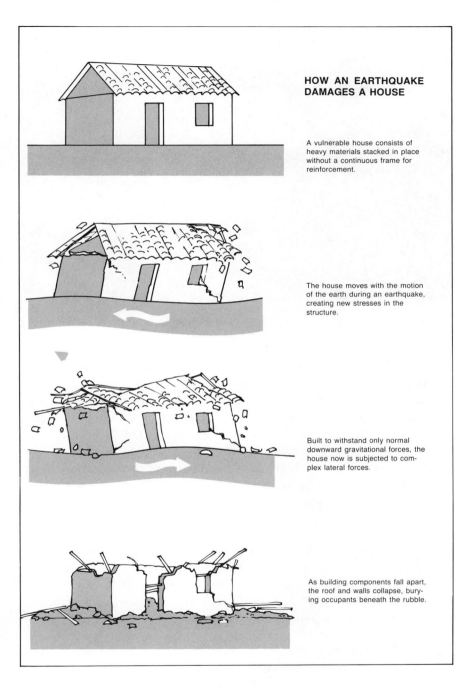

HOW AN EARTHQUAKE DAMAGES A HOUSE

A vulnerable house consists of heavy materials stacked in place without a continuous frame for reinforcement.

The house moves with the motion of the earth during an earthquake, creating new stresses in the structure.

Built to withstand only normal downward gravitational forces, the house now is subjected to complex lateral forces.

As building components fall apart, the roof and walls collapse, burying occupants beneath the rubble.

Subsidence caused by liquifaction (Kingston, Jamaica).

Secondary effects.   Often as destructive as the earthquake itself are the resulting secondary effects such as landslides, fires, tsunamis, and floods. Landslides are especially damaging and often account for the majority of lives lost. During the 1970 earthquake in Peru, the total number of deaths exceeded 70,000, with 50,000 injured. Of those killed, 40,000 were swept away by a landslide that covered the town of Yungay. Similarly, in the Guatemala earthquake of 1976, most deaths that occurred in Guatemala City were caused by the collapse of the unstabilized hillsides where thousands of urban squatters had settled (Office of Emergency Preparedness 1972).

Of far more concern are tsunamis, the large seawaves caused by an earthquake abruptly moving the ocean floor. The waves move at a high velocity and can cross thousands of kilometers before they run up on shore. At sea, their low wave height gives little evidence of their existence; however, as they approach land, their velocity decreases and their height increases. In this way a 5-meter crest moving at 600 kph in the open ocean becomes a devastating 30-meter-high wave moving at 50 kph when it reaches shore (Hendley 1978).

Tsunamis are dangerous because areas far from the earthquake's epicenter can be struck without warning. There are instances of earthquakes in Chile creating tsunamis that struck in Japan. The tsunami hazard is

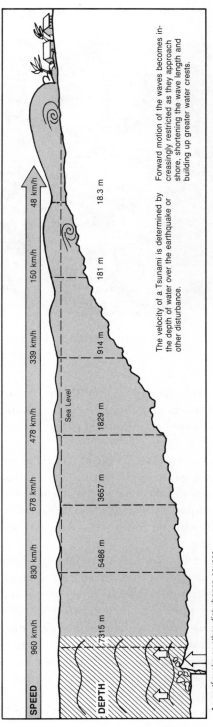

| SPEED | 960 km/h | 830 km/h | 678 km/h | 478 km/h | 339 km/h | 150 km/h | 48 km/h |

An earthquake or other disturbance causes a column to form above the ocean floor which radiates outward.

DEPTH: 7315 m, 5486 m, 3657 m, 1829 m, Sea Level, 914 m, 181 m, 18.3 m

The velocity of a Tsunami is determined by the depth of water over the earthquake or other disturbance.

Forward motion of the waves becomes increasingly restricted as they approach shore, shortening the wave length and building up greater water crests.

DESCRIPTION OF A TSUNAMI

A highly vulnerable hillside settlement (Lima, Peru).

especially dangerous for countries in the Pacific Basin and the island countries like the Philippines and Indonesia, where hundreds of remote, low-lying islands with poor communications cannot be given adequate warning.

The risk of fire immediately after an earthquake is often high because of broken electrical lines and gas mains. In recent years, officials in most of the world's major cities have installed devices that shut these services down automatically if an earthquake strikes. Yet the threat still exists in many of the smaller cities and the squatter settlements of the larger cities where open fires are used for cooking.

One fact is crucial: earthquake losses are largely preventable. Approximately 90 percent of the loss of life in all earthquakes is the result of building collapse. Until recently, this was unavoidable; but more is known about the nature of earthquakes and their effects now. We have engineering techniques to make new structures reasonably earthquake-resistant at a small additional cost, and we are rapidly developing techniques to make older buildings safer. Even structures made of materials such as adobe and brick in the poorest settlements of the Third World can be made relatively safe to substantially reduce the loss of life.

The human contribution to natural disaster goes beyond the construction of unsafe buildings, however. The pressures of increasing population density have led people to settle in areas that are difficult to develop safely, such as mountainous regions, active fault zones, and areas of artificial fill. The rapid growth of urban centers in developing countries is due largely to the imbalance of economic systems, and the increased vulnerability is directly related to the poverty that forces people to move to these vulnerable sites. Reducing earthquake vulnerability in these areas means dealing also with the socioeconomic roots of poverty, and thus is relief directly related to the development of that particular society.

TROPICAL CYCLONES: CAUSES AND CHARACTERISTICS

Tropical cyclones (known as hurricanes in the North Atlantic and South Pacific, cyclones in the Indian Ocean, and typhoons in the North and Western Pacific) are among the most awesome events of nature. Every year these violent storms, with winds of over 120 kph, bring destruction to coastlines and islands lying in their erratic paths. Stated simply, cyclonic storms are giant whirlwinds in which the air moves in a large tightening spiral around a relatively calm center of extreme low pressure (the "eye"), reaching maximum velocity in a circular band extending outward 30 to 50 kilometers from the edge of the eye. Near the center, winds may gust to more than 300 kph, and the entire storm can dominate the ocean surface for tens of thousands of square kilometers.

Much is known about how a cyclone forms. In order to develop, a cyclone must have a warm sea and calm air. The warm air rises—heavy, humid, and full of water vapor. Its place is taken by air rushing in from the sides and, because of the earth's rotation, this moving air is given a twist, so that the entire system begins to revolve. The warm rising air meets cooler air and releases its water vapor in the form of rain. It takes a tremendous amount of energy for the air to lift the water in the first place, and now this energy is released in the form of heat. This increases the rate of ascent of the air and a continuous cycle begins to develop. More water is released and thus more heat; the more water and heat released, the faster the cycle goes. This cycle becomes the engine that drives the beast, and gradually it goes faster and faster and the air mass becomes much larger.

Because the wind system is revolving, centrifugal force tends to throw the air outward so that the pressure in the center becomes very low, thus forming the eye of the storm. The pressure on the outside is very high, so the wind moves faster in an attempt to fill that low pressure area. The faster it moves, however, the more the centrifugal force throws it outward. Soon there are very fast circular winds and, when they reach 120 kph, the system becomes a cyclone or hurricane.

The system then begins to move forward like a spinning top. This brings it into contact with more warm sea and air, and the process becomes self-

HOW A HURRICANE FORMS

An atmospheric disturbance forces warm moist air of the prevailing Easterlies to rise. As the air cools, water vapor condenses and falls as rain; heat energy is released, and winds intensify.

The storm grows as air spirals inward, rises, and is exhausted from the top by high level winds. Surface air converges at an increasing rate toward the low pressure at the storm center.High winds, heavy rain, and storm surges occur as the storm becomes a mature hurricane.

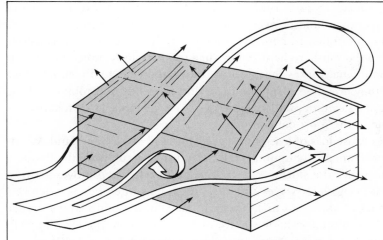

Wind blowing into a building is slowed at the windward face creating high presure. The air flow
separates as it spills around the building, creating
low pressure or suction at end walls, roof and
leaward walls.

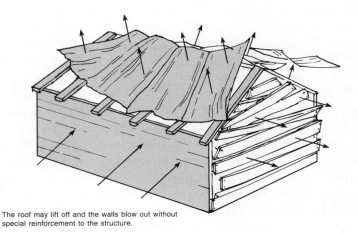

The roof may lift off and the walls blow out without
special reinforcement to the structure.

HOW A HURRICANE DAMAGES A BUILDING

31

sustaining. Once a cyclone is formed, it will continue to move and expand until it passes over land or over an area where the sea is cooler.

In the northern hemisphere, cyclones generally move in a northwesterly direction; in the southern hemisphere, in a southwesterly direction. Little is known about what makes these storms move and change direction, other than that they are affected by the high altitude winds and rotation of the earth. Scientists cannot predict where a cyclone will strike land, making this hazard one of the most dangerous.

Cyclones cause loss of lives, houses, crops, food stocks, and land. Winds do the most damage to buildings, but most deaths result from the flooding that accompanies the storm. As a cyclone approaches and moves across a coastline, it brings huge waves and raises the tides sometimes as much as 5 meters or more above normal. This rise may come rapidly and produce flash flooding in the coastal lowlands, or it may come in the form of giant waves, known as a storm surge (popularly called tidal waves). Waves and currents erode the beaches and barrier islands, undermine buildings, and wash away roads and irrigation ditches. The torrential rains that accompany cyclonic storms can also produce flooding and mudslides.

The most dramatic effect of cyclones is the damage they cause to houses. Contrary to popular belief, few houses are blown over. Instead, they are pulled apart by winds moving swiftly around and over the building. The wind lowers the pressure on the outside and creates suction on the walls and roof. Because the houses explode, few people are killed even when the structure is completely destroyed. Most deaths and injuries in cyclones are caused by flooding and flying debris. This is important to consider when developing environmental policies and housing reconstruction plans.

As in the case of earthquakes, most deaths in tropical cyclones are more directly attributable to human activities than to the storm itself. We can make houses wind-resistant. We can give low-lying areas extensive protection from flooding. With simple planning, we can avoid areas vulnerable to the action of waves, erosion, flooding, and mudslides. Even if hazardous areas must be occupied, there are measures we can take to reduce the vulnerability of people living in the structures and settlements.

Mudslides in hilly or mountainous areas are usually a direct result of human activity. Heavy rains quickly supersaturate hillsides that have been deforested or stripped for farming, and immense landslides result. In 1974, Hurricane Fifi struck Honduras. Little wave or wind damage was recorded, but large loss of life occurred in the massive mudslides caused by the torrential rains. The largest number of people killed were in squatter settlements located in the flood plains of the Ulma River, where the basic political and economic conditions (that is, failure to resolve the land

STORM SURGE

As a tropical storm forms, winds increase and atmospheric
pressure drops.

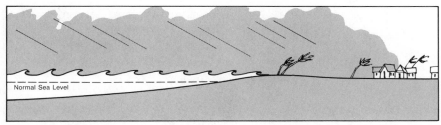

Decreased atmospheric pressure causes the sea level to rise.

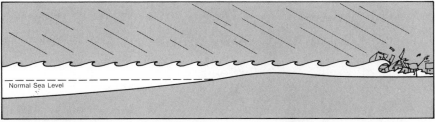

As the storm approaches land, winds pile up water to raise
the sea level even higher, and the sea sweeps inland.

distribution issues that create squatter settlements) contributed to the
disaster.

Ironically, a widely promoted disaster preparedness measure has also
caused casualties. Public officials often encourage people to move to
churches and schools for safety, without realizing the potential problems
inherent in these structures. Buildings with large, open rooms generally are
not reinforced to withstand high winds or flooding. In the case of Hurricane
David in August 1979, there was little advance warning for the residents of
the small island of Dominica, and no churches or schools were open.
Although more than 95 percent of the structures received substantial

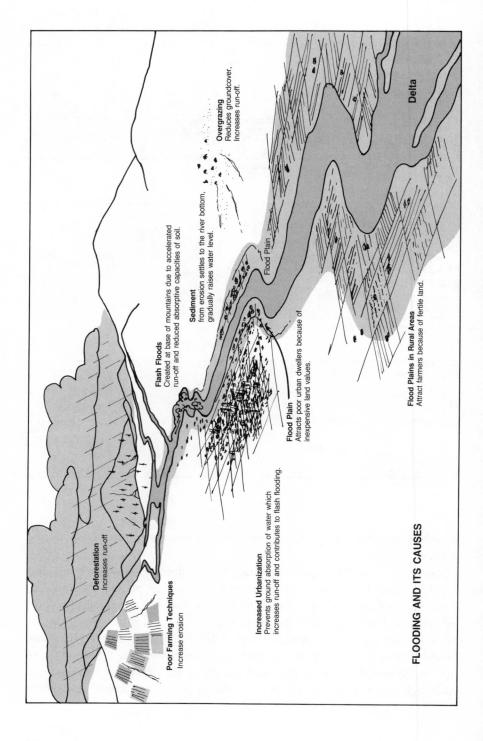

Deforestation
Increases run-off

Poor Farming Techniques
Increase erosion

Flash Floods
Created at base of mountains due to accelerated run-off and reduced absorptive capacities of soil.

Sediment
from erosion settles to the river bottom, gradually raises water level.

Overgrazing
Reduces groundcover, Increases run-off.

Increased Urbanization
Prevents ground absorption of water which increases run-off and contributes to flash flooding.

Flood Plain
Attracts poor urban dwellers because of inexpensive land values.

Flood Plain

Delta

Flood Plains in Rural Areas
Attract farmers because of fertile land.

FLOODING AND ITS CAUSES

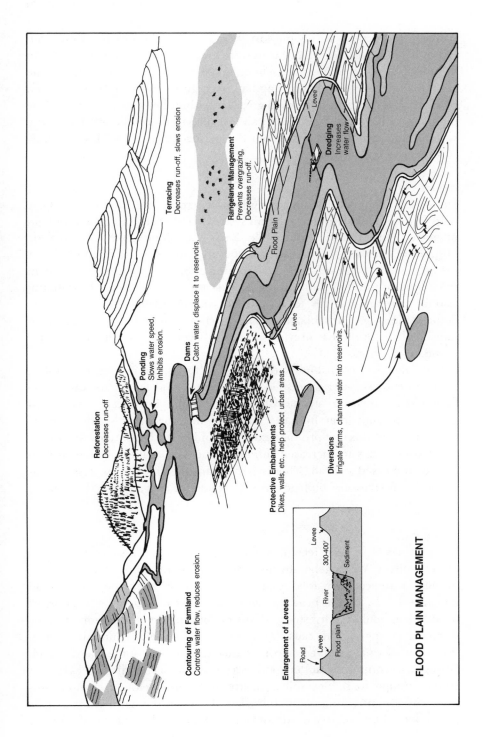

Reforestation
Decreases run-off

Contouring of Farmland
Controls water flow, reduces erosion.

Ponding
Slows water speed,
Inhibits erosion.

Terracing
Decreases run-off, slows erosion

Dams
Catch water, displace it to reservoirs.

Rangeland Management
Prevents overgrazing,
Decreases run-off.

Flood Plain

Levee

Dredging
Increases
water flow

Protective Embankments
Dikes, walls, etc., help protect urban areas.

Levee

Diversions
Irrigate farms, channel water into reservoirs.

Enlargement of Levees

Road
Levee
River
Levee
300-400'
Flood plain
Sediment

FLOOD PLAIN MANAGEMENT

damage, fewer than 40 people lost their lives. In the nearby Dominican Republic, however, over 1,200 lives were lost, almost 60 percent of them in the collapse of churches and schools—400 from the destruction of one church alone. Here prior warning had been given and people encouraged by the civil defense authorities to go to larger buildings for protection. The high loss of life can be attributed almost directly to public officials acting without adequate knowledge about the performance of buildings in hurricanes.

FLOODS

Floods kill. They kill by destroying houses, crops, and food stocks. They strip farmland, wash away irrigation systems, and erode large areas of land or make them otherwise unusuable. Each year, floods take an increasing number of lives and an increasing amount of property. In fact, flooding is the one natural hazard that is becoming more of a threat rather than remaining constant or diminishing. Floods are caused not only by rain, but also by human changes to the surface of the earth such as farming, deforestation, and urbanization. These actions increase the runoff from rains. Thus, storms that previously would have caused no flooding today inundate vast areas.

Not only do we contribute to the causes of floods, but reckless building in vulnerable areas, poor watershed management, and failure to control the flooding also help create the disaster condition. Ecologists have found evidence recently that human endeavors may be directly affecting the weather conditions that produce extensive and heavy rains. Irrigation of dry lands contributes to increased humidity and evaporation, which in turn lead to increased rainfall. This is particularly heightened in desert areas where large lakes are built to provide water for irrigation or for nearby settlements.

DROUGHTS

Drought has long been recognized as one of the most insidious causes of human misery. While generally associated with semiarid or desert climates, drought can occur in areas that normally enjoy adequate rainfall and moisture levels. In the broadest sense, any lack of water for the normal needs of agriculture, livestock, industry, or human population may be termed a drought. The cause may be lack of supply, contamination of supply, inadequate storage or conveyance facilities, or abnormal demand. Drought, as commonly understood, is a condition of climatic dryness that is severe enough to reduce soil moisture and water below the minimums necessary for sustaining plant, animal, and human life. Drought is usually accompanied by hot, dry winds and may be followed by damaging floods.

THE DROUGHT CYCLE

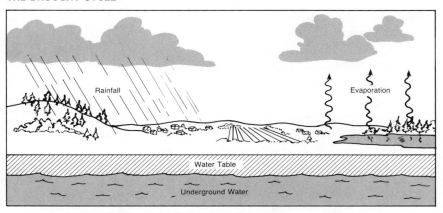

NORMAL HYDROLOGICAL BALANCE. Water supply is adequate to meet demand. The community grows and land use intensifies.

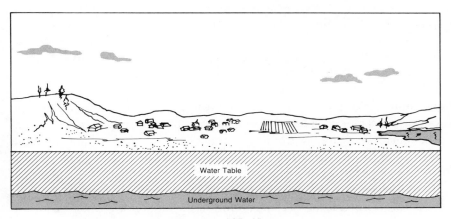

DROUGHT. Meteorological changes reduce rainfall, while urbanization, overgrazing, deforestation, and farming reduce water retention of the soil. The normal hydrological balance is broken. The topsoil erodes and the water table is lowered making recovery difficult. Food production and drinking water are reduced and people migrate out of the area.

The basic causes of drought are still not clearly understood. It is generally believed that droughts are a consequence of changing global weather patterns. These may be triggered by a number of factors, including the interrelationship of the earth's rotation, solar radiation, heat transfers to the earth's surface, minute matter in the earth's atmosphere, variations in topographic relief on the earth's surface, and the earth's thermal conductivities.

Economic activities can also contribute to the development of drought conditions. In the early 1970s, overgrazing led to the rapid expansion of the Sahara Desert southward, creating widespread drought in the Sahel region. Similarly, poor cropping methods and improper soil conservation techniques often contribute to drought conditions.

Drought is accompanied by reduced cloud cover, which increases exposure of land to solar radiation, resulting in increased transpiration and evaporation rates. These conditions add to the potential severity of the drought. When conditions become very dry, above-normal moisture is required to replenish moisture reserves in the soil, streams, and lakes. This situation tends to perpetuate drought and, once established, is very difficult to reverse.

The effects of drought depend on its severity and duration and the size of the affected area. The impact depends on the level of socioeconomic development. Societies that are more developed and economically diversified can better adjust to a drought and can recover more quickly. The poor regions, especially those reliant on any crop or pastoral economics, are most severely affected.

Drought effects can be classified as primary and secondary. Primary effects follow directly from the lack of water: decreased food production and impairment of agricultural economies, damage to land, loss of plant and animal life, reduction of human consumption and hygienic use of water, proliferation of insects, and damage to the natural environment. Secondary effects follow from the primary ones: economic loss, radical population shifts, and post-drought erosion and flooding.

The worst effect of drought is the loss of food. Any period of abnormal dryness lowers soil moisture and subsequently reduces crop production. Crop failures of substantial magnitude set in motion a chain reaction of human suffering and economic difficulties. In the developing countries, crop shortages can lead to famine that, without timely and well-managed aid, can cause large numbers of deaths.

In recent years there has been some debate as to exactly how much human endeavors affect drought and drought conditions. While there is no doubt that the basic condition is weather-related, the severity and length of time the drought lasts are affected by human actions. Poor cropping patterns, overgrazing, the stripping of topsoil, poor conservation techniques, depletion of both surface and sub-surface water supplies, and, to an extent, unchecked urbanization, all have an effect on the creation of drought conditions and contribute to the relative severity of the drought.

This knowledge has led to some rather unsettling discoveries. In the Sahel (Africa) in the 1960s, several development programs introduced stronger and more durable breeds of cattle. The objective was to increase meat production and to decrease cattle losses, thereby reducing the economic hardships for herdsmen. Some studies have indicated, however, that these newer cattle were one of the primary causes of the overgrazing that led to increasing desertification, which in turn contributed to the chain of events that led to the drought and famine of the 1970s.

OTHER HAZARDS

There are, of course, many other natural hazards occurring each year. Among these are fires, tornadoes, landslides, and volcanoes. Depending on the magnitude of the phenomenon and the size of the affected population, it may or may not be considered a major international disaster. Each has various primary and secondary effects, and each in turn is affected to some extent by those human actions that contribute to the creation of a vulnerable condition. As we have seen, there is no disaster that is not directly affected in some way by human endeavors.

Classification of Disasters

Disasters are classified as rapid on-set or cataclysmic, and long-term or continuing. In a cataclysmic disaster, one large-scale event causes most of the damage and destruction. Following this event, there may be a tremendous amount of suffering and chaos, but things soon begin to improve. In a long-term, continuing disaster, the situation after the event remains constant or may even deteriorate as time passes. Cataclysmic disasters include earthquakes, volcanic eruptions, cyclonic storms, and floods. Continuing disasters include droughts, crop failures, and prolonged civil strife. The damaged area in a cataclysmic disaster is usually relatively small, while the area affected in a continuing disaster may be extremely large.

Cataclysmic disasters destroy buildings and entire human settlements. Loss of life is sudden and therefore dramatic.

In terms of food and food distribution, cataclysmic disasters are normally more disruptive than destructive. For example, they may disrupt the transport and marketing systems. They can disrupt or damage irrigation systems and, to a limited extent, they may destroy food supplies. But the extent of destruction depends on the season, the location of the disaster, and the total area affected. On the other hand, while continuing disasters disrupt transportation and distribution networks, they can also bring them to a complete halt and ultimately destroy the system itself.

Phases of a Disaster

Disaster specialists have consistently made efforts to classify the time periods of a disaster. Among the standard classifications used are: the pre-disaster period, the warning phase, the emergency phase, the rehabilitation phase, the recovery phase, and the reconstruction phase. These phases are ordinarily used to describe actions and activities by agencies. They are artificial and easily exaggerated. There are several agencies, for example, that define the emergency period in terms of the number of days it takes them to develop and execute a program, rather than in terms of the needs of the victims.

After most disasters, three phases can be identified according to what actually happens in the affected community: the emergency phase, the transitional phase (also called by many the rehabilitation phase), and re-construction.

The emergency phase is characterized by actions that are necessary to save lives. They include search and rescue, first aid, emergency medical assistance, restoration of emergency communication and transportation networks, and in some cases, evacuation from areas still vulnerable to further disaster. Other actions taken during the emergency phase include initial disaster assessment and emergency repairs to critical facilities.

The transitional phase initially includes people's returning to work and the permanent repair of infrastructure, repair of damaged buildings, and other actions necessary to help the community return to normal as quickly as possible. This phase coincides with the period in which emotional recovery normally occurs. In many ways, the recovery period is the most difficult for the victims. During this time, depression may set in as people finally realize the full extent of losses. Limited outside intervention during this phase can be of great assistance in helping victims to recover. Assistance in the form of cash or credit, activities that produce jobs, and constructive projects are among the more appropriate types of aid.

Reconstruction is characterized by the physical reordering of the community and the physical environment. During this period, people reconstruct housing and other buildings, and repair roads and other community facilities; agriculture returns to normal. The time span is often very difficult to define. It may start fairly early, even during the recovery period, and may last for many years. The reconstruction of housing in particular is an activity that takes many years to complete.

It is difficult to set time limits on these three phases or accurately to define the limits of each, even for one specific type of disaster. For example, the emergency phase of a hurricane or a flood may be only a few days, or as long as a week. A volcano may precipitate an emergency period of only a

When the Guatemalan earthquake disrupted normal city services, this woman was forced to draw her drinking water from a broken water line. (Photo: Laffont/Sygma)

few days or up to a month. An earthquake may have continuing aftershocks after the first major tremor, thus prolonging the emergency for a number of weeks, as was the case in China in 1976. A drought and a resulting famine can last for months or even a year or more. And of course wars and the refugee crises they can initiate may last for many years.

The best way to identify the various phases is to examine what is happening in the disaster-affected community. An agency can then initiate activities that are appropriate to that phase. If response is not related in this way to community actions, the aid provided may come at a time when the community is not prepared to deal with it properly. One of the most common mistakes is the provision of housing reconstruction assistance during either the emergency or the transition period, rather than during the appropriate reconstruction phase. In Guatemala, scores of relief agencies rushed to provide housing reconstruction assistance within the first few months. Approximately six months after the programs began, most were phased out; however, reconstruction activities for the vast majority of the people had not yet begun. Many Guatemalans preferred to continue to reside in small temporary buildings until the earth tremors had ceased and until they had accumulated adequate materials and cash to pay for reconstruction of permanent dwellings. While there is no doubt that the relief agencies did make a contribution to providing housing for large numbers of the people, nonetheless only a few programs (notably Programa Kuchuba'l and the Save the Children Alliance Program) remained in operation during the critical time that most people in the rural areas rebuilt their own homes.

The graph on page 43 shows the peak reconstruction periods as measured by requests to a relief agency for housing assistance after the Guatemalan earthquake. It illustrates that activity was directly related to the seasons and reached its peak several years after the earthquake had passed. This shows that the reconstruction period varies in intensity and duration.

There is a danger in trying to define these phases, especially if agencies see their roles in terms of a particular phase. For example, an agency that sees itself as an emergency relief organization tends to limit its involvement to what it defines as the emergency phase. Because the emergency is rather short-term, two things normally result. First, the agency expands its definition of the emergency period to span several months; it then delivers emergency equipment and resources long after the actual emergency needs have passed. Second, the agency tends to push its employees and counter-parts to develop programs and have them completed, or at least have resources committed, before the end of the arbitrary emergency period. As a result, the local staff is forced to rush into a confused and disorganized situation, gather information that may not be accurate, and develop

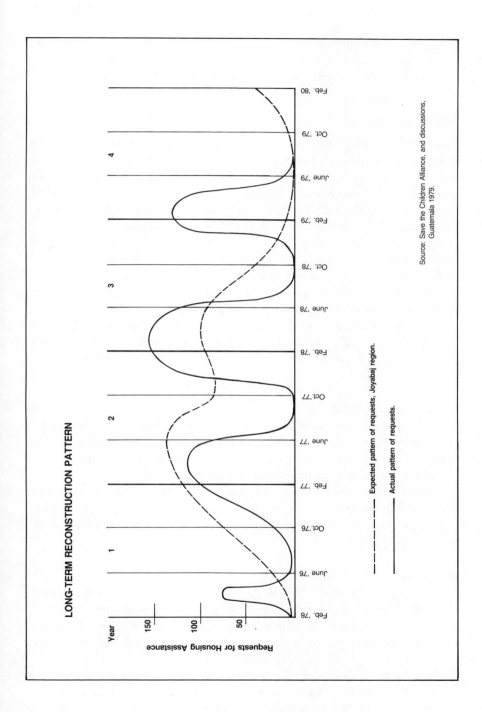

LONG-TERM RECONSTRUCTION PATTERN

Year

Requests for Housing Assistance

150

100

50

Feb. '76 | June '76 | Oct.'76 | Feb. '77 | June '77 | Oct.'77 | Feb. '78 | June '78 | Oct. '78 | Feb. '79 | June '79 | Oct. '79 | Feb. '80

1   2   3   4

– – – – Expected pattern of requests, Joyabaj region.

————— Actual pattern of requests.

Source: Save the Children Alliance, and discussions,
Guatemala 1979.

43

programs that either ignore the local coping mechanisms or take key leaders away from other activities more appropriate for the time period. The usual results are programs that are poorly conceived and executed.

Effects of Disasters

"No two disasters are alike" is a common saying among relief officials. Yet it is surprising how many agencies respond to disasters as if they were all alike. Over the years, it has become standard practice to supply certain goods to every disaster area. Among the best-known items are tents, clothes, high-protein foods, milk powder, and blankets. Each of these, of course, may be useful in specific situations. Yet a close examination shows that each is appropriate only in a limited number of situations. An agency's standardized responses often reflect a lack of understanding of the differences between disasters and of the disruptive effects and consequences of each. The responses are also reinforced by myths that have evolved over the years regarding what is appropriate for disaster aid.

Each type of disaster can have a number of disruptive effects. These in turn cause generally predictable problems and needs of four kinds: environmental, medical, social and economic, and administrative and managerial.

ENVIRONMENTAL EFFECTS

Disasters can have any number or combination of four effects: destruction and damage to homes and buildings; decreased quantity or quality of water supplies; destruction of crops and/or food stocks; and the presence of unburied human bodies or animal carcasses.

These environmental effects vary considerably from disaster to disaster. For example, earthquakes affect buildings but not usually crops, while hurricanes may affect both. Table 2-1 lists each of these effects and the hazard that produces them.

MEDICAL EFFECTS

In his study of disaster epidemiology, Karl Western (1972) lists four possible medical effects of disasters: traumatic injuries, emotional stress, epidemic diseases, and indigenous diseases affected by the disaster. Table 2-2 indicates the patterns of injury resulting from natural and man-made disasters; table 2-3 indicates the patterns of disease.

These tables may produce a few surprises, especially when one thinks of the standard practice of rushing massive medical aid to a disaster-striken community. Table 2-2 shows that while some disasters do create a need for surgical assistance, the period of need is extremely short. Thus by the time

Table 2-1 Environmental Effects of the Major Natural Hazards

HAZARD	EFFECTS	CONSEQUENCES
Earthquake	Tremors (ground shaking	Damage buildings, dams; cause avalanches; can collapse underground structures such as caves and tunnels.
	Liquifaction	Buildings on surface sink into soil.
	Ground failure	Landslides; settlement.
	Ground rupture (horizontal displacement)	Damages buildings on the rupture; breaks utility lines in the ground; may alter flow of subsurface streams; offsets streams, roads, and bridges.
	Tsunamis (seismically generated sea waves)	Flooding and impact damage from giant waves destroy manmade structures and crops; scour land; salinate wells and standing water.
Tropical Cyclone	High winds	Damage buildings and other manmade structures; destroy some standing crops, especially basic grains; damage orchards and other trees.
	Intense rains	Cause flooding, which damages human settlements and may force evacuations; cause landslides; damage certain crops, especially tubers; may cause excessive erosion.
	Storm surge	Causes rapid flooding, which damages human settlements and forces evacuation; scours and erodes topsoil; deposits salt on fields; may increase salinity in subsurface water table; destroys most crops.
Volcano	Blast	Destroys timber, crops, houses, bridges.
	Lava flow	Inundates all in its path; causes grass and timber fires; may force evacuation of human settlements.
	"Bombs" (ejected lava and other large materials)	Can damage structures they hit; may start fires; may force evacuation of human settlements.
	Ash fallout	Can destroy crops; damages machinery; can render croplands temporarily unusable (but restores nutrients over long term); may force evacuation of human settlements and destroy animal habitat; creates respiratory problems; can clog waterways.
Flood (Can be caused by unusually intense rainfall or by changes to earth's surface such as deforestation upstream)	Inundation	Results in damage to human settlements; forces evacuation; erodes topsoil; may change course of streams, rivers; destroys most crops; deposits silt in some downstream areas that may be beneficial.

Table 2-1 *(cont.)*

HAZARD	EFFECTS	CONSEQUENCES
Drought	Reduced cloud cover; increased daytime temperatures; increased evaporation rates; increasing likelihood of dust and sandstorms	Dramatic reduction of surface water; severe crop losses; soil erosion. Food shortages; increased hunger and malnutrition. Losses to livestock. Population shifts and migration.

most aid from outside the country can be marshaled and sent to the disaster area, the need has passed.

Table 2-3 makes clear that there is almost no actual immediate threat of epidemic arising from a disaster itself. While numerous secondary threats exist, in actuality few of these occur. If a communicable disease does break out, with proper epidemiological surveillance methods the source of outbreak can be quickly identified, the disease isolated, and an epidemic prevented, all by a very small staff using established epidemiological procedures. In no case in recent memory has there been a need for mass immunizations following natural disasters.

Table 2-4, also from Western's study, lists the most serious communicable diseases that follow disasters and the most effective methods for prevention and control. The public health measures are listed in order of priority. From this table it is clear that immunizations are generally regarded as the last defense against the disease. In most developing countries, people have been exposed to many of the endemic diseases and have built up some degree of natural immunity. Often these natural immunities are best left intact. Mass immunizations—which often require multiple dosages over a scattered period of time and which have only a short-term effect—may actually increase the people's vulnerability to disease once the medical relief program has ended.

Often the most effective means of combating disease is through environmental engineering rather than medical methods. Yet most disaster assistance has focused on meeting medical needs of victims and has generally ignored environmental needs. Many agencies perceive disasters in terms of a medical emergency and try to develop their response accordingly, rather than to carry out public health measures dealing with the environmental elements of the disaster. For this reason, few foreign agencies have any medical impact on disaster recovery, as the needs they are prepared to meet are nonexistent or have disappeared by the time the agencies arrive.

Table 2-2 Patterns of Injury and Surgical Needs in Disasters

INJURIES EXCEED DEATHS	SURGICAL NEEDS	PERIOD NEEDED
Warfare	High	Continuously
Tropical cyclones (without damaging storm surges)	Moderate	First 72 hours
Tornadoes	Moderate	First 48 hours
Fires	Moderate–low	First 24 hours
DEATHS EXCEED INJURIES		
Landslides	Low	First 72 hours
Avalanches	Low	First 72 hours
Volcanic eruptions	Low	First 72 hours
Tsunamis	Low	First 72 hours
Tropical cyclones (with damaging storm surges)	Moderate	First 72 hours
Floods	Low	First 72 hours
Earthquakes	High	First 72 hours
FEW OR NO SURGICAL NEEDS		
Famines		
Insect swarms		

SOURCE: *The Epidemiology of Natural and Man-Made Disasters: The State of the Art,* Karl Western, London School of Hygiene and Tropical Medicine, University of London, 1972. Page 81.

Table 2-3 Patterns of Disease Resulting from Disasters

DISASTER TYPE	ACTUAL IMMEDIATE EPIDEMIOLOGICAL THREAT	SECONDARY EPIDEMIOLOGICAL THREAT
Cataclysmic disasters		
Earthquakes	None	None
Tropical cyclones (without storm surge)	None	Waterborne,* vectorborne† diseases.
Tropical cyclones (with storm surge)	None	Waterborne diseases (except cholera), vectorborne diseases
Floods	Waterborne diseases	Waterborne, vectorborne diseases
Tornadoes	None	None
Fires	None	None
Tsunamis	None	Waterborne diseases (except cholera), vectorborne diseases
Landslides/avalanches	None	None
Continuing, long-term disasters		
Warfare	None	All waterborne, personal contact,‡ and vectorborne diseases a possibility due to overcrowding
Drought/famine	Malnutrition	Malnutrition increases susceptibility to all diseases, but particularly measles, diarrhea.

*Waterborne diseases: typhoid, paratyphoid fevers, sewage poisoning, cholera, schistosomiasis, leptospirosis
†Vectorborne diseases: louseborne typhus, plague, malaria, viral encephalitis, relapsing fever
‡Personal contact diseases: shigellosis, diarrhea, skin infections, hepatitis, measles, whooping cough, diptheria, influenza, tuberculosis

Table 2-4 Communicable Diseases That May Follow Disasters and the Most Effective Methods of Prevention and Control

DISEASE	PUBLIC HEALTH MEASURES
Water and/or Food-Borne Diseases	
Typhoid and paratyphoid fevers	Adequate disposal of feces and urine
Food poisoning	Safe water for drinking and washing
Sewage poisoning	Sanitary food preparation
Cholera	Fly and pest control
Schistosomiasis	Disease surveillance
Leptospirosis	Isolation and treatment of early cases (typhoid and paratyphoid fevers, cholera)
	Mass immunization (typhoid fever and cholera)
Person-to-Person Spread	
Contact Diseases	
Shigellosis	Reduced crowding
Nonspecific diarrheas	Adequate washing facilities
Streptococcal skin infections	Public health education
Scabies	Disease surveillance in clinics
Infectious hepatitis	Treatment of clinical cases
	Immunization (infectious hepatitis)
Respiratory Spread	
Measles	Adequate levels of immunization before the disaster
Whooping cough	Reduced crowding
Diphtheria	Disease surveillance in clinics and community
Influenza	Isolation of index cases
Tuberculosis	Immunization of selected groups in the population (example: children—measles)
	Continued primary immunization of infants (diphtheria, whooping cough, tetanus)
Vectorborne Diseases	
Louseborne typhus	Disinfection (except malaria and encephalitis)
Plague (rat flea)	Vector control
Relapsing fever	Disease surveillance
Malaria (mosquito)	Isolation and treatment (no isolation for malaria)
Viral encephalitis	

SOURCE: *The Epidemiology of Natural and Man-Made Disasters: The State of the Art*, Karl Western, London School of Hygiene and Tropical Medicine, University of London, 1972. Page 90.

Table 2-5 Immediate Social and Economic Consequences of Disasters

	SHORT-TERM MIGRATIONS	PERMANENT MIGRATION	LOSS OF HOUSING	LOSS OF INDUSTRIAL PRODUCTION	LOSS OF BUSINESS PRODUCTION	LOSS OF CROPS
CATACLYSMIC DISASTERS						
Earthquake			X	X	X	
Cyclone			X	X	X	X
Flood	X		X	X	X	X
Tsunami			X	X	X	X
Volcano	X		X			X
Fire	X		X	X	X	X
LONG-TERM, CONTINUING DISASTERS						
War	X	X	X	X	X	X
Drought/famine	X					X

Table 2-5 shows the immediate social and economic consequences of disasters, some of which are easy to see; the more profound social and economic upheavals and changes they bring are more difficult to identify and monitor.

ECONOMIC, SOCIAL, AND POLITICAL CONSEQUENCES

Economic impact.   Disasters disrupt rather than destroy economies. During an emergency, people must leave their jobs and devote their time to disaster-related activities, such as search and rescue, or to caring for survivors. During this period normal economic activities are severely curtailed, even if the sources of employment are unaffected by the disaster. This period is short-lived, however, and in the later phases of a disaster economic activities quickly assume a high priority for both businesses and victims alike. Whether or not an economy can recover quickly depends on the losses sustained. Physical damage to businesses and industry may temporarily halt some activities, but most enterprises can operate at reduced levels even with the loss of equipment. Often the workers in a damaged factory can be put to work helping to repair or rebuild the facility. In any case, the loss of jobs is usually only temporary.

Of far more concern is the impact of disasters on persons who are participating only marginally in the economy, people such as subsistence farmers, small shopkeepers, fishermen. After a disaster it is not uncommon for many small enterprises to fail. For the owners, a disaster can wipe out not only their investments but also their savings.

Several observers have noted that boom economies often develop after a widespread disaster such as an earthquake or hurricane where there is

DAMAGE TO INFRASTRUCTURE	DISRUPTION OF MARKETING SYSTEMS	DISRUPTION OF TRANSPORT	DISRUPTION OF COMMUNICATIONS	PANIC	LOOTING	BREAKDOWN OF SOCIAL ORDER
X	X	X	X		X	
X	X		X		X	
X		X	X			
X			X			
	X					
X			X	X		X
X	X	X	X		X	X

Table 2-6 Effects of Natural Hazards

	EFFECTS ON LAND SURFACE	EFFECTS ON STRUCTURES
Earthquakes	Fissures on surface	Damages buildings, roads, dams and bridges
	Landslides	Buries surface structures, temporarily dams rivers causing localized flooding
	Liquifaction of soils	Damages buildings
	Collapses underground caves, tunnels	May damage structures on surface, may change underground streams
	Avalanches	Damages buildings, roads, dams, and bridges
Cyclonic Storms	High winds	Damages buildings, power lines, towers
	Flooding (rain and run-off)	Damages buildings, bridges
	Flooding (storm surge)	Damages buildings, roads, bridges extensively
Droughts	Dry soils	No major damage
	Windstorms	Minor damage
	Desertification	No major damage
Floods	Erosion	Undercuts foundations
	Mudslides	Buries buildings and damages other manmade structures
	Silting	No major effect
Tsunamis	Flooding	Destroys or damages buildings, bridges, irrigation systems
Volcanoes	(Blast)	Destroys or damages buildings, other surface structures
	Lava flows	Buries buildings, sets fires
	Ash deposits	No major effect
	Localized fissures	Damages buildings, dams, bridges

major physical reconstruction. Long-term effects are not yet known, but at least one study indicates that if low-income victims are given priority in job hiring, boom economies can be a means of adjusting some of the losses (*Human Organization* 1979).

The effects of a natural disaster on the economy of a community are difficult to quantify, and surprisingly little attention has been given to economic reconstruction needs. This is in major contrast to post-war reconstruction efforts, such as the Marshall Plan, where great emphasis is

EFFECTS ON AGRICULTURE	EFFECTS ON TREES
None	None
Loss of crops on affected area, usually minor	Loss of timber on affected area, usually minor
None	None
Localized loss of irrigation usually temporary	None
Localized crop losses	Localized timber losses
Damage to standing crops especially grains	Widespread loss of timber
Damage to standing crops in flood areas	Minor losses along streams
Extensive damage to crops, irrigation systems; leaves harmful salt deposits, scours topsoil, contaminates wells	Loss of trees near shoreline
Kills crops	Kills some trees
Erodes topsoil	Minor damage
Covers farmland with sand, alters cropping patterns	Kills trees, increases scrub growth
Destroys crops, changes cropping patterns	Reduces forests
Localized crop losses	Localized timber losses
Improves soils	No major effect
Localized destruction of crops; minor salt water contamination of soils, wells	Loss of trees along shoreline
Minor damage	Widespread timber losses near eruption
Buries crops and renders land unusable	Destroys forests and starts forest fires
Destroys crops, makes land temporarily unusable pollutes streams	Kills trees
No major effect	No major effect

placed on helping business and industry to rebuild. (To an extent, this may be due to the fact that insurance is available to protect industry from most disasters, while it does not cover war risks.)

An interesting approach to earthquake reconstruction was taken by the People's Republic of China in the aftermath of the Tangshan earthquake in 1976. Here the government decided to concentrate on rebuilding the industry first rather than giving housing equal or top priority. The reasoning was that if jobs were provided, people would be better able to cope and could later participate financially in the new housing schemes. The planners felt that this approach would give them time to explore all the options for physical planning, especially siting choices, and give them a chance to replan a safer city.

While the Chinese certainly have far more control over reconstruction than do most other countries, the general approach bears watching.

The impact on land.   Each type of natural disaster has its own effects on land values. After an earthquake, land values normally increase, especially in urban areas, and surprisingly even in marginal areas. This is because of increased demand for "safe" land from people who have lost their land or who live on sites still threatened by aftershocks. Since earthquakes have no effect on agriculture, agricultural lands will usually experience the same increase in price as urban land.

As a general rule, land values decline following the eruption of a volcano. Agricultural land will on an average lose more in value than urban land, especially if ash fallout is extensive.

Land values following cyclones vary depending on the type and extent of damage. If a storm surge has struck, the value of the land inundated usually declines, especially if large salt deposits remain. Beachfront property also declines in value, in both urban and rural areas. Sites that prove safe, that is, above the flood level, or that were protected from high winds (by hills or manmade structures), may increase in value. In general, however, land values decline.

Small marginal farms usually cannot survive economically following a cyclonic storm. In Andhra Pradesh, for example, following the 1977 cyclone, a high proportion of the small farmers (those who owned two acres or less) were forced to sell their land because they could not afford to rehabilitate it and reinstall the irrigation systems. This may result in a substantial increase in the number of people migrating to urban areas, creating a housing shortage.

Floods have little effect on land value in rural areas, but in urban areas, flood plains are usually considered undesirable for housing and other types of development. Therefore, the land will have less value than other sites. In the less developed countries (LDCs), undesirable or low-cost lands attract squatter settlements, which are extremely vulnerable to disasters. Unless alternate land is offered at a reasonable price, these hazardous settlements proliferate. A disaster striking an area such as this will have little effect on land values, but the survivors often require new land in exchange for the sites that have been flooded.

Land issues are of special concern in disasters because in many cases they have been a major factor in disaster vulnerability. As mentioned above, a

Displaced disaster victims invade surrounding lands for living space following the Guatemalan earthquake.

large percentage of squatter settlements and other housing occupied by low-income people is situated in areas that are particularly vulnerable to disasters. Often people move to this land because they cannot afford safer, more suitable sites or because large landowners refuse to sell more suitable sites. Thus when a disaster occurs, a disproportionately high percentage of the people affected are those living on these sites.

Disasters typically exacerbate land problems. It is usually obvious that those disproportionately affected were living on vulnerable sites. People soon undertake political action to provide suitable sites for those made homeless and landless by the disaster, as well as for those still living in areas vulnerable to secondary disasters. Typical here are land "invasions" (illegal occupations for the purpose of developing land), political demonstrations, and land acquisition activities by humanitarian organizations.

Failure to address land issues can affect a proposed reconstruction program. Self-help housing programs are not likely to be successful unless people are either landowners or have long-term leases or agreements to occupy the land. New sites offered must not be vulnerable to secondary or future disasters.

A unique problem often arises after disasters that is related to land ownership. Relief organizations often distribute reconstruction materials without distinguishing between landowners and tenants. Does the landless

victim who accepts this material and uses it in the reconstruction of a
permanent house then own the structure? In many cases, especially in Latin
America, the ownership of any permanent structure is automatically
conferred on the landowner. There have been cases where the disaster
victims purchased reconstruction materials from relief agencies and rebuilt
their houses only to be evicted upon completion of the building.

Social and political impact.   Disasters often highlight the social struggles in a
society and underscore the inherent inequities within a political system.
Earthquakes and hurricanes, for example, affect a disproportionately high
percentage of the poor in developing countries, for it is they who live in
unreinforced, poorly built structures, often located on marginal lands. A
disaster makes it very evident that the poor are vulnerable because they are
poor, and this can lead to profound political and social changes within a
society: many governments destabilize in the years immediately following a
disaster. In the Sahel drought, every government fell, many directly as a
result of dissatisfaction with relief efforts.

The case often cited is of the chain of events leading to the independence
of Bangladesh. In 1970, a tropical cyclone generated a massive storm surge
that swept across the barrier islands and the delta regions of East Pakistan,
killing as many as half a million people. The failure of the Pakistani
government to respond to this disaster with massive aid highlighted many
of the inequities inherent in the relationship between East and West
Pakistan. Using the disaster as a rallying point, a major political movement
took control of the Pakistani government in the general election that
followed several months later. The West Pakistani clique in power refused
to relinquish control and, within a short period of time, civil war erupted.
Fierce fighting and reprisals against the Hindu minority led to a massive
exodus of refugees from East Pakistan into eastern India. The burden
placed on the Indian government by these refugees led India to invade East
Pakistan to help create the independent state of Bangladesh. The fighting
during this period, plus the massive dislocation of people both inside
Bangladesh and outward to India, disrupted agriculture and set in motion
the beginning stages of a famine.

Students of this period point out that the cyclone and storm surge set in
motion the sequence of events by underscoring the inequities in the
treatment of the poorer eastern sector by the more afflent West Pakistan.
They argue that other events could easily have initiated the same sequence,
but in fact it was the disaster that provided an event of such magnitude that
political inequities could not be ignored.

Disaster relief efforts may also play a part in heightening awareness of
social problems and may fuel repression by reactionaries within a society.

In the aftermath of the Guatemalan earthquake, many outside relief agencies chose to work in the Indian communities, largely ignored by their own government. Relief and reconstruction activities provided opportunities for the Indians to develop leadership and contact with the development agencies, many of which stressed conscientization (developing an awareness of the roots of one's poverty). This led to growing demands for change. That these demands threatened the oligarchy ruling Guatemala, there can be no doubt. As early as the summer of 1976, only five months after the earthquake, relief workers in several programs were warned privately by the military that they were being watched and should not raise the Indians' expectations too much. Whether the disaster created the unrest by highlighting the social disparities in the country and the government's inability to deal with the situation, or whether it was simply one of the contributing factors that led to the virtual civil war that erupted four years later, one thing is clear. Prime targets for assassination by right-wing death squads have been the leaders of the reconstruction programs.

ADMINISTRATIVE AND MANAGERIAL EFFECTS

Administrative problems in disasters are made more difficult by four factors, which increase in importance with the extent of the disaster.

Effects on community leadership.   The loss of leaders due to death or injury can impair disaster response. Yet there is rarely a heavy loss of national leaders even in earthquakes and cyclones, because they live in better or stronger housing and thus are rarely injured. Leaders at the provincial or national level are slightly more exposed, while leaders at the village level are usually more vulnerable.

Since disasters often isolate communities and require them to rely on local leadership, a key element of a disaster plan should be to provide safe shelter for local leaders and their offices.

Disruption of formal organizations.   When a disaster strikes, large formal organizations are most disrupted. Small, community-based organizations are generally better able to function, even with loss of leaders. In Guatemala hundreds of villages were isolated by landslides and forced to rely on their own leadership and resources until the national government could reach them. They did so remarkably well.

When formal organizations are disrupted, there is often a breakdown of clear lines of authority. In the emergency period, this can actually be beneficial, because it allows nonformal ad hoc organizations to develop quickly in order to solve specific problems. In his study *The Disaster Community* (1961), Charles Fritz points out that people band together in times of disaster to overcome common hardships. This results in the rise of local leaders and increases the efficiency of local organizations in dealing with the immediate aftermath of the disaster.

In short, no one stands on formality and things get done simply because they have to.

Damage to critical facilities and lifelines.   Widespread disasters can destroy or damage facilities that may be critical not only for responding to the disaster, but also for maintaining a safe environment and public order. Among these are communications installations; electrical generating and transmission facilities; water storage, purification, and pumping facilities; sewage treatment facilities; hospitals; police stations; and other public and private buildings.

The temporary disruption of communications is a critical problem for disaster managers. Damaged facilities make it more difficult to gather information and transmit it to decision makers. It is interesting to note how many emergency operations plans rely heavily on telecommunications. Yet no provision is made to protect these facilities from hazards.

Disruption of transportation (and isolation of resources).   During the initial stages of a disaster, almost all surface means of transportation within a community are disrupted. Bridges can be knocked out; roads can be cut by landslides or floods; rubble can block streets and highways. This can present a two-fold problem: First, rescue and other emergency vehicles are restricted. Second, unless adequate thought is given to positioning, vehicles and equipment may be isolated. In a recent hurricane in the Caribbean, most trucks designated to carry sand and sandbags to help combat localized flooding during hurricanes were prevented from responding by flood waters that cut off the only route from their parking lot to the area they were supposed to protect.

All of these administrative and managerial problems can be overcome through adequate pre-disaster planning. We will deal later with some measures that can reduce the impact of these problems.

EFFECTS OF DIFFERENT TYPES OF DISASTERS ON RESPONSE

Table 2-7 lists appropriate responses according to the type of disaster for both local authorities and foreign intervenors in the initial period, as well as during the later stages. It is my assessment based on personal experience of needs in various types of disasters. Initially, most of the needs are met by the local authorities and indeed by the victims themselves. In the cataclysmic disasters, there is very little that foreign intervenors can do, other than to support the work of local authorities with cash or to help re-establish basic services and critical facilities. This is not to say that most agencies do not in fact try to intervene at this stage, but the truth of the matter is that such intervention is usually wasted. It arrives too late and only adds to the general confusion rather than bringing order into the situation.

In continuing or long-term disasters, however, both the initial and secondary response by local authorities and foreign intervenors should be the same. However, foreign intervenors can also provide technical assis-tance in such specialized fields as earthquake and wind engineering. In a supportive role, intervenors can offer credit to groups that otherwise would be ineligible through the credit and loan schemes of the local government. The secondary response ideally is a partnership between local authorities and the foreign intervenor, so that more people can be served more rapidly and gaps left in the local aid coverage can be filled by foreign aid.

In the particular case of war, where refugees have gone from one country into another, foreign intervenors are often called upon to respond in lieu of the local government. This may be for a variety of political reasons, as well as the local government's inability to deal with the situation in economic terms. In many war situations, a role unique to the foreign intervenors can arise, namely, refugee repatriation or relocation to a third country.

Table 2-8 lists appropriate types of aid for communities struck by various types of disasters. The table is an oversimplification, as many of the issues relating to the provision of aid will be discussed later. It does, however, give a brief overview as to basic aid requirements following each major disaster type. It assumes, of course, that the actual relief item is culturally appro-priate. For example, short-term feeding does not mean the sending of "junk foods" from the U.S. to a disaster in Africa; and emergency shelter does not mean providing a Western architect's idea of an instant house to a society that is perfectly capable of building an adequate structure from indigenous materials.

To make certain that the most important myths and misconceptions are thoroughly deflated, here is a summary of what disasters are not and what aid is not needed.

1. Earthquakes do not cause loss of crops. The victims therefore do not require massive food aid.
2. Earthquakes do not create conditions for epidemics.
3. Earthquakes do not create a need for clothes or other material goods. (These items may be buried, but they can be recovered.)
4. Earthquakes do not necessitate migrations of people; therefore refugee camps are not necessary.

Disasters and Development

Table 2-7 Response to Disasters (Ideal)

TYPE OF DISASTER	INITIAL RESPONSE BY LOCAL AUTHORITIES	INITIAL RESPONSE BY FOREIGN INTERVENORS
CATACLYSMIC		
Earthquake	Search and rescue; medical assistance; disaster assessment	Cash; assistance in reopening roads, reestablishing communications, contact with remote areas; disaster assessment
Cyclone	Evacuation; search and rescue; medical assistance; disaster assessment; provision of short-term food/water; water purification; epid. surveillance; provision of temporary lodging	Cash; assistance in reopening roads, reestablishing communications, contact with remote areas; disaster assessment; assistance with water purification
Flood, tsunami	Evacuation; search and rescue; medical assistance; disaster assessment; provision of short-term food/water; water purification; epid. surveillance; provision of temporary lodging	Cash; assistance in reopening roads, reestablishing communications, contact with remote areas; disaster assessment; assistance with water purification
Volcano	Evacuation; search and rescue; short-term feeding; emergency shelter	Cash
Fire	Evacuation; search and rescue; short-term feeding; emergency shelter	Cash
CONTINUING/LONG-TERM		
War	Medical assistance; food (including intensive and supplementary feeding); water; emergency shelter; protection; sanitation	Medical assistance; food (including intensive and supplementary feeding); water; emergency shelter; protection; sanitation; provision of medicines
Drought/famine	Medical, nutritional services, water (on site, if possible); epid. surveillance	Medical, nutritional services, water (on site, if possible); epid. surveillance

*Assumes refugees are in refugee camps outside their own country.

SECONDARY RESPONSE BY LOCAL AUTHORITIES	SECONDARY RESPONSE BY FOREIGN INTERVENORS
Repair/reconstruction of infrastructure, housing, public buildings; jobs; credit; assistance to business	Repair/reconstruction of housing; jobs; credit; technical assistance; assistance to small business and institutions
Repair/reconstruction of infrastructure, housing, public buildings; jobs; assistance to agri. recovery (loans, seeds, farm equipment, animals), small business, fishermen	Repair/reconstruction of housing; jobs; credit; technical assistance to agri. recovery, small business, and institutions
Repair/reconstruction of infrastructure, housing, public buildings; jobs; assistance to agri. recovery (loans, seeds, farm equipment, animals), small business, fishermen	Repair/reconstruction of housing; jobs; credit; technical assistance to agri. recovery, small business, and institutions
Relocation, credit, financial assistance to victims; assistance to agri., small business	Relocation, credit, financial assistance to victims; assistance to agri., small business
Repair/reconstruction of infrastructure, housing, public buildings; jobs; assistance to agri. recovery and small business	Repair/reconstruction of housing; jobs; credit; technical assistance
*Food (incl. supplementary feeding, feeding of school-age children); housing; sanitation; social services; typing; legal services; nutritional surveillance	*Food (incl. supplementary feeding, feeding of school-age children); housing; sanitation; social services; typing; legal services; nutritional surveillance; resettlement assistance
Reestablishment of agri. sector (loans, seeds, farm equipment, animals); technical assistance; nutritional surveillance	Reestablishment of agri. sector (loans, seeds, farm equipment, animals); technical assistance; nutritional surveillance

Table 2-8 Appropriate Aid

CATACLYSMIC DISASTERS	CASH	EMERGENCY SHELTER	TEMPORARY LODGING	IMMUNIZATIONS	SHORT-TERM FEEDING (NORMAL FOODS)	LONG-TERM FOOD AID
Earthquake	X				X	
Cyclone	X		X		X	
Flood	X		X	X	X	
Tsunami	X				X	
Volcano	X		X		X	
Fire	X		X		X	
LONG-TERM, CONTINUING DISASTERS						
War	X	X		X	X	X
Drought/famine	X			X	X	X

*Depending upon the climate

5. Emergency shelter is rarely needed, even after earthquakes. People can build adequate emergency shelter from the rubble and usually do so long before emergency shelters or tents arrive.
6. Tropical cyclones do not cause outbreaks of cholera. Cholera must be endemic to the community before the cyclone strikes. If a tidal wave (storm surge) accompanies the cyclone, chances are the threat of disease will be *lessened*, because cholera is neutralized by salt water.
7. Hurricanes that are not accompanied by tidal waves do not pollute water supplies.
8. Massive food aid is rarely required following a cataclysmic disaster such as a hurricane.
9. Used clothing is almost never needed; it is almost always culturally inappropriate and, though accepted by disaster victims, it is almost never worn.
10. Blankets can be useful but, if needed, can be found locally and need not be imported.
11. *Foreign* intervenors should not directly intervene immediately after cataclysmic disasters. Their assistance is most effective in the reconstruction period, not the emergency phase.
12. Most needs are met by the victims themselves and their local governments and agencies, not by foreign intervenors.

INTENSIVE FEEDING	SUPPLEMENTARY FEEDING	SURGICAL AID	MEDICAL SUPPLIES	CLOTHING	BLANKETS	LOANS OR CREDIT	AGRICULTURAL ASSISTANCE
		X			X*	X	
					X*	X	X
					X*	X	X
					X	X	X
					X*	X	X
		X			X*	X	X
X	X	X	X		X*		X
X	X		X			X	X

3
The Borracho Hurricane

In order to see how each part of the disaster relief system works or does not work, I have constructed a fictitious disaster and described events as they often occur. All the events and actions of the agencies are based on actual occurrences.

A hurricane has been chosen for this exercise because it enables us to look not only at post-disaster actions, but also at activities that occur prior to a disaster when there is a warning period. While each type of disaster is unique, the following scenario is typical of all sudden natural disasters. Although based on actual occurrences, the examples here are intended for educational purposes only and do not reflect on the ability or capacity of any individual or agency. Most agency names are fictitious.

The Setting: The Republic of Borracho is a small, heavily populated country situated on the coast of a major landmass in the Tropics. The land bulges out into a shallow gulf, and coastline forms 60 percent of its border. Isolated fishing villages dot the coast, but most of the fertile coastal plain is inhabited by farmers who work small subsistence rice paddies. The remainder of the countryside is mountainous, and here small farmers strive to eke a living from eroded hillsides denuded by years of deforestation.

The poverty of the mountains has driven thousands of families to the capital, which lies on the south coast of the country. Many families live in squalid shanty towns scattered throughout the city, and many have recently been moved to Puerto Esperanza, a controversial new town built on a marshy area several kilometers from the capital. Puerto Esperanza, touted by the government as a model community and criticized by the opposition as an instant slum, is less than one meter above the high-tide level.

CHRONOLOGY OF EVENTS FOR
THE BORRACHO REPUBLIC HURRICANE

August 27:

Ships passing through the Central Tropics report a rapid drop in baro-metric pressure to weather stations nearby. The weather stations pass this information to the International Hurricane Tracking Network (IHTN), which soon verifies the formation of a tropical depression and notifies the surrounding countries.

August 28:

Satellite observation and aircraft monitoring indicate that the depression has become a tropical storm.

In Borracho, the chief weather service forecaster follows procedure and notifies the director of the Emergency Preparedness Committee (EPC). The forecaster also reviews the difference between a hurricane watch (a first-stage alert given 48 hours before a hurricane is expected to strike) and a hurricane warning (posted when the hurricane is only 24 hours away). The director of the EPC notifies a few key government personnel and suggests that preliminary actions be taken in case a hurricane should develop. The government press agency is instructed to contact the weather bureau each hour to get an update on the storm information. One hour later, a synopsis of the storm is broadcast over the national radio system.

The public takes little notice of the storm, which is still more than 1200 kilometers away.

August 29:

Satellite photos and reconnaissance flights through the storm indicate that it is now a full-fledged hurricane. The IHTN alerts governments of the countries in the region and various international organizations including the United Nations Disaster Relief Office (UNDRO) and the League of Red Cross Societies.

The International Emergency Assistance Agency, an aid ministry of one of the countries that has helped Borracho to improve its disaster prepared-ness capabilities, offers expanded assistance should the hurricane strike.

At 2:00 P.M., the director of the EPC calls a meeting to bring members up-to-date on the hurricane's progress and projected direction. By 4:00 P.M., the scheduled time of the meeting, only half of the committee members have been located, and the meeting is postponed until 7:00 P.M.

Later the meeting convenes with only seven of the twelve members present. The weather service forecaster repeats his briefing. The committee asks him to predict the hurricane's path, which he refuses to do. One of the committee members goes into another room and telephones the International Hurricane Tracking Network. He is given a more detailed briefing and a description of the projected hurricane track. The briefer at the IHTN adds that in his own estimate the hurricane is not likely to strike Borracho because it is moving in a direction that will take it north of the country. The committee member returns and tells the committee what he has learned. The committee decides not to issue a statement because it would alarm the public.

Elsewhere, the monthly meeting of the Association of Humanitarian Agencies in Borracho (AHAB) is being held. At the end of the meeting, one of the members asks what plans are being made to prepare for the hurricane. The chairman replies, "Borracho doesn't have hurricanes."

August 30:
The hurricane intensifies and begins to move in a westward direction. The radio gives hourly reports on its position and notes that it has changed direction and is now moving toward the northeastern coast of Borracho.

At 10:00 A.M., another meeting of the EPC is called. The weather service has indicated that it will issue a hurricane watch that afternoon unless the storm changes direction. The committee begins to draw up its operational plans. The first item is to find a strong building with good communications to use as an emergency operations center.

Word leaks to the press that a hurricane watch will be issued later that day, and the announcement is carried in the hourly newscast on the national radio system. When the weather service is contacted for verification of the story, the forecasters deny that a watch has been set. The denial is reported on the radio the next hour.

During the afternoon, meetings are held at various government ministries to prepare for the hurricane. The protection of equipment critical to the operation of each ministry is given a high priority. Building materials and sandbags are requested from the public works department to protect installations in the low-lying and exposed areas, but available supplies are soon exhausted. Precautionary measures along the coast are fairly extensive; little attention is given to areas further inland.

The Borracho Red Cross reviews its plans for dealing with the disaster. It has a series of guides issued by the League of Red Cross Societies to serve as a model for its own activities. As staff review the guides, it becomes clear that most are for actions that should have been taken long ago, and there is little that can be done before the disaster strikes. Nevertheless, at the end of its meeting, the director notifies the government that "the Red Cross is ready."

In a large government hospital in the capital city, the administrator goes through his checklist. The backup generator is ready; the staff have been alerted; and a number of patients have been discharged early so that extra beds will be available in case of an emergency. One problem is found, however. The stockpile of drugs for diseases that the hospital administrator suspects might occur following a hurricane is low and in some cases, drugs are missing entirely. The administrator contacts the EPC, which in turn contacts the International Emergency Assistance Agency and asks that these medicines be sent immediately.

In the country that formerly ruled Borracho, which has a large Borrachian immigrant community, there is growing interest in the hurricane. The news media, sensing this interest, prepare to dispatch reporters to Borracho to cover the hurricane.

August 31:

At 1:00 A.M., the storm intensifies again. At 1:15 A.M., the weather service issues a hurricane warning.

The prime minister calls the EPC to check on its activities. The director assures the prime minister that everything possible is being done. At the same moment, the EPC is trying to develop an evacuation plan and to find a list of buildings designated as hurricane shelters to give to the news media.

At dawn, the citizens of Borracho awake to hear the radio announce the hurricane warning. The newspaper publishes the newly found list of buildings designated as hurricane shelters, some of which no longer exist. The EPC then goes on the radio with a "new" list of shelters and urges persons in low-lying areas along the coast to evacuate.

Within several hours, the police in the Rio Dulce area (a broad, low-lying river delta region) report that they cannot reach several fishing villages on the coast because rising tides have cut off the roads. The police request trucks and boats to help evacuate these villagers. The Borracho Defense Force sends several convoys of trucks carrying assault boats to help.

As a precautionary measure, the EPC recommends that residents of Puerto Esperanza be evacuated as soon as possible.

By noon the only signs of the approaching hurricane are the rising tides along the upper portions of the eastern coast. Winds are now gusting, and there are intermittent rain showers.

Members of the EPC are running out of time. Hundreds of details remain, and each minute someone thinks of some new precautionary measure that should be taken. One of the problems facing the committee is what to do about numerous complaints of profiteering in the sale of emergency supplies. At 2:30 P.M., the director asks the prime minister to declare such practices illegal, which he does in a newscast 30 minutes later.

At 3:00 P.M., the EPC receives a call from the International Emergency Assistance Agency informing it that it is impossible to deliver the requested medical supplies due to the proximity of the storm.

At 4:30 P.M., the foreign news teams arrive and begin their live televised reports. The first story describes the profiteering and shows pictures of several well-armed store owners defending their property against looters.

At 5:00 P.M., the weather service announces that the hurricane's course has now changed, putting it on a track for the central and southern portions of the country. The impact is predicted for the early morning hours of the following day. Winds are now gusting up to 60 kilometers per hour.

The EPC receives the news with great anxiety. Most of the preparedness activities have focused on the northern regions, not the south. Warnings are quicky issued to evacuate Puerto Esperanza.

Twenty minutes later, the prime minister goes on the national radio and television to issue a plea to all persons in low-lying areas to evacuate as quickly as possible. He suggests that those who cannot escape should seek shelter in churches and schools.

At nightfall, the column of army trucks arrives in the delta. Thousands of families have waited until the last moment to leave and are now trying to walk out of the area. The main road is packed with thousands of evacuees. After two hours, the trucks are unable to move any further.

In Puerto Esperanza, the sea level is one meter above normal. Water is coming across the road that separates the community from the sea, and large breakers are quicky eroding the roadbed. Vehicles attempting to evacuate have stalled. The residents of Puerto Esperanza begin moving away from the sea on the only other road that links the area with higher ground, but this road is also low and crosses two streams that are now flooding. At 10:00 P.M., a bridge collapses and the people are stranded.

Word of the plight of Puerto Esperanza is flashed to the EPC. It orders an army engineering battalion to attempt to evacuate the people. The army sends a truckload of small boats to the fallen bridge but, by the time it arrives, the surface is too rough and the plan is abandoned. Twenty-five hundred families begin scrambling to their rooftops. Two thousand people will not make it to safety.

Midnight:
Communication from the capital to outlying areas is lost.

At 2:00 A.M., passage of the eye of the hurricane is recorded at Puerto Blanco, 45 kilometers north of the capital. Winds in the capital reach a peak of 200 kilometers per hour.

Aftermath:

By dawn on September 1, the winds have subsided to 100 kilometers per hour, and a few people are beginning to venture outside to see the damage. By 10:00 A.M., winds are still gusty, but it is possible to leave shelters and other structures without too much danger.

In the capital, wind damage is severe. Almost every house has been damaged somewhat. The slums have suffered heavily, with total destruction of buildings as high as 85 percent in some areas. Casualties exceed the capacity of the hospital by 200 percent. A major disaster is reported at Puerto Esperanza, but has not yet been verified. No news has yet been received from the rural areas, and the Defense Force reports that contact has not been reestablished with the trucks sent to evacuate the delta.

At noon, the prime minister orders a helicopter to take him, the director of the EPC, the Red Cross chairman, and several cabinet ministers over the affected area. In their flight over the capital, the prime minister is shocked at the extent of the damage. As the helicopter moves over Puerto Esperanza, the extent of the devastation and loss of life is shockingly apparent. The few survivors cling to the tops of the few buildings that have survived the storm. As the helicopters of the prime minister's party swoop low overhead, all aboard see frantic gestures for help.

As the prime minister's helicopter returns, he is informed that a tidal wave has swept approximately 45 kilometers into the delta region. Overflights report that whole villages have vanished.

At the Emergency Operations Center, reports are fragmented and confused. The death toll and damage are reported high in all parts of the affected area. It is difficult to discern a pattern because the reports are not submitted in any standard form or classified according to priority. The Emergency Preparedness Committee is barraged by reporters clamoring for information. Members of the EPC decide that their first action should be to conduct an extensive survey of the damage. Their second action is to appoint the Red Cross as coordinator for all emergency relief.

On Embassy Row, ambassadors are beginning to receive cables asking if offers of aid should be made. One ambassador is upbraided for not sending an immediate disaster assessment and a request for aid.

By nightfall, more contingents of foreign press arrive. By the next day, their reports will have made Borracho the number one news story in the world.

At 8:00 P.M., the EPC meets with representatives of the voluntary agencies and the foreign embassies. The director of the EPC reports on casualties and damage and lists the pledges of aid and assistance that have been received from other governments. The agencies ask for instructions, but it soon becomes clear that no reconstruction plans or activities have been prepared. The EPC's apparent indecision and lack of leadership is reported to the prime minister.

All through the night, casualties continue to arrive at hospitals and aid stations in the affected zones.

Overseas, donations of relief goods are collected at voluntary agencies, churches, and the consulates of Borracho. Donations are especially heavy from communities with large numbers of Borrachians.

In Geneva at the headquarters of both UNDRO and the League of Red Cross Societies, lists are established to record all major donations. They are to be updated daily and sent to a long list of voluntary agencies and foreign ministries.

September 2:
At 7:00 A.M., the prime minister announces that he has taken personal command of the emergency operations and reconstruction and has appointed a new Disaster Relief Committee to take over from the EPC. He calls on the international community for help. He orders the army to patrol the city to prevent looting.

At 7:30 A.M., the Red Cross sends a telex to the League of Red Cross Societies requesting tents, clothing, medicine, and food.

In the foreign ministry, offers of assistance are pouring in. At the airport, the first flights of relief goods are arriving. They consist of tents, medicine, blankets, and military ration packs.

At 10:00 A.M., a local doctor reports a possible case of cholera. The prime minister orders mass innoculation of all persons in the disaster area.

At 11:00 A.M., hospitals appeal to the prime minister's office for assistance in replenishing medical supplies. The prime minister passes this request to the governments that have offered assistance. At the same time, the airlift of medical supplies requested prior to the emergency is arriving at the airport.

The voluntary agencies and churches hold a meeting at the damaged headquarters of the Association of Humanitarian Agencies in Borracho to decide what to do. After hours of discussion, they decide to donate all money received to the government and all materials to the Red Cross. Churches report that spontaneous donations of clothing are heavy and ask the Red Cross to arrange for helicopters to carry the donations to the mountains. The Red Cross agrees and diverts several helicopters from search-and-rescue operations. The director of the Red Cross will later lose his job over this decision.

At Red Cross headquarters, the first accurate casualty reports from outside the capital are beginning to arrive. Heavy losses are reported in the delta. The largest number of casualties occurred when churches and schools used as shelters collapsed or were flooded. In one church alone, 400 people are reported dead.

The Red Cross, severely constrained by lack of resources and with no real organizational infrastructure outside the capital, asks for a meeting with the government to clarify responsibilities. At this meeting, it is decided that the Red Cross will continue to have responsibility for relief coordination in the capital and that the government will reassume responsibility for all other areas.

In the industrialized countries, televised reports of the devastation have begun to arrive. The most vivid reporting is about the tragedy of Puerto Esperanza. The story depicts the ineptitude of the government and ends with a statement that, unless massive international assistance is received, survivors will starve to death. Overnight, relief agencies report donations in excess of half a million dollars.

Realizing that the telecast has had a major impact on donations, the director of a voluntary agency with a program in Borracho contacts the network and asks that the organizations working there be identified.

Several agencies decide to send their disaster officers or senior personnel to the area to assess needs and to coordinate emergency activities.

At UNDRO a decision is made to dispatch someone to assist in coordination and disaster assessment.

September 3:
The airlift of aid continues. The majority of aid is provided by foreign governments, many of which have stockpiles of relief goods. Shipments from nongovernmental agencies also begin to arrive. Some of these materials, especially aid from governments, come from stockpiles, and these are sorted, bundled, and well-marked. Other materials are simply packed according to size, with each bundle containing a hodgepodge of different materials, which must be sorted upon arrival in Borracho.

By midmorning, the Defense Force is besieged with politicians clamoring to use military helicopters to fly over the disaster area to see the damage.

By noon, groups of villagers from remote highland areas begin to filter into aid stations to report massive destruction and heavy loss of life due to landslides and flooding in the denuded mountains.

Overseas, more news stories arrive daily with scenes of death and destruction in Borracho. The voluntary agencies (volags) that do not have programs in Borracho feel public pressure to get involved. For years Alpha Organization, a medium-sized international development agency, has wanted to initiate a program in Borracho, but did not have the money. The overseas program coordinator argues that the hurricane has provided an

Stages in a disaster: *a* A satellite photo reveals a storm system. *b* The morning after, a storm has become a disaster for the inhabitants of this village. *c* A relief agency comes in to distribute supplies. *d* Sometimes, however, the aid is neither appropriate nor distributed soon enough to those who need it most. *e* Victims construct temporary housing out of available materials.

ideal opportunity to begin a program because funds can be raised not only for relief but also for development activities. Alpha decides to initiate an appeal and begins to recruit a staff for the Borracho program.

September 4:

After press reports of looting the previous night, the government slaps a nighttime curfew on the disaster area.

Now that certain roads have been re-opened, the government begins distribution of relief goods outside the capital. Supplies had been confined to deliveries of food and medicine by helicopter, but now truck convoys are able to take larger amounts and a wider variety of aid to the rural areas.

At the airport, a call goes out for volunteers to help sort relief materials. The sheer volume of the material and the confusion caused by poor packaging require several thousand people working at the airport and at other sorting centers.

Throughout the affected area, a tremendous salvage effort is taking place. People are busy trying to gather up as much building material as possible, especially the tin roofs found wrapped around trees, curled on the ground, or lying intact. Thousands of makeshift shelters have been built out of the rubble. Several foreign press correspondents assigned to do a story about the need for tents ask a group of victims to stop hammering so that their sound man can record an interview with a relief official arriving with a shipment of tents.

Overseas, the voluntary agencies are queried by the press about their plans for relief and reconstruction. Privately many of the staff are worried that more detailed programs have not been formulated. In order to speed things along, several agencies send additional staff to get things moving.

September 5:

At midday, the absence of clouds allows high-flying reconnaissance planes to photograph the area.

Helicopters arrive from the overseas military bases of a friendly government. Their first activity is to airlift a complete field hospital to the delta region.

Throughout the day, massive aid continues to arrive by air. Supplies are unloaded from military and commercial transports and transferred to helicopters for delivery to the rural areas.

In the capital, the Disaster Relief Committee calls a meeting of relief agencies. To reduce duplication of effort, the government asks each agency to take responsibility for relief and reconstruction in one particular sector. A list of communities is placed on the board and each agency selects one to assist. Several voluntary agencies that have worked in the country for many years are not present at the meeting (later referred to as the "lottery"), and the areas where they have had extensive experience are assigned to other agencies. No attempt is made to verify the qualifications or capacities of any of the new agencies present at the meeting.

September 6:
Reports of corruption and favoritism in the distribution of relief supplies are reported in the press. The prime minister asks the churches to form committees to oversee the distribution of relief goods in each community.

During the day, three different voluntary agencies call coordination meetings in separate locations.

At midday, the government calls for more volunteers to help sort and package incoming relief goods. The total number of people involved in sorting materials now exceeds 4500.

In the early afternoon, the prime minister visits Puerto Esperanza and promises massive aid in a rousing "phoenix from the ashes" speech broadcast on national radio and issues an appeal for cooperation from all political parties and factions in the reconstruction effort. Two hours later, the leader of the opposition calls a press conference where he notes "massive corruption" and vows to make equality of aid an issue in the next election.

September 7:
At 10:00 A.M., the Disaster Relief Committee calls a coordination meeting between the government and voluntary agencies to discuss housing reconstruction.

At midday, the UNDRO official arrives and offers to coordinate foreign assistance. The DRC agrees and that afternoon the UNDRO representative calls a coordination meeting for the next day.

That evening, a radio station operated by a group of evangelical missionaries resumes operation. Church leaders tell disaster victims that it is their sins that have brought calamity to Borracho and calls for a national of prayer.

September 8–14 (Week Two):
Throughout the week, aid continues to pour in. At the airport, aid is classified into two categories: the well-marked and -packaged aid arriving from governments and the more experienced relief agencies, and the so-called junk aid, which includes individual contributions and gifts thrown together and shipped with few, if any, markings. Many packages are irrelevant to the needs of the people of Borracho. Workers chortle amongst themselves about electric frying pans, cans of smoked oysters, used nylon

stockings, odd lots of shoes, and instant mashed potatoes (which are inadvertently used by a number of women as a laundry detergent).

During the morning, a group of visiting congressmen arrive on a fact-finding mission. They demand helicopters to fly over the disaster-stricken area. Later that day, an interim aid agreement between their government and Borracho is signed.

During the week, numerous coordination meetings are held—some under government sponsorship, others at the instigation of one or more of the voluntary agencies, and one called by UNDRO.

Early in the week, photographs from the high altitude reconnaissance flights arrive and are given to the government; Borracho, however, has no photo interpreters.

During the week, the relief agencies in Borracho are offered large donations from foundations, intergovernmental organizations, and their own governments. Most of the donors are anxious that the money benefit the victims as soon as possible; therefore they attach a restriction that the money be spent within thirty to ninety days.

Daily, new relief agencies (some "instant agencies," such as Friends of Borracho) arrive. They are assigned areas of responsbility by the DRC. Expatriate volunteers also start to arrive. Among this group are several doctors who pester local medical officials for assignments and interpreters.

Also arriving are a number of manufacturers' representatives from companies that produce small prefabricated buildings. Each claims to have the "ultimate solution" for rebuilding low-cost housing. Some houses are touted as temporary and others as permanent. The DRC, unable to choose among them, decides to hold a housing fair where the manufacturers can set up their units and show them to the public. The people's preferences will be determined and a housing system will be selected.

At a meeting of the DRC, many village relief committees report long lines for food at distribution centers. The same day, the government is offered a huge food-aid package of surplus commodities. There is one restriction: the food must be given away. Despite some opposition from farmers and cooperatives, the government signs the food-aid agreement.

At midweek, the hospital administrator reports a new problem. Parents have been arriving to look for small children evacuated from the mountains by helicopter. The DRC asks a voluntary agency to help reunite families.

Several embassies in Borracho advise the volags that they have money for housing reconstruction and they will accept proposals if they are submitted within one week. Proposed projects must be completed within sixty to ninety days.

Several embassies also offer the volags surplus food commodities to distribute. The food must be given away or distributed in food-for-work schemes.

At a meeting of the DRC, several agencies point out that the distribution of free aid to the victims can be counterproductive. The chairman of the DRC reacts firmly, saying that to ask victims to pay for food or other aid would be against the humanitarian principles of disaster relief, and he orders that all aid be given free to the victims. Several local development groups argue that this will create dependencies, but the government is adamant.

In the private sector, architects and engineers offer their services to voluntary agencies as advisors. At first the agencies are excited at the prospect of having this technical assistance, but they soon discover that few of the professionals are familiar with the traditional housing built by the majority of the people in the country and that their idea of low-income housing is far too expensive for most of the agencies, not to mention the victims themselves.

Housing is rapidly becoming a major issue. The chairman of the DRC appeals for rapid housing action, citing the approaching rainy season (five months off). He states that it is government policy that all housing must be made of "permanent materials" that are hurricane-proof. A few agencies point out that the cost of permanent construction will limit the number of people who can be served and that so-called permanent materials require more sophisticated reinforcement for safety. The government, however, refuses to change its policy.

September 15–21 (Week Three):
During the third week, emphasis begins to shift away from emergency relief activities to concern about interim recovery and longer-term reconstruction needs.

Foreign military engineers arrive with heavy equipment to help repair roads and bridges, and most of the roads are soon reopened.

Helicopter pilots report fewer cargoes and are withdrawn. The prime minister, sensing a change in mood, appoints a National Reconstruction Committee to coordinate long-term recovery, but announces that the Disaster Relief Committee will remain active until all relief needs have been met.

By this time, a central volag coordinating committee, acting under the leadership of the Association of Humanitarian Agencies in Borracho, has evolved. It is subdivided into various "topic" committees to deal with issues such as housing and agricultural recovery.

Late in the week, groups of international banking officials arrive for talks on reconstruction loans to the government. The prime minister orders the Finance Ministry to give top priority to refinancing the national debt.

Insurance adjusters complete their initial reports. The business community is pleased that most claims will be paid promptly and that the insurance companies have been lenient. The businessmen begin to hire construction workers to help rebuild. The wages for carpenters and masons skyrocket and even tradesmen with limited skills find there is no lack of jobs.

There are reports that a boom economy is developing and prices are climbing at an astounding rate, especially for materials and tools that will be used in reconstruction. The government, fearful of creating a black market, hesitates to establish price controls.

The Disaster Relief Committee is informed that relief goods, including food from the food-for-work programs, are showing up in local markets. The government issues an order banning such sales.

Local farmers protest the distribution of free food, and farmers' organizations report that, if the food donations continue, farmers who have been able to salvage some of their crops will have no market for them.

Housing reconstruction and agricultural recovery are proving difficult for some of the volags. They cable their headquarters for permission to hire several noted specialists recommended by a local university. Fearful that the hiring of consultants will add to overhead costs that donors would criticize, the headquarters decide against hiring the specialists.

The National Housing Bank announces low-interest loans for housing repair and replacement, with special criteria to enable the poor to apply.

The field director of Beta Aid, a voluntary agency, reports difficulties in setting up the reconstruction program outlined in his initial proposal and requests an extension of the ninety-day limit. The donor refuses, citing public pressures to act quickly. In order to speed the program, the field director hires workers from another region, chooses a simple design for all the houses, and begins to mass-produce them. The Beta program will later be praised among the foreign agencies as a model of speed and efficiency, but condemned by local people as a program that built slipshod housing and failed to employ people in the disaster area in need of work and cash.

Overseas, Borracho no longer retains front-page interest, and voluntary agencies note a sharp decline in donations.

September 22–28 (Week Four):
At the beginning of the week, the UNDRO representative submits his final report on the disaster and then leaves the country. The coordination meetings, now poorly attended, are reduced to biweekly affairs. The prime minister declares that the emergency is over and lifts the curfew.

The government announces a change in policy on the distribution of relief goods and agrees to allow sales of certain items. It also goes on record as encouraging the subsidized sale of building materials. It is left to the agencies to establish eligibility requirements. In the countryside, the differing programs and varying levels of assistance provided by each agency lead to complaints by the disaster victims. The National Reconstruction Committee (NRC) considers setting uniform reconstruction policies. After much discussion, it decides not to set the policies, fearing that the voluntary agencies and their donors will resent such a move.

New agencies continue to arrive. Those already operational report a large number of visitors "touring" the programs for ideas and advice. Some agencies complain that visitors are taking up excessive amounts of their time.

In some areas, agencies form consortia to work together, but in other cases, rivalries develop and agencies become bitter critics of each other.

Many programs report a sudden loss of staff. Until now volunteers filled the majority of positions and carried out almost all of the relief work. As relief efforts wind down, volunteers leave to return to their normal work. Among the first to go are farmers and unskilled laborers. Some offer to continue working if the agencies will pay a decent wage, but the agencies refuse to do so, believing that people should not be paid for helping themselves. As the defections increase, however, the policies of the agencies change and a number of workers are retained at minimal wages.

In a remote mountain village, ECHO International (a newly arrived agency) calls a town meeting and, through interpreters, tells the people that ECHO has been assigned to help rebuild the village. It orders the people to stop rebuilding until the agency decides what to do.

News media in Borracho report that reconstruction programs are inadvertently helping only landowners and homeowners, because renters will not rebuild houses for fear that the owners will then force them out. The issue of the land tenure pattern and the need for land reform are not mentioned.

Overseas, news accounts also mention reconstruction inequities. Several agencies are accused of not reaching the poorest of the poor. One agency that has elected to concentrate on rebuilding and improving traditional housing is criticized for rebuilding slums. Other news reports criticize the aid programs for inadvertently supporting a corrupt, nonrepresentative government.

October–March:

Aid continues to arrive. The local relief committees have been re-formed as reconstruction committees. Food aid is now arriving in ever increasing quantities. There is continuing opposition to the food program, however, especially from the Agricultural Ministry. Its fears that farmers would not replant are coming true. The ministry thus proposes a system of price supports, but the only farms eligible are the larger farms along the coast.

Continued complaints over inequities in aid lead the government again to consider establishing uniform reconstruction policies. After much debate, the NRC decides to develop a "model approach" and recommend that agencies use it as a guide. The agencies completely ignore it.

A group of landless tenant farmers, left homeless by the hurricane and led by community organizers from the opposition party, occupies a large tract of undeveloped land at the edge of the capital. The government, fearing the political consequences of evicting it, agrees to acquire the land and sell it to the families. To keep the incident from being repeated, the government announces that people involved in the occupation will not receive financial assistance or materials for housing reconstruction. A church agency offers to provide building materials in defiance of the government. Other landless families then embark on similar "invasions."

At a meeting of the NRC, a group of low-income families from a large town in the Rio Dulce region protests that the agency assigned to its community has not been seen since the day after the "lottery." A check by the NRC reveals that the organization, Wings of Deliverance, is not a registered charity but a tax shelter created by several businessmen to justify a trip to Borracho. The total contribution of Wings of Deliverance is one thousand dollars.

As reconstruction progresses, the government realizes that its policy on permanent housing is unrealistic and agrees to permit reconstruction programs to rebuild traditional housing as long as the resulting construction is "safe." The Housing Bank, however, refuses to grant loans to people working with traditional materials.

Other problems complicate reconstruction. Land costs escalate. Small farmers unable to recover sell their land and move to the towns. In the capital, it is especially hard to find adequate housing. The number of land invasions increases.

At a meeting of the NRC, the secretary reports on a survey of housing reconstruction programs. Forty-five nongovernmental organizations are involved in housing reconstruction. Twenty-nine are located in the capital or the immediate vicinity, ten are located along the highway connecting the capital and the delta, and the other six are located in the mountains. The report also shows that only 35 percent of the total area affected by the hurricane is receiving reconstruction assistance. Therefore the government must establish a housing program to fill the gaps.

The prime minister orders the Ministry of Housing to begin constructing housing projects for disaster victims. Puerto Esperanza, where the reconstruction efforts have been very slow, is selected as the site for the first of the new housing projects.

Overseas, Borracho is gone from public consciousness. Funding for volag reconstruction projects must now compete with other projects or get by on the remainder of the donations raised during the emergency.

Returning home, a relief organization prepares a ten-page "evaluation" of its program that consists mainly of a brief description of the hurricane, a summary of the materials donated, and a picture of its disaster officer with the prime minister.

Midyear:

Six months after the disaster, all but a few foreign agencies have departed, claiming to have completed reconstruction of their assigned areas. The NRC surveys indicate that work is incomplete. Sixty percent of the urban residents and 85 percent of the people in the rural areas are still without replacement housing.

Midyear marks the end of the first post-disaster harvest. Observers notice a resurgence in housing demand, as people now have the time and capital to rebuild. However, only a few agencies remain to provide technical or financial assistance. Even among those agencies that want to stay, funds for continued operations are not available. To help meet the new demand, the government seeks a loan from the International Bank to finance other reconstruction activities. After two months, the loan is approved in principle, but funds cannot be made available until the next fiscal year, further delaying reconstruction.

In the agricultural sector, surveys indicate that decreased agricultural production necessitates continued food aid for another year. A report by the Agricultural Ministry that the number of small farmers has declined by seven to ten percent, and that a significant portion of the land formerly devoted to growing rice in the delta region is now used to produce cotton and other cash crops, goes unnoticed.

•   •   •

Having now experienced the Borracho hurricane, what was wrong in the various responses? Keep this scenario in mind as you read further. You may also wish to return to this chapter after you have finished the book.

4
Community Reaction to a Disaster

COPING MECHANISMS

In order to understand how a society responds to a disaster, it is necessary to understand more about a little-known subject, namely, how a society "copes" with an unusual or stressful situation. In every society there is a variety of internal social structures that help individuals and families through difficult periods. These are known as coping mechanisms. In a disaster, they become collective instruments for organizing action on behalf of the disaster victims. The relationship of individuals and families within this system may be either formal or informal. Generally, the relationship has been worked out over generations. Each person knows how to react and use the various mechanisms available. Examples of coping mechanisms are: the family, the extended family, religious organizations, and clans. They can include more formal organizations such as villages and local governments. In Latin America the *patron* system would also be included. Coping mechanisms have been classified by anthropologist Margaret Kieffer (1977) as either internal or external.

Internal Mechanisms

SOCIAL UNITS

The most basic coping mechanism is that of the family. In its simplest form, the nuclear family consists of parents and their children. Extended families consist of more than one nuclear family that are related by kinship, share a common residence, or are joined together in economic activities with an authoritative or ceremonial head. Social units are the strongest of all the coping mechanisms. Kinship is a strong bond, and even when members of a family unit move away from a community, there remains a strong

80

association and obligation to those remaining. In time of need, people may look to their family for support if a strong social tie remains.

In a disaster, the primary means for coping are the social units. Families first help members of their own family, then relatives, then neighbors. In the immediate emergency period, assistance includes searching for and rescuing victims, transporting them to nearby medical facilities, recovering belongings and erecting emergency shelter, providing temporary lodging to those who have lost their homes or are still threatened by the disaster, providing immediate food supplies, clothes, and blankets if they are required, and the mutual sharing of salvage and repair work. The comforting of each other during this time is one of the most important aspects of coping.

In the transition phase, it is the social unit that is most looked to for emotional recovery. During reconstruction, family and friends offer a combination of money and labor to help the victims or each other to restore homes and agriculture.

RELIGIOUS INSTITUTIONS

Examples include local religious institutions such as churches, mosques, temples, and the social organizations affiliated with them, such as men's and women's societies and social service organizations. Religious institutions help individuals to cope in a number of ways. During the emergency period, many people look to religious organizations for leadership, and this is probably their most valuable function. Religious institutions and leaders also provide much in the way of emotional support and comfort to the victims. More functional assistance includes provision of shelter and burials. In some areas, churches are called upon to ensure that emergency aid is distributed equitably. In Dominica, following Hurricane David, the Dominican Christian Council was asked to supervise much of the early distribution of relief goods.

During the transitional phase, religious institutions continue to provide leadership and social services, and many take on such additional roles as lending money, providing small cash grants and material aid to meet individual needs, and serving as consignee for relief goods. In Jamaica, following the 1979 floods, many churches that owned land in the disaster-affected area loaned or leased it to flood victims so that they could plant crops and cultivate them while waiting for the flood waters to recede.

In the reconstruction period, direct involvement of most religious organizations tends to fade, except for the leadership role. Religious organizations are, however, an excellent contact for outside groups, allowing them entry into the community. They thus serve as a major focal point for long-term reconstruction actions.

Survivors of the Guatemalan earthquake turned to the church to cope with the disaster. (Photo: Ron Sawyer)

POLITICAL ORGANIZATIONS

At the village level, the number of political organizations is fairly limited. These include local formal or informal government (a mayor or town council, or village chief and village elders), local chapters of the major political parties, and the local offices of the provincial or national government. Political parties play a major role in disasters only if the party structure is the de facto government of an area, such as is the case in many socialist countries. The degree to which local offices of provincial or national governments can play a part in disaster response depends on the degree of autonomy that is granted and, of course, the leadership qualities of the persons within each of the government agencies.

Following disasters, the internal political organizations provide a variety of assistance to disaster victims. During the emergency, the local government provides leadership, supervises the distribution of relief goods, organizes and supervises evacuations, and provides equipment and tools. If the situation demands, the local government can also be called upon to provide order and protection.

During the transitional phase, the government continues to provide leadership and, in many cases, serves the additional important function of providing information. At the same time, government concentrates on those areas that are normally within its special responsibility; that is, the restoration of community services, especially the repair and reconstruction of critical facilities and lifelines. Governments also often provide land to disaster victims, either for temporary occupation or permanent resettlement.

During the reconstruction period, the government again provides leadership and also planning services. Local governments aid or serve as a point for the distribution of the national or provincial government's assistance to victims. For example, local governments may run a credit scheme for the national government.

ECONOMIC SYSTEMS

There are three such systems: informal, interpersonal economic relationships; patronage; and mutual assistance organizations such as cooperatives, labor unions, guilds, or federations. In the villages, a relative or friend within the community may make loans to an individual. The *patrón* in rural Latin American communities is usually a person or organization that employs a large number of peasants or *peónes*. It benefits the *patrón* to help his *peónes* recover quickly from a disaster, as it helps to keep up production. Aid from a *patrón* may be in the form of time or money, although recovery will rarely be to a level above what the *peón* had known before.

Mutual aid groups such as cooperatives are becoming more and more prevalent in the developing countries. They may be of a type formed within the community itself, or an affiliate of an organization with regional or national membership. The greatest number of these organizations are agricultural cooperatives and labor unions. In a disaster, these organizations provide leadership as well as some degree of financial security. Members of the organization often band together during the transition and reconstruction phases to help each other out in various reconstruction activities. These organizations can be the source of loans and grants to individual members and, in rural areas, are often among the first to be able to provide seeds, tools, and fertilizers for agricultural recovery. In recent years, international relief organizations have looked increasingly to co-operatives as their counterparts in the delivery of disaster assistance.

Local economic organizations usually play a major part only in transition and reconstruction phases. During this time, their contributions are one of the most important factors in the conclusion of a successful post-disaster program.

External Mechanisms

External mechanisms include social organizations, church-related groups, political organizations, economic institutions, social and economic development organizations, and in some cases, the national government.

The effectiveness of external organizations depends largely upon their ability to understand and deal with the cultural constraints within the host society, their view of development, and their ability to communicate effectively with the victims.

These groups may become involved during any phase of a disaster. Organizations with a wide national base can be among the most effective in assessing and providing early emergency aid. Many international relief agencies have found national groups to be effective counterparts for channeling disaster assistance.

Summary of Mechanisms

Margaret Kieffer (1977) has devolved several generalizations about coping mechanisms. The following are among her most important observations.

1. In any coping situation, that which is most familiar will enhance the coping mechanism and its ability to operate.
2. The less complex rural cultures have shorter recovery periods.
3. In more complex situations, alternatives at the internal level are diminished; conversely, external mechanisms are more applicable to the urban settings.
4. In the rural communities, external mechanisms will be more efficient and effective if they operate through an existing internal mechanism.
5. The more contact a traditional culture has had previously with modern culture, the more readily will it accept assistance.
6. *Strong external influence may act, often inadvertently, to break up internal coping mechanisms and their effectiveness.*

The effects of intervention on coping mechanisms are the subject of the next chapter.

CLASSES OF VICTIMS

For present purposes, there are three classes of disaster victims. First are primary victims—those persons living within the disaster-affected area who have suffered injury, the loss of relatives, or damage to their property.

Secondary victims are those residing within the affected area or on the border of the affected area, who suffer economic loss due to the disaster or to actions resulting from relief operations. Examples of secondary victims are those involved in economic activities dependent upon goods or crops destroyed by disaster, or shopkeepers with stores inside the disaster area who are not able to sell their goods either because of lack of cash on the part of the victims or because materials that are normally sold have been supplied without charge by relief agencies.

Tertiary victims are those who are indirectly affected, who live in the same country but not necessarily in the disaster-affected area. For example, people receiving development aid suddenly lose this aid because resources are reallocated for the disaster victims. This occurred in Andhra Pradesh, India, following the 1977 cyclone. Within the region, water was allocated evenly during the main growing season to three different irrigation systems. After the summer season, there was only enough water left to supply one sector for a second crop. Thus the water was supplied to each system once every three years. The cyclone struck two of these sectors just before the summer crop was to be harvested. Though it was not the turn of either sector to receive water for a winter crop, the government decided to shift the water allocation to one of the affected sectors, so that those who had lost their crops would be able to plant again and thus recoup some of their losses. The farmers in the sector that was to have received water that year thus had to share the burden for the disaster. Many were small farmers already living a marginal existence, and the reallocation of the water cut heavily into their economic livelihood.

COMMON MYTHS ABOUT VICTIM BEHAVIOR

Earlier we looked at some of the common myths about the cause and effects of disasters, especially as they relate to victims' needs. There are, however, a number of other myths that shape the perception of international agencies and the donor public that should be reviewed and debunked.

The first of these myths is that victims are totally helpless in disasters. As we have seen, this is not the case. The victims always have a variety of resources upon which to draw, and each society has many ways of dealing with disaster. It has often been pointed out that the lower on the socioeconomic scale, the more self-reliant the family is; the more self-reliant, the easier it is to cope with disaster.

The second myth, and one that is perpetuated by the relief agencies, is that disasters are situations that require outside assistance in order for the victims to cope. Here is an example of the type of headline that often appears:

VICTIMS CAN'T COPE
WITHOUT YOUR HELP

This is a gross distortion of the actual fact. Outside assistance has the potential to be helpful if provided in the right way, but Third World societies have coped without outside assistance for centuries, and until aid is provided in a culturally sensitive manner, its benefit will continue to be limited.

Myth number three is that disasters wipe out indigenous coping mechanisms—that somehow the disaster creates a condition where local organizations (both formal and informal) are not capable of operating properly. Research has shown that, contrary to popular belief, a crisis reinforces local coping mechanisms and that local organizations often work better in times of crisis than in normal periods. As we shall see later, the true danger is that aid programs that ignore local coping mechanisms often disrupt the latter's ability to function properly and in some cases damage them by undermining their credibility within the community.

A myth believed by many people, probably generated by Hollywood, is that victims respond to disasters with abnormal behavior. It is a commonly held view that disasters incite panic, hysteria, rioting, and shock and leave victims too dazed to deal with the situation. Numerous sociological studies have shown that this is not the case. Even in times of war, people usually react deliberately both during and immediately after the disaster. While it is true that much confusion reigns and social organization may be disrupted, very quickly there is a coming together that results in spontaneous action by the refugees as they look after their own interests. Abnormal behavior is the extreme exception, not the rule.

A corollary to this is that grief traumatizes disaster victims to the point where they must be led into activities in order to save themselves. While it is true that grief and shock often follow the loss of close relatives in a disaster, grief is something that must be worked out individually and something that relief agencies are rarely prepared to deal with. Coping with grief is an individual process. It is doubtful that any relief program, however well-intentioned, could help victims overcome their losses simply by providing material aid.

II
Intervention

5
Disaster Assistance: Some Concerns

The disaster and the havoc that it causes form only one part of the picture. The ways in which agencies respond to disasters and the implications of that response for the development of the affected countries are of major concern, for inappropriate responses, constituting a second disaster, occur frequently.

The popular concept of disaster assistance is as follows. Soon after a disaster strikes, resources are marshaled and shipped in. Foreign agencies work hand-in-hand with local government, relief committees, and societies to provide organization and matériel to replace disaster losses. After several months, reconstruction begins and soon things return to normal. Disaster assistance is seen as humanitarian assistance, and humanitarian assistance is viewed by most as above question. After all, if one is trying to help, how can that be bad?

If there were no further concerns, there would be no need for this book. But there is a far greater range of issues to be considered, the implications of which are just becoming more clearly understood. Unfortunately, many relief and development agencies have not yet even identified these issues, much less begun to come to grips with them.

EFFECTS OF INTERVENTION ON COPING MECHANISMS

It is imperative that an intervenor attempting to conduct a relief or reconstruction program first identify the various coping mechanisms that exist and understand their role in society. Otherwise the relief program could damage the coping mechanisms or substantially reduce their effectiveness. This is especially the case with external coping mechanisms. As they play a major role in the society even in normal times, the danger is that the intervenor, in order to attain short-term goals, will have an overall negative effect on society in the long-term. Many development programs depend upon these coping mechanisms and on the self-reliance that they encourage.

Unfortunately, most intervenors do not understand the role played by coping mechanisms in a culture. Many cannot identify them, nor do they make an attempt to do so.

As outsiders, they are not familiar with the society and how it works. Even agencies working in the area prior to a disaster, who are familiar with some of the coping mechanisms, may not have seen how they work collectively to respond to a disaster.

Intervenors are often blinded to the long-term implications of a program by the more obvious short-term emergency needs created by the disaster. In a very real, humane attempt to respond urgently to these needs, they often do not take the time to explore and identify what is currently happening in the community.

Intervenors operate without the social and anthropological data and background that is needed to identify coping mechanisms. Even in the more sophisticated relief agencies, there are few full-time staff members capable of conducting an analysis of the disaster-affected society and providing information that can be used for planning programs. While agencies have attempted to retain sociologists or anthropologists for short-term analyses, these efforts have usually fallen far short of providing the type of information that program planners can use to develop a program.

Thus a major problem confronting any intervenor is how to identify the coping mechanisms that exist in the society and how to relate outside help to these built-in disaster response systems. Furthermore, outside assistance must be provided in such a way as to encourage a collective response using these mechanisms. Failure to do so can create a large number of problems that may ultimately damage or destroy the mechanisms as a means of coping. Intervention can do this in any one of the following ways.

First, it can undermine the authority and prestige of local leaders. When a major relief program with resources of material, staff, and equipment is established, it creates an instant alternative to local resources. If local leaders are not involved, their prestige may be affected and they may eventually lose authority.

Intervention can become a disincentive to self-help. In many communities, the expectation of aid has delayed reconstruction efforts. In Guatemala, following the 1976 earthquakes, a study of three villages showed that when one village, which was rather small and isolated, learned of the massive relief efforts being undertaken in nearby communities, it delayed initiating activities that the people were perfectly capable of undertaking themselves (Rosene 1977).

Even within a single community, intervention can become a disincentive to self-help. In the village of San Andres Itzapa, Guatemala, an intervenor "adopted" the village to provide reconstruction assistance and ordered a halt to all local activities until the intervenor could decide what it was going to do (Rosene 1977). While this is an extreme case, the very presence of an outside agency and curiosity about what it intends to do, especially if no local leaders are involved in the decision-making process, can in itself be a major disincentive.

Massive intervention can undermine confidence in the coping mechanisms, especially external ones. It can do this in one of two ways. First, local agencies with only limited resources can come to be perceived as ineffective. The experience in Guatemala provides a good example of this. Local agencies could offer only a limited amount of materials for housing and shelter. The foreign agencies, on the other hand, could provide whole houses. Thus many Guatemalans began to deride the local agencies for their limited resources and capabilities.

Second, local agencies are often judged by the standard of the intervenor rather than on the basis of their own contributions.

Few intervenors are familiar with the development issues within a community prior to their intervention. Thus they stand a good chance of reinforcing the status quo and patterns of underdevelopment. Researchers have noted that following disasters, the victims often become more dependent on local *patróns*, especially lending institutions and community power brokers, than they were prior to the disaster (Rosene 1977). Basic problems within a community are often exacerbated by the disaster, but the ability to deal with the disaster collectively has been reduced and the power transferred from indigenous coping organizations to an oligarchy or an organization seeking vaster control over the society. In a recent disaster in the Caribbean, a foreign relief agency formed a committee made up of residents of the community whom they perceived as leaders to handle the relief and reconstruction program. Just prior to the disaster, however, the people in the community had formed a social and political movement to wrest power from precisely the same group of people and had begun to take economic and political control of the community. The actions of the relief agency, which were taken primarily because these "leaders" spoke the language of the intervenors, led to the oligarchy regaining control of the community through the way in which it distributed the reconstruction and relief aid.

Relief efforts may obscure underlying political realities. Often, contradictions and inadequacies within a society are brought to light in a disaster and its aftermath. Just as disaster relief may hinder a positive adjustment to natural hazards, it may also hinder appropriate social and political adjustments. In many cases, the very offer of bilateral relief is based on political and economic considerations. Here massive disaster relief has served to obscure perception of social realities and inhibit a process of positive adjustment.

Even when the intervenors try to use the local coping mechanisms, their intervention can often still be disruptive. Simply overloading the abilities of a local group and its staff is a common problem. The old saw that the best way to kill an organization is to give it too much money appears to have validity in disaster practice. A corollary, of course, is to give too much work or to expect too much from the members of the local group. Overloading an organization in this manner only makes it appear weak and ineffective.

Finally, intervention can wipe out the development efforts of indigenous organizations almost instantly. One of the primary goals of development efforts is to encourage self-reliance on the part of the people. Yet a massive relief program that does not take development questions into consideration can create disincentives to self-reliance, can establish dependencies on outside organizations, and can foster doubts on the part of the people about their own ability to control their lives and destinies. The chaos left behind when intervenors do not fully consider the implications and impact of their programs can delay, and in some cases even inhibit, further development work. Following the 1977 cyclone in Andhra Pradesh, the development organizations coming into the area reported difficulty in developing economic and agricultural programs due to the animosity resulting from the ways previous relief programs had been conducted (ARTIC 1978).

The development issues most overlooked by intervenors are, in summary:

1. *The need to facilitate cooperative actions.* It has been frequently shown that if a society is to develop socially or economically, it must attain a degree of sophistication in conducting cooperative activities. Many agencies overlook this connection, and some of their programs have reduced the possibility of cooperative action in future programs.
2. *Participation in decision making.* An agency that offers a pre-determined plan or one prepared without the full participation of the disaster victims misses the opportunity to increase the people's ability to make choices and to help them attain self-confidence in decision making. In essence, this represents a continuation of one of the major obstacles to development.
3. *Dependency relationships.* The degree of dependency on institutions or resources beyond the control of a low-income population is a major contributor to social and economic underdevelopment. The dependency relationship may involve leadership, money, or materials. Depen-

dency relationships are normally very one-sided in favor of the provider. Many relief and reconstruction programs have been shown not only to maintain the dependency relationships but in some cases to establish new ones (Taylor 1977).

4. *Political reform.* Foreign intervention often ignores fundamental political problems within a society and therefore tends to exacerbate the pre-disaster situation.

5. *Political reform and land tenure.* Few agencies recognize the long-term impact of relief programs, especially in the field of housing, on land tenure.

6. *Fostering unrealistic expectations.* It has been pointed out that many relief programs have led to unrealistic expectations on the part of the recipients. The provision of free housing for a relatively small number of people following the Andhra Pradesh cyclone created the expectation that everyone who had lost a house would soon be receiving a *pukka* (brick and cement) house from either the government or a relief agency. In fact, it was impossible for the government to provide housing of this type for even one-tenth of the total number of affected families.

It should be clear now that relief and reconstruction programs cannot be viewed or carried out as separate or distinct operations. They must be conducted in the same manner as development programs.

It is apparent that many organizations, including some of the most progressive development groups, fail to make this connection and, prompted by the urgent post-disaster needs, concentrate their energies on rapid delivery of relief items. The approaches that they would normally use in development (such as extensive citizen participation, support of existing social systems, development of local initiatives) are all put aside in the belief that the disaster requires an immediate response and the development approach is too slow. Organizations that normally encourage "bottom-up" decision making suddenly take on a "top-down" orientation.

Yet normal development approaches cannot be discarded in emergencies. Experience has shown that they must be used in developing and executing all relief and reconstruction projects. Organizations that disregard the development approach can set back or even wipe out years of progress toward development.

THE NATURE OF THE AGENCY-VICTIM RELATIONSHIP

The first and most important set of issues that agencies need to deal with concerns the way in which they relate to the victims. The interrelationship between agency and victims is the major factor determining whether a relief

program succeeds. But even further, it is also the major factor determining
the impact the relief program will have on the society.

Almost from the very beginning of intervention, the first question that
arises is one of accountability. Ask staff members of almost any relief
organization to whom they are accountable, and they will probably reply to
their home office, to their accountants and, almost always, to the agency's
donors. Some may respond that they are also accountable to the government of the country in which they are working. A few may even say that they
are accountable to their counterpart agency in the country. But where in
this list is the victim? If this is truly the helping relationship that most
agencies would like to achieve, why has the victim been left out?

The lack of accountability does not translate to a lack of concern for the
well-being of the people in the affected community. But without at least
some accountability to the victims, agencies come to feel that they have
almost free rein in developing their programs and are not responsible for
either the consequences or the impact (not that many agencies ever even
consider that the impact might possibly be negative).

The concept of accountability to the victims of a disaster is a concept long
overdue in relief practice. Without accountability, programs inevitably
become paternalistic in nature or end up serving the needs of the donors
and the agencies rather than the needs of the victims. Unfortunately,
accountability requires a complicated and time-consuming approach to
problem solving, rather than a streamlined, simple one.

Paternalism is often the most difficult thing for relief agencies to come to
grips with. In any cross-cultural situation (whether involving persons from
agencies in the advanced nations and someone from the Third World, or
persons from different ethnic or socioeconomic classes within a society),
there is potential for paternalism to be either expressed or felt. Paternalism
may be overtly expressed, but more often it takes subtle forms. This is not
to say that it is intentional; but the fact remains that it is there. For example,
the people within the relief or reconstruction program are more often
designated as recipients than participants.

If a relief program is set up by intervenors from outside the community
and all decisions are made by the intervenors, what message is expressed to
the people in the community? What they may infer is that they are not able
or trusted to handle their own needs. Certainly a demonstration of massive
response points to the inadequacy of the local government and its agencies;
and the more decision making that is removed from the local community,
the more the feeling of helplessness is accentuated. The central question in
determining whether a program is paternalistic is deciding whether it

supplements and complements the existing community processes, or ignores them altogether. If it ignores them, the chances are that there is an assumption of inadequacy and the program is subtly reinforcing the feeling of helplessness on the part of the victims.

In an extreme case, this feeling of helplessness can pervade an entire culture. The situation in Bangladesh is often cited as typifying the problems of paternalistic aid. In 1970, when a massive storm surge and cyclone swept inland from the Bay of Bengal, killing over 250,000 people, massive relief efforts were mounted within the country. The following year, a fierce civil war broke out, displacing 20 million people, disrupting agriculture and commerce, and bringing the country to a complete standstill.

Following the war and achievement of independence for Bangladesh, further relief efforts were mounted by the international community to help the country recover. So extensive were these efforts that relief agencies provided assistance in almost every field, and foreign advisors could be found in virtually every ministry from agriculture to health. Bangladesh was proclaimed an "international basket case" and in the five years after the civil war, millions of dollars worth of material aid, food, and technical assistance were given to the country.

Despite the aid, tremendous food shortages existed within various sectors and aid agencies continually called upon the world community to respond to the needs of Bangladesh. Soon almost everyone believed that Bangladesh as a nation was totally helpless and gradually starving to death. The people in Bangladesh began to feel the same way. The more aid came in, the more they "realized" how helpless they were! In this situation, many of the Bengali professional class "bailed out" and emigrated; those that chose to stay constantly talked about how bad things were and how more aid was needed. Soon those Bengalis who were in charge of various programs designed to reverse the declining situation began to believe that they could not find Bengali solutions and that they themselves were inadequate for the tasks at hand. It became commonplace within the government to assume that everyone was starving and that the situation was totally hopeless. Bangladesh became a self-fulfilling prophecy.

A special set of problems in the agency-victim relationship occurs when the intervention results in the first extensive contact an isolated rural community has with outsiders. In the past two decades, there have been few areas untouched by such intrusions; but in many parts of the world, the influence and impact have been limited. When a disaster occurs in a remote area and massive outside aid is brought in, the villagers may have access for the first time to modern goods and services. For example, some villages in Africa had their first contact with modern medicine, education, and mechanization with the coming of relief aid during the Sahel drought.

The way in which this aid is provided can affect the way the recipients come to perceive not only the goods and services involved, but also the delivery mechanisms. If the first contact is one in which everything is given away and no return is asked, either in the form of work or cash, might not the recipients begin to believe that these services should be provided indefinitely on the same basis? A further concern is whether continued delivery over a long period of time can create a feeling of dependency.

For the development agency providing long-term aid, the agency-victim relationship can be especially difficult. Many agencies that have worked for years to develop local leadership and to foster community participation in decision making rush to provide massive aid like everyone else. If the agency succumbs to the "disaster syndrome" and drops its development approach in favor of charity, it stands a good chance of wiping out much of what it accomplished in its previous work. In the eyes of the people, the agency suffers "image reversal" when it abandons development goals for a welfare approach.

Unfortunately, even if an agency continues to use development approaches, it runs the risk of being adversely affected by competing relief programs. For example, World Neighbors had been working in the Central Highlands of Guatemala (in the communities of San Martín, Chimalte-nango, and San José Poaquil) for many years prior to the 1976 earthquakes. During this time, it had worked to develop local leadership, to form cooperative savings and loan institutions, and to encourage self-reliance in a variety of community concerns. After the earthquake, it was only logical that the organizations already present in the community should be relied upon as a basis for reconstruction efforts. Furthermore, it was decided that the reconstruction program should support and improve community processes and foster a spirit of self-reliance. But notice what happened when other agencies joined in.

One of the components of the reconstruction program was the distribution of corrugated metal roofing sheets (known locally as *lamina*) to assist people in reroofing their homes. The *lamina* was sold at a subsidized price. The people benefited from the lower cost, more people could be served, and no one was given charity. (For those who could not afford to buy, work programs were established so they could earn credits toward the purchase price.)

The program became operational in a very short period of time and, within a matter of weeks, thousands of families had been able to purchase the *lamina* at reduced prices. Soon, however, a number of other programs in adjoining areas began to provide the same material free or for minimal labor. Several months later, other reconstruction programs began offering not only free *lamina* but also, in some cases, free houses. The result was that the people who had originally purchased the *lamina* began to complain that World Neighbors was trying to take advantage of them. Only after much effort was the agency's relationship with the people of the community restored.

THE ECONOMIC IMPACT OF DISASTER RELIEF AND RECONSTRUCTION

A relief or reconstruction program is essentially an economic system superimposed on a community that has been affected by a disaster. Take, for example, the provision of material aid. In order to get the goods to the people, an entire network is set up to provide storage, transportation, and distribution to and within the community. The capabilities of logistical systems and the range of goods provided expand yearly. No longer are just food, clothing, and blankets provided to disaster victims; often an entire range of goods that would make a department store owner envious are shipped to the scene. When the distribution system is set up, it is almost always controlled by the relief agency acting through its representatives in the community.

When disaster strikes a community, the economic systems of the community are also affected. Physical facilities may be destroyed or damaged, and the distribution of goods and services disrupted. If the community is to return to normal, it is essential that these systems be restored as quickly as possible. But just as these systems are struggling to recover, new systems in the form of relief and reconstruction programs appear and compete directly with them. A recent example occurred on Fiji. One island group was severely affected by an intense hurricane that destroyed much of the agricultural production of the country and approximately 80 percent of the housing. Massive relief efforts were organized by the government. To qualify for the relief, family members had to show that they were unemployed as well as being disaster victims. During the period that the aid continued, the normal economic systems (such as small stores, material suppliers, and their respective distribution networks) were bypassed. The aid, in effect, became a competing system. Thus the victims were denied much-needed capital that would have enabled them to recover more quickly. Several of the smaller stores eventually closed, and a number of suppliers put off reordering stock.

Thus the relief program delayed recovery of the normal economic systems within the community. When the program was due to terminate, it was not surprising that program staff found that the food program had to be continued because there were still inadequate supplies in local stores. In short, the relief program created a dependency situation that was contrary to the objective of a quick return to normalcy.

This adverse impact relates not only to the distribution of goods, but also to the effects on local labor. This is especially the case in the housing sector. When a relief agency develops a housing program that provides a permanent replacement structure built with either pre-fab techniques or self-help or voluntary labor, the carpenters and masons who are an essential part of the normal building process are often circumvented. In order for these men to survive, they often must leave the community to find work. In Guatemala, there was an exodus of skilled masons and carpenters to the capital. While this was due in part to the good salaries offered in Guatemala City, there is no doubt that many also were faced with the lack of job opportunity resulting from various reconstruction programs set up by relief agencies.

The important conclusion to draw is that humanitarian issues like meeting fundamental human needs for survival and emotional recovery dominate only the emergency period. In the succeeding phases, the issues are essentially economic. Housing, reconstruction, agricultural recovery, the restoration of jobs, small businesses, and government services—all are questions of economic revival. Programs that do not help restore the existing economic systems within a community are, in hard reality, a waste of time and effort.

DISINCENTIVE EFFECTS OF RELIEF AND RECONSTRUCTION

Only recently have people begun to study the disincentive effects of relief and reconstruction programs. As yet, there is very little concrete evidence either to support or to refute the contention on the part of many relief strategists that a mishandled relief program can have extensive disincentive effects not only on the recovery of the disaster-affected community, but also on long-term development.

This area is too important to ignore. We must have more data. Yet the gathering of data is often very difficult because of the challenge it makes to our underlying assumptions about humanitarian assistance. A typical disincentive chain goes like this. First, immediately following a disaster, large amounts of food aid are brought in. A distribution system is set up by the relief agency, which operates through local working groups or committees. The food is then given away to the disaster victims. In the meantime, because the food distribution system is apart from the normal system, local merchants cannot sell the foodstuffs that they have and must lower their prices in order to compete with the free food that is being distributed. If the food aid program is providing the same items that are normally sold by the stores, the suppliers will be severely affected and unable to move much of their own stock. The result is that they will not be able to offer a good price to local farmers to resupply goods that are usually sold and, in order to keep their profit margins up, they will pay less to farmers for the goods that they do purchase.

Marginal farmers, who grow only one crop, will be hit hardest. In practice, one of two things happens: either farmers sell out and leave the land, or the next year they are forced to plant less than in the previous year due to lack of capital to purchase seeds and fertilizers.

This disincentive chain can be affected by factors at any link and, of course, the final results often depend on the particular country and other environmental/economic aspects beyond the disaster. It has been noted, however, that in cases where massive food aid has been provided after disasters, agricultural production, adjusted for disaster-induced losses, has still shown a decline.

In considering the disincentive effects of post-disaster aid programs, it is important to remember that in the immediate aftermath of a disaster, there often is a very real need for the materials being distributed. The question is not basically one of need, but rather the manner in which the need is met.

THE "SET BACK" PROBLEM

"Set back" is difficult to define in absolute terms. It is something that happens following a disaster that can be perceived only by those who were involved in long-term development work before the disaster occurred and who are witness to the changes brought about by the disaster itself and the recovery process. The term "set back" has been coined to describe the negative consequences to development of post-disaster intervention. It is caused by the failure of intervenors to consider fully the impact of disaster assistance.

In a broad sense, the set back problem represents the loss of an opportunity to use the disaster to resolve basic problems. In some cases, it even represents the imposition of new obstacles that must be overcome in order to attain pre-disaster development objectives. Following earthquakes or hurricanes, for example, many relief agencies rush to initiate housing reconstruction projects. Many have no experience in the housing sector and do not know how to build safe houses. Instead of taking advantage of a situation that has eliminated much of the previous unsafe housing and provided intervenors with a unique opportunity to start from scratch, scores of housing programs systematically rebuild thousands of structures each year that actually increase the vulnerability of their occupants to the very disasters that destroyed the houses in the first place.

COMPETITION FOR DEVELOPMENT FUNDS

Relief and reconstruction efforts compete with development programs for available funds. In countries where disasters occur frequently, they can create an enormous financial burden unless adequate steps are taken to mitigate their effects. Fiji provides a good example. In the 1970s, the country was repeatedly struck by hurricanes, which forced the government to commit a large portion of the foreign aid received to reconstruction. In the early 1980s, roughly 20 percent of the foreign aid was spent on overhead costs alone for reconstruction efforts from four separate hurricanes (Cuny and Perez 1982). In the housing sector, failure to plan for mitigation of periodic disasters has had a profound effect. Not only have the disasters added to the overall demand for new housing, but the government's decision to replace the lost houses with expensive prefabricated buildings has added to the overall cost of reconstruction. Because the replacement houses are not hurricane-resistant, should another hurricane strike the same areas, the government would be placed in the position of having to rebuild houses not yet paid for. This would require funds and other resources that might otherwise have been devoted to social and economic development programs.

THE EXPECTATION OF AID: A DISINCENTIVE TO INITIATIVE

Highly publicized relief efforts in recent years have led many countries to expect similar efforts in their behalf should a disaster strike. Often countries or communities that are perfectly capable of dealing with a disaster themselves postpone taking effective action until they determine what aid they might receive. In some cases, governments and local agencies have advised people not to do anything because it might make them ineligible for disaster benefits. This attitude is of major concern for both relief and development agencies because it places a larger burden on the relief agencies and gives a disproportionate share of the decision making to the outsiders.

6
Change after Disasters

It is a common adage within the relief and development community that disasters have the potential to introduce change and to improve the society during the reconstruction period. Often after a disaster, one hears government or relief agency staff talk about the possibility of rebuilding a model society and describe the tasks ahead much in the terms of a phoenix rising from the ashes. That such a desire is felt and expressed is certainly laudable. If millions of dollars will suddenly be available, why not use them to rebuild a better community?

Unfortunately, the record of success in producing the phoenix has not been overly noteworthy. For the disaster victim, recovery means returning to normal, and normal usually means whatever existed before the disaster. The success ratio of these attempts to use disasters as opportunities for change has been rather low, even in the more industrialized nations where more extensive resources exist.

This poor showing does not mean that a number of opportunities for modest change are not present. But usually these opportunities require a subtle approach, patience, and a long-term commitment on the part of the agency.

There are three generally recognized ways in which change can be introduced following a disaster. The first is known as "invisible change." This approach is often used in dealing with housing or material aid. It refers to the process of making an improvement of some sort that does not outwardly affect the appearance or performance of an item or a particular activity. One example of invisible change is found in the improvement of traditional building techniques to enable adobe housing better to withstand the forces of earthquakes. In Guatemala, Programa Kuchuba'l introduced a variety of methods designed to make the traditional adobe houses more earthquake-resistant. Included were better methods for strengthening the walls using vertical columns and tying the columns together by means of wire cross-bracing. Both the posts and the cross-braces were covered by a thick stucco and were therefore invisible. To someone who had not seen the housing construction process, the houses would appear to be very traditional.

A second approach is known as the "substitute method" and is often used when introducing new varieties of crops. The provision of a new type of seed—one that is stronger or that resists various pests, but that requires no basic change in normal cropping patterns—can be substituted following a disaster such as a hurricane or flood where crops have been affected.

The "building block method" is the third approach: an agency begins to introduce change slowly by first working to re-establish a semblance of normalcy, and then introducing limited innovations. An example is the establishment of an Integrated Rural Development Program (IRDP) in Guatemala by the Save the Children Alliance following the 1976 earthquakes. Earlier, the Alliance had considered establishing a development program in Guatemala. When the earthquakes struck, rather than jumping in immediately to set up an IRDP, the organization chose instead to concentrate first on a limited number of reconstruction objectives. The first sector chosen was housing. During the first few months, a housing reconstruction team was formed and began to build a skeleton organization in the community where it planned to conduct the IRDP.

For its initial housing efforts, the Alliance chose to use the same invisible change approach initiated by Programa Kuchuba'l. After the program had been established and the invisible goals attained, staff added additional activity areas (such as public health, agriculture, and adult education). They also chose to build up the normal system before introducing the next level of change. Not only did each component of the overall program use the building block approach, but the program as a whole used this method to establish a presence in the community.

These approaches represent ways in which an agency can intervene subtly in a situation where people's primary motivation is to get back to normal as quickly as possible. However, disasters may also create a demand for change in certain sectors. Demand change is simultaneously both the easiest and the most difficult type of change to respond to with an adequate program. An agency must first identify the source of the demand and probe its depth. Following the Andhra Pradesh cyclone, there was a tremendous call for improved housing to withstand hurricane-force winds. This demand was interpreted by many of the relief agencies as being unanimous on the part of the people living within the affected communities. What the populace had in mind was improved traditional housing or *pukka* structures made of brick that were common to the area. Many of the agencies interpreted the demand as being so strong that people would be willing to have non-traditional housing as long as it was made of *pukka* materials. Because it was cheaper to build duplexes and larger multifamily houses than to build single-family *pukka* structures, some agencies proposed housing schemes using multifamily designs. Others proposed one-room, single-family units intentionally designed to be rather small so that the available resources could be stretched as far as possible.

In both cases, the agencies overestimated the willingness of the people to sacrifice their traditional houses (which met the functional needs of the families) in order to move into the safer *pukka* structures provided by the agencies. Today, many of the agencies' housing units stand vacant, while immediately next to them, a traditional building has been erected and occupied.

The lesson here is that even where people are demanding change, agencies must determine in advance how much will actually be accepted.

LESSONS FROM THE PAST

Let's review some of the lessons from past experience and the findings of the major research in disasters. For brevity, I am presenting them in an abbreviated form and placing them in two broad categories: General Aspects of Intervention and Aid and Assistance.

General Aspects of Intervention

Lesson 1: Relief and reconstruction operations should be conducted within the context of development.

Lesson 2: The process through which a family obtains disaster assistance is more important than the actual aid received.

Lesson 3: The people can do it and they known how.

Lesson 4: The people consistently prefer private and informal solutions over public and formal ones, even when the latter may objectively be more adequate.

Lesson 5: When properly executed, intervention can provide a strong stimulus to recovery and a base for positive changes.

Lesson 6: The rehabilitation system may constitute a more powerful agent for change than the impact of the actual disaster (Bates et al. 1963).

Lesson 7: Activities should be appropriate to the phase of the disaster.

Lesson 8: "Organizations that [arrive] on the scene soon after the impact . . . [are] successful to the degree to which they [fit] themselves into the rescue pattern already established by the local groups" (Form and Nosow 1958).

Lesson 9: The role of intervenors is to support activities that local individuals or organizations *cannot* carry out themselves.

Lesson 10: The lack of uniform reconstruction standards or policies (or failure of all intervenors to agree on basic approaches to relief) creates undue competition and leads to inequitable distribution of assistance.

Lesson 11: Massive relief can be counterproductive.

Lesson 12: The anticipation of large-scale assistance by foreign agencies makes local organizations reluctant to take relief measures.

Lesson 13: Aid may inadvertently be provided in such a way as to inhibit the recovery process and create dependence.

Lesson 14: Relief efforts may obscure underlying political realities (Cuny et al. 1982).

Lesson 15: Disaster relief may hinder the victims' own efforts to better prepare for a recurrence of the disaster.

Lesson 16: Despite the availability of local resources and solutions appropriate to post-disaster needs, there is a strong and growing demand at all levels in the Third World for "Western" (that is, highly technological) responses.

Aid and Assistance

Lesson 1: The subject of disaster assistance has been viewed predominately from the standpoint of the intervenors. Thus many of the common relief approaches have evolved in ways that facilitate delivery of relief assistance. If agencies are to provide effective aid, they must view disaster assistance from the standpoint of the victims and *their* requirements.

Lesson 2: Many post-disaster needs can be determined based on the natural hazard, season, and location.

Lesson 3: "In almost every disaster, outside agencies underestimate the basic resources still available in communities" (Quarantelli and Dynes 1972).

Lesson 4: Material assistance following disasters generally:
   a. is far in excess of actual needs;
   b. is in proportions larger than needed or usable;
   c. requires services and facilities that could be used for more essential tasks;
   d. often causes conflicts among relief agencies;

    e. adds to the problem of congestion;

    f. in some cases may disrupt the local economy (Dynes 1970).

Lesson 5: Relief materials from within the disaster-affected country are more likely to be compatible with normal use patterns than those delivered from a different culture; and the most useful materials provided by intervenors are those purchased in or near the disaster area.

Lesson 6: Re-establishment of the local economy and job security is usually more important for disaster victims than material assistance.

Lesson 7: Assistance provided by international relief agencies rarely plays a major role in the actual *emergency* phase.

Lesson 8: It is unrealistic to assume that foreign assistance sent to a disaster area will be applied in the emergency phase. Therefore, the emphasis on speed or "emergency response" should be changed to developing a response relevant to needs at an intermediate or advanced phase of recovery.

Lesson 9: Contributions from external donors are most effective in pre-disaster and reconstruction phases (Cuny et al. 1982).

Reconstruction is a complex process and often involves sophisticated techniques and activities with which local groups will need assistance. Providing assistance at this point is a meaningful role that intervenors can play.

POSITIVE ASPECTS OF INTERVENTION

Previous problems and consequences notwithstanding, there are of course positive aspects to intervention. Disasters often precipitate dynamic social and economic change, and intervention can play a part in shaping that process by providing expertise and resources not otherwise available at key points during the post-disaster period. Intervention can support coping mechanisms rather than harm them. Resources and new opportunities can strengthen existing institutions and help them better serve the community. And intervention can provide an opportunity for new leadership to emerge and for new groups to form to meet needs not adequately served by existing groups or effectively handled by established leaders. Intervention can also provide an alternative means of attaining development progress when existing organizations or leaders impede change.

Examples of intervention with positive results can be found in every disaster. There are hundreds of examples of families and even whole communities benefiting from aid they received: new and safer houses, new jobs and businesses, and expanded opportunities.

But what is important is the collective impact of the response. This is much more difficult to measure, but again, some positive examples can be found. One of the most noteworthy occurred in the aftermath of widespread famine in the Bihar region of India in the 1960s. Until then the principle staple of the people was rice. When periodic droughts hit the region, the irrigation systems could not supply enough water to grow the rice, and thousands of small farms went out of production. An international team of experts was assembled by the Government of India and the U.N. Food and Agricultural Organization (FAO) to develop an integrated reconstruction plan for the area. The team decided that one way of reducing vulnerability to droughts was to try to convert a large percentage of the riceland to the production of wheat, which requires less water and can better withstand dry periods. At the time, wheat was relatively unknown in Bihar, so a public education program was established to introduce the crop to farmers and create a demand (and taste) for flour among the general populace. At the time, the program was quite controversial, and many observers doubted that it would be successful. Yet today wheat accounts for a significant amount of the grain produced in the area (some years as much as 45 percent) and the number of people affected by famine has been reduced.

7
The Relief System

DEFINING THE SYSTEM

Much has been written recently about the foreign aid organizations and their role in international development in the Third World (Eugene Linden *The Alms Race* 1976; Denis Goulet *The Uncertain Promise* 1977; John G. Sommer *Beyond Charity* 1977). While the workings of these organizations and their interrelationships in normal circumstances are similar to the patterns that occur after disasters, there are enough differences to warrant closer examination.

The relief system consists of donors and intervenors. At the upper levels of the system, those who collect and channel resources to those active in the field are collectively known as the donors. Intervenors are the organizations that carry out the activities in the affected countries. In the middle levels of the system, some organizations are both donors and intervenors (for example, AID). An organization that is a donor in one disaster may be an intervenor in another. Generally, however, roles are firmly established.

What is generally referred to as the "international relief system" can be divided into five tiers: the first three represent the international level, the fourth the regional or country level, and the fifth the project level. Into these tiers are fitted a complex network of organizations, each of which has a specific role or resources to offer following a disaster. If the system is viewed theoretically as a multi-tiered funnel for collecting resources and channeling them into a disaster-affected community, it is possible to visualize the workings and interrelationships at each level.

The Five Tiers

Starting at the top are the individuals and companies that contribute funds or matériel; these are the primary donors. It is impossible for donors to deliver directly to the victims; therefore, they must donate to an organization that either works in the community or can in turn pass on their gift to an organization that is on the scene. The organizations that receive the gifts, including churches, governments, and foundations, form the second tier.

The second-tier organizations have a number of options in distributing the donations. They can pass them on to the groups in the next level, composed of the international relief and development organizations (known collectively as voluntary organizations or volags), or to international intergovernmental organizations such as the United Nations or the Organization of American States (OAS), or they can bypass this level and give directly to the fourth tier, the local government and nongovernmental organizations. In practice, most funds are passed directly from second-tier to third-tier groups.

Page 109 shows the tiers, the patterns of donations, and the interrelationships of the various organizations. For example, churches normally give to volags in the third tier rather than to lower levels in the system. Governments donate to all levels, depending on the disaster and the political implications of the aid. Foundations contribute to volags, international organizations, and sometimes directly to local nongovernmental organizations, but almost never to the local government. At the third tier, volags and international organizations often support each other. For example, many volags give money directly to specialized UN organizations such as UNICEF, while many of the UN organizations (such as the UNHCR) contract the volags to carry out their programs. Similarly, volags often donate to regional organizations and vice versa, and even laterally to other volags.

The volags serve as a conduit for funds to three of the groups in the fourth tier. First, they support their own field offices and the projects that their staff develops. They also fund other international volags or the local nongovernmental organizations in the affected country. Often, too, they provide funds to missionaries through organizations in the third tier or directly to those in the fourth tier. Volags often also fund each other in the third tier and the UN or regional intergovernmental organizations. In fact, volags have a record of funding just about every type of organization in both the third and fourth tiers, except local governments. Thus, in effect, volags often become not only operating agencies but also de facto foundations. OXFAM U.K. and OXFAM America acted as a foundation following the 1976 Guatemalan earthquake by funding another volag, World Neighbors, which was in turn supporting a variety of projects in the earthquake zone.

The fourth tier represents the first group of organizations in the affected country. It comprises the host government, local nongovernmental organizations, and the offices or field representatives of the foreign volags and

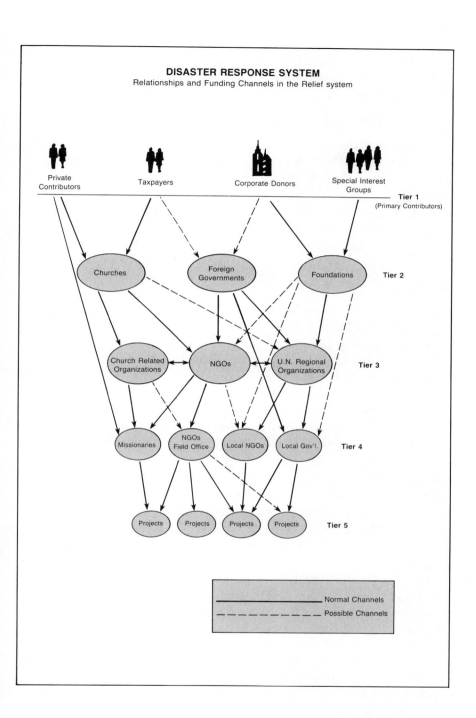

DISASTER RESPONSE SYSTEM
Relationships and Funding Channels in the Relief system

Private
Contributors

Taxpayers

Corporate Donors

Special Interest
Groups

Tier 1
(Primary Contributors)

Churches

Foreign
Governments

Foundations

Tier 2

Church Related
Organizations

NGOs

U.N. Regional
Organizations

Tier 3

Missionaries

NGOs
Field Office

Local NGOs

Local Gov't.

Tier 4

Projects

Projects

Projects

Projects

Tier 5

———————— Normal Channels
— — — — — — — Possible Channels

missionaries. Their interrelationships are not as complex as at the international level, for here there is a competition for funds. Here too the decisions are made on how the funds will be spent inside the country, and such decisions are critical for the outcome of the overall relief and reconstruction program.

The final level the resources must go through before reaching the victims is the project level. This fifth tier represents the operational level at which the funds are dispersed and the point at which the victims' needs are resolved.

Most of the organizations in tiers 2 through 4 are both recipients and donors. In terms of the relief system, all organizations in these tiers, and many in the fourth tier, are collectively known as donors.

Motivation

Who are the donors and what motivates them? The individuals and families in the first tier make their donations either spontaneously or in response to a request from an organization in one of the lower tiers. Donations are voluntary and humanitarian concerns are the prime motivation.

Corporations and business organizations are also in the first tier and make donations to second- and third-level organizations, but their motivations are more varied. Humanitarian interests, of course, are a factor, but there are also issues of self-interest that come into play. A corporation with operations in the disaster-affected country cannot ignore a disaster and must demonstrate its concern and goodwill to the victims and host government. It can do this indirectly, by funding the voluntary organizations or the local nongovernmental organizations providing disaster relief or a foundation that will make the choice for the company. Or it can do it directly by setting up small-scale projects that benefit the company's workers or their communities. For example, many corporations have offered low-interest loans to their workers for housing reconstruction.

Corporations may contribute funds to support the national objectives of their own government, especially if these are thought to lead to gains for the corporations in the future. Thus, if a disaster is seen as creating a potential for political instability, governments and corporations alike may offer substantial aid to a wide range of institutions in the affected area.

This combination of self-interest and humanitarian concern on the part of corporations need not be considered negative. As an example of indirect aid, Programa Kuchuba'l received an early boost with a donation of $10,000 from the Philip Morris Company, which enabled it to produce a large number of training aids that were used throughout the program. If a corporation becomes directly involved in relief efforts, the results are usually mixed. Even the best-intentioned corporate relief programs often fall short of their objectives, usually because the corporations are not attuned to all the issues involved. A corporation in Guatemala that produced building materials spent approximately half a million dollars for a housing program that benefited only 100 families. Within several months, most of the low-income families who had moved into the project had sold the houses and left, claiming that the cost of maintaining and running the houses was beyond their means.

The objectives of the churches, governments, and foundations that make up the second tier are more complex. For the churches, humanitarian concerns dominate, but concern about the impact of the disaster on missionary works and a measure of opportunism also prevail. What better chance than a disaster to demonstrate the goodwill and humanitarian efforts of an organization and to establish or expand a presence in a community where previously the denomination had little influence? Churches donate primarily to the relief and development organizations of their own denomination, to affiliated ecumenical groups, or their own missionaries. Occasionally, church donations will be channeled to the voluntary organizations. In some cases, churches will also donate to the United Nations, especially UNICEF and the World Food Programme, and to other intergovernmental organizations that have a specific program for the disaster-affected area.

Foundations play a limited role among the second-tier organizations and serve primarily as a conduit for corporate and private funds to other organizations. Usually the foundation has a specific interest in a particular country or a particular activity such as agriculture or housing. Foundations are among the organizations most responsive to their donors, especially the large corporations that provide funds (and often direction). The foundations are normally motivated by the wish to achieve a certain set of goals outlined by the founders and donors; these cover a wide range. Generally they can be described as humanitarian or are related to economic development or certain political objectives.

Of all the organizations in the second tier, governments are usually the most influential and powerful. And at the same time, their actions are often the most difficult to define. They are motivated by myriad factors including humanitarian, geopolitical, and economic objectives, by treaties or other prior contacts, and, regrettably, by military objectives. Unfortunately, many of the military objectives are obscured by the true humanitarian objectives and vice versa. In some cases the political and economic objectives can be linked to humanitarian goals. If aid is provided quickly to the government of a country affected by a disaster, continuity and stability can often be ensured, and a timely donation of economic aid can keep an economy from being affected too adversely. Principal businesses and industries can be restored quickly, which benefits not only the recipient but also the donor government. Usually, however, the primary political objective is to maintain or attain influence.

In order to carry out their post-disaster objectives, governments donate to almost every type of organization on the next two tiers. It is the local government with which the donor government has its primary relationship and to which it directs the primary flow of aid. This arrangement can be both a constraint and an opportunity, depending on the capabilities of the host government.

The second pattern of government funding is for the donor to give to the voluntary organizations in its own country that have contracts or programs in the affected area. These donations have drawn much criticism in recent years. Many organizations are so heavily funded by their governments that they become, in effect, an arm of the government's foreign policy. The ready availability of cash and material has "hooked" many organizations, and they are almost totally dependent upon their foreign aid ministeries for support. There has been growing concern that this alliance undermines the credibility of the volags and reduces their ability to be innovative and to operate independently. The implications of this connection cannot be overemphasized. If the national government of the volag does not want it to conduct a relief program in the affected area, it can bring a tremendous amount of pressure on the volag to stay clear. And if it wants a volag to become involved, it can, similarly, make things very easy for the agency. While a few agencies have been able to remain independent of their governments and provide true humanitarian aid without regard to political consequences, the number is unfortunately rather small and dwindling. On the other hand, there can be no doubt that, because governments make extensive resources available to volags, a much wider range of services can be offered. The question facing the volags, then, is where to draw the line and how to accept the government's aid without becoming a pawn in a political game where the true agendas are often hidden.

Governments also contribute to the relief programs of international organizations. Specialized agencies of the United Nations command a large portion of these funds. They are a handy conduit for governments and allow a government without an extensive foreign aid program to make a contribution without actually having to decide the details of how the money is to be spent in the field. Such transfers of funds are effective in that they assure that special problems will receive at least some attention and countries that would not otherwise receive attention will get at least some. For the more influential countries (such as the U.S., Canada, and the U.K.), contributions to these organizations are done more *pro forma* than anything else.

On the third tier are the volags and the intergovernmental agencies that act as service agencies, and it is here that overall policy and planning for the international relief effort of the nongovernmental organization occurs. Actions at this level are shaped by a variety of factors. Humanitarian concerns are, of course, the prime motivator. When a disaster strikes, most agencies feel compelled to do something, especially if they have programs in the disaster-affected area. The *raison d'être* of many organizations is to respond to disasters, or at least to respond to human needs in times of crisis. Therefore, they must become involved.

For others, disasters appear to provide an opportunity not only to serve other people but also to expand the range of services and the influence of the organization. Often this is coupled with an opportunity for growth, especially if the disaster is on a large-scale, commanding much public attention. The greater the tragedy and the more extensive the media coverage, the greater the opportunity for a successful appeal. Therefore many organizations, for reasons of self-preservation, start up disaster relief programs.

Some volags enter a disaster to support the political objectives of their own government. During the Vietnam War, several volags began programs to aid refugees and to help war victims in direct support of the American (and indirectly of the South Vietnamese) government.

There is a special factor motivating *development* organizations in disasters. This is called "development through disaster opportunity." Several organizations perceive disasters as a radical event that will speed up the development process. They reason that disasters create an atmosphere for change and that, with a massive influx of money and material, opportunities exist to have a significant impact on the society. Organizations often choose this moment to begin their development programs, entering first with a relief program, then moving to a reconstruction and later a development program. (Such was the case with the Save the Children Alliance following the Guatemalan earthquake).

The intergovernmental organizations that make up the second group on the third tier, like the volags, have the dual role of being both operational agencies and providing funds. Their primary task is to support the relief and reconstruction operations of their member governments. Thus the primary involvement is with the governments of the disaster-stricken areas. In some cases they do provide funds to volags.

The actions of international organizations are guided by the concerns of their member governments—not only the recipients of aid, but also the most influential donors. Thus their objectives are often more political and economic than humanitarian, and occasionally the objectives have military overtones.

The final members of the third tier are church and missionary organizations. If the organization is denominational, the objectives are usually quite clear and reflect the policies and aims of the membership of that particular religious group. If the organization is ecumenical, however, it may operate under a confusing set of instructions. It must deal with a variety of internal contradictions and myriad philosophies. The ecumenical movement in relief and development is probably too young to be evaluated conclusively; yet at present it is apparent that these organizations often spend more time trying to determine what is acceptable to each of the member religious groups than what is appropriate for the victims. Ecumenical organizations also become entangled in many of the same snares as the nondenominational voluntary agencies. They too are often heavily funded by their national governments. It is always difficult for these organizations to draw the fine line between humanitarian service and political complicity. There can be no doubt that the ecumenical movement offers one advantage, however, namely, the ability to generate extensive resources and to provide a single entity for their distribution.

The fourth tier is made up of the local government, the local nongovernmental organizations (NGOs), the field offices or representatives of the international voluntary agencies, and the missionaries working in a particular country. This tier is classified as both the second level of the relief system and the lowest level of the donor community and can also be considered either as intervenors or as coping mechanisms. Nonetheless they are donors, crucial because they actually have face-to-face contact with the ultimate recipients of the donations: the disaster victims. As with the organizations of the upper tiers, the organizations of the fourth tier have rather clearly defined funding patterns. The government usually gives funds to its own agencies for projects and to the nongovernmental organizations of its own country. Local NGOs generally support their own projects and no one else's. Missionaries similarly fund their own projects or people with whom they have had contact.

Only the volags have a diverse funding pattern and may fund the activities of any of the other three groups (although, if they have their own projects, the bulk of their funding will go to these).

At this level, where face-to-face contact with the victims occurs, aid would seem to be offered for the best of motives. Yet even here, politics and economic objectives often intrude. Governments have been known to show favoritism in the distribution of relief supplies. Local NGOs often support community groups for political as well as humanitarian reasons. And even missionaries have been found using aid as a means of furthering their own religious objectives.

KEY ACTORS IN THE RELIEF SYSTEM

While the entire relief system, especially at the donor level, is composed of hundreds of different organizations, only a relative handful can be considered key actors. What makes these organizations "key" is a combination of the resources they command, the contributions of money, goods, or technology that they can make, or the influence they wield as "pacesetters" relative to the state of the art.

U.S. Government

No other country responds more fully to disasters than the U.S. It responds to some extent at all phases of a disaster and is extensively involved in predisaster planning, mitigation, and preparedness. The U.S. is one of the largest sources of funds for disaster relief and operates throughout the Third World.

In the initial stages of a disaster, assistance is coordinated by an office in the State Department. The Office of U.S. Foreign Disaster Assistance (OFDA) sends representatives to the affected area to help the American Embassy officials on site determine what the requirements are and how the U.S. Government can best respond. If the country has an AID Mission, it will be responsible for coordinating the American Government's actions on site. The Mission may decide simply to provide funds or matériel or a combination of both. If it has an existing program, such as one in housing or agriculture, it may redirect the personnel from that program to the disaster area. Normally, however, the AID Missions prefer to fund the American voluntary agencies active in the country or to provide the funding directly to the host government.

Because the United States is a major power, there are, of course, many political ramifications to the aid that it provides. Critics have often pointed out that the American aid programs in general tend to support the status quo in the developing countries. In addition, they often criticize the programs for being a mechanism for distributing American goods and thereby providing an indirect subsidy for American agriculture and manufacturing interests. The food programs of the U.S. Government, in particular PL-480 Title II, have drawn the bulk of this criticism in recent years.

The response of the U.S. in any one disaster is normally dependent upon its relationship with the affected country. If the country is considered "friendly" or strategically important, the aid provided following a disaster can be massive. Typical responses include the sending of Disaster Assessment Teams (DAST) and the immediate provision of a small cash grant to the host government. Within the next few days, several plane loads of relief supplies will be forwarded, including water tanks, family-sized tents, and an initial donation of PL-480 food stuffs.

The U.S. Embassy can arrange for private donors to ship relief supplies at government expense to the affected area and can make available a wide variety of resources to the American and often other agencies working in rehabilitation and reconstruction. If the disaster is particularly severe, OFDA will approach Congress for a large appropriation to help in reconstruction and will notify the host government and the American voluntary agencies that it will entertain proposals for the use of these funds.

If substantial clearance and road repair activities are required, teams of military engineers, complete with supporting equipment, may be offered to help restore roads, repair bridges, and reestablish communications.

If extensive search and rescue is required, and there are adequate American military resources nearby, helicopters and small aircraft can be put at the immediate disposal of the host country. Following the 1970 earthquake in Peru, an American helicopter carrier was diverted to the Peruvian coast, where the entire complement of helicopters was assigned for several weeks to assist in the relief and rescue operations (a highly visible, if not cost-effective response).

While these vast resources may seem impressive, especially to the local people, their effectiveness and cost-benefit ratio must seriously be questioned. Could not the money be better spent to stimulate local response using more appropriate technology and emphasizing participation of the victims?[1]

Government Aid Outside the U.S.

The second group of key actors among governments includes the United Kingdom, Canada, France, and Sweden. All have large and extensive aid programs in their own right, and each has extensive contacts among the disaster-prone countries in the developing world. The U.K. and France are often tied to their former colonial territories by a combination of sentiment and economic interests and thus can be counted on to respond in these areas quickly and on a large scale. Canada and Sweden, on the other hand, are a bit more selective with their aid programs as they do not have the same

1. Furthermore, the victims often see the use of American military equipment and personnel as threatening. American officials providing humanitarian assistance are often unaware of the connotations of a massive response that relies on military capabilities.

resources to offer, but can be counted on in a wide variety of situations. Sweden and Canada both are newcomers to the aid game, not having been colonial powers, and therefore often find that their aid is more acceptable in political terms than that of the U.K. or France, which are often constrained by the same limitations as the U.S.

Following a disaster, all of these countries respond in much the same way as the U.S., offering a combination of direct and indirect assistance, cash and material aid, and military personnel and equipment to help in the immediate emergency relief.

The U.K. and France each have a considerable number of private organizations that are normally involved in development or relief activities and can work through these groups. Canada and Sweden, on the other hand, do not have a large number of nongovernmental organizations operating overseas and therefore their aid tends to be more direct.

Smaller Government Aid Programs

The third key group includes West Germany, Holland, Japan, and Saudi Arabia. Each of these has relatively small aid programs, and the programs of Japan and Saudi Arabia are highly regionalized. The Dutch are one of the up-and-coming supporters of international development and relief activities and are generally unique in that they often fund private organizations from other countries.

These governments normally provide financial assistance only and rarely become operational in a disaster. Occasionally they provide material and in a few cases have provided military equipment, such as aircraft or engineering equipment, if it has been requested by the host government. As more private groups develop in these countries, the support they receive will likely follow the patterns shown for other European governments and the U.S. The continued growth and development of the European Economic Community, with its associated international development and aid programs, will provide another arm of assistance for each of the European countries. Whether the overall effort will be to expand or reduce each country's individual response remains to be seen.

There are, of course, many other governments that provide assistance following disasters and indeed, virtually every government close to the affected area or with religious or economic ties makes some form of contribution.

Communist Bloc Aid

The USSR, China, and Cuba, as well as many of the Eastern European nations, also provide disaster relief, though aid from these countries varies greatly in quantity and quality. Normally they provide cash, though on occasion they have donated food or agricultural equipment and have replaced industrial equipment lost in the disaster. Probably their best-known relief operation outside of their normal client states was in Peru following the 1970 earthquake. The Russians organized a massive airlift of food and medical supplies and were involved in the reconstruction of housing around the town of Huaraz.

Cuba's disaster aid program is typical. When its neighbors in the Caribbean are struck by earthquakes or hurricanes, Cuba usually offers a rather small amount of aid. In Nicaragua following the 1972 earthquake, Cuba donated several planeloads of relief supplies including water puri-fication equipment and medicines. It also offered a team of public health workers and a medical field hospital, which proved to be very effective. Political considerations, however, did not allow the Cubans to remain on site for longer than several weeks, and their aid program soon ended.

In recent years the Chinese have become more active in post-disaster assistance; previously they have been involved only with their immediate neighbors and a few countries that were client states in Africa. Chinese relief aid is generally limited to the provision of technical assistance and funds. Since China's own experience with severe earthquakes in 1976, it has shown much interest in sharing information with countries with similar earth-quake problems. It is expected that China will become a major participant in international relief and reconstruction efforts.

It is difficult to assess the aid provided by Communist countries. The political rhetoric surrounding the aid often obscures the true impact of the assistance, and because it is given in a highly political environment, it is not likely that effective evaluations will be carried out.

Intergovernmental Organizations

The intergovernmental organizations are often key participants in the international relief system. The UN, of course, is the largest, and in various types of disasters, its specialized agencies have major assignments in the overall relief effort. For example, in droughts, the World Food Programme is often designated as the lead agency; in refugee situations, the UNHCR is normally assigned the coordinating role. Within the UN system, almost half its agencies have some responsibility in disasters. There are even special UN agencies created to handle long-term aspects of disasters. UNRWA, the United Nations Relief and Works Agency, was created to handle the Palestinian situation. If an operation lasts for more than a year, a UN special operation will normally be created, with one of the UN agencies designated as the lead agency, as was the case in the Sahel during the drought of the 1970s.

The UN Disaster Relief Office (UNDRO) was established in the 1970s to coordinate the various relief and reconstruction efforts of the UN system and to stimulate prevention and preparedness measures. In the immediate post-disaster period, the UNDRO office in Geneva serves mainly as a coordinator for information on donations and, in the field, as a convenor of coordination efforts among foreign donors. In recent years, UNDRO has placed increased emphasis on its preparedness activities.

UNDRO has had difficulty in defining its role and implementing an effective program. An evaluation of the office in 1980 by the Joint Inspection Unit of the UN found "implementation . . . has been hampered by [the] imprecise nature of [UNDRO's mandate] and [its] inability to establish a leadership role; by problems in determining UNDRO's functions in 'other' disasters; [by] the proper mix of relief co-ordination, preparedness and prevention work; [by] the extent of an 'operational' role; and [by] the appropriate initiation and termination of its relief efforts" (Allen et al. 1980).

The UN specialized agencies can provide a wide variety of resources ranging from technical assistance to food. UNICEF and the World Food Programme often have their own staffs within a country who are capable of formulating and conducting a relief program. UNDRO normally works through the resident representatives of the UN Development Programme, or may send a member of its staff to the affected country to help carry out the disaster assessment and coordination role.

The European Economic Community (EEC) is rapidly expanding its disaster assistance, serving primarily as a conduit for funds and material to Third World countries that do not have large bilateral assistance agreements with EEC member countries. In the future, this role is likely to expand.

Oil-producing nations have become major aid givers since the 1973 oil price increases. The Organization of Petroleum Exporting Countries (OPEC) now supplies more than 25 percent of all aid to the Third World, but as yet little of this aid is for disaster assistance. OPEC members have set up two multilateral development banks that are likely to become major resources for reconstruction financing (New Internationalist 1979).

Another key agency among international organizations is the World Bank. The Bank is unique in that it is a lending institution and works only with governments. It can provide funds by offering credit or soft loans, often supporting them with a wide range of technical assistance. The World Bank grew out of the American aid program to Europe following World War II, and much of its program is still structured in the same manner. The World Bank normally becomes involved only in reconstruction. If it has an ongoing program in the disaster-affected area, the World Bank may increase its level of support during the emergency or transition phase; however, this is rare. The World Bank normally spends its funds on projects that will make a contribution to longer-term development. Favored projects are in the agricultural, small business, and housing sectors.

Regional Organizations

The importance of regional organizations in any specific situation depends on the organizations involved and on the location of the disaster. For example, the Caribbean Development Bank could be considered a key organization by governments in that region, though in the overall picture, bilateral aid from the major powers would generally prove to be much more important. Regional organizations rarely have extensive post-disaster aid programs and can generally offer only loans, financial assistance, and occasionally technical assistance.

Volags

Even though the voluntary agencies do not make a large contribution in terms of the amount of resources, they are often "key" simply because they are more flexible and can experiment in terms of both the style and content of their programs.

The volag system has two levels. The first provides coordination at the international level. The League of Red Cross Societies (LORCS), the World Council of Churches, Caritas Internationalis, the International Committee of the Red Cross (ICRC), and the International Council of Voluntary Agencies (ICVA), to name a few, serve their member groups by collecting and disseminating information and relief materials, and by providing technical assistance to them. These organizations handle the majority of the appeals and serve as "traffic directors" for much of the material aid that goes from the industrialized countries to the developing countries. The World Council of Churches serves the ecumenical movement made up of the mainline Christian organizations in the West. Caritas serves as co-ordinator for the Catholic relief organizations, while the League co-ordinates the relief efforts of the various national Red Cross Societies. The League monitors relief operations and sends delegates to work with the various national societies to help carry out relief operations.

In Geneva, coordination is done through a committee called the LORCS-Volag Steering Committee (Brown 1979). Composed of the League, CRS, Lutheran World Federation, OXFAM, and the World Council of Churches, the committee provides a forum for exchanging information about disasters and for coordinating appeals. The committee has undertaken several joint disaster preparedness activities and has published several disaster preparedness guides and manuals.

In addition to the steering committee, a regular monthly meeting of the League and the other relief agencies, including both governmental and private agencies, is held at the LORCS Secretariat to exchange information and reduce overlap during current disasters.

Each of the coordinating bodies has its own reserve of funds and, sometimes, matériel, which it can commit immediately when the disaster occurs. It launches an appeal to other member organizations and affiliates as soon as a local organization requests assistance. It may provide aid to assess the needs, but its primary role will be to record and coordinate the assistance dispatched.

There are many problems associated with the role of coordinator. The staffs represent many different countries and, therefore, the coordinator must be sensitive to many nationalistic concerns—a sensitivity that tends to constrain many organizations. They are also in the difficult spot of being the focal point for appeals and must pass them on to the donors, inadvertently endorsing the appeals, whether they are appropriate or not. While organizations can attempt to investigate requests, normally they cannot pass judgment on them and are therefore often unjustly criticized when inappropriate aid arrives. It has been pointed out that an effective role for these organizations is disaster preparedness; namely, working with affiliates in the disaster-prone countries to identify effective responses and the appropriate assistance.

Worldwide, there are more than one thousand different organizations that might respond to a disaster. Of these, only a few are considered key, because at least one can be counted on to respond in any disaster. Among these are CARE, Catholic Relief Services of the United States, Church World Service (also of the U.S. and a World Council of Churches affiliate), OXFAM, the various national organizations of Save the Children and Terre des Hommes, and World Vision. Of these, the first three are the largest relief organizations in the world, and the resources they command give them an influential role in any operation in which they participate. Each is involved in both relief and development works, and one or the other is generally involved in almost every country in the Third World. CARE has its own programs administered by a professional staff, supplemented in disasters by volunteers. CRS and CWS usually operate through local counterpart organizations, though in a few cases they do have their own programs. Their interests are not restricted to any one sector, and they have entered housing, agriculture, small business, and many other fields, both in normal and in post-disaster times. The programs of the "Big Three" have often been criticized as being too closely linked to U.S. policy[2] and, indeed, in many post-disaster situations the U.S. State Department has relied on these agencies heavily. In some cases, they are designated as the official U.S. relief agency for a particular disaster, especially if the U.S. has no AID Mission in the country. The quality of the performance of these agencies is mixed and often depends on whether or not they had a program in the affected area prior to the disaster and therefore a good base upon which to build. Criticism of these programs has centered on the fact that they often tend to be more responsive to the needs and requirements of the U.S. Government than to those of the disaster victims. For example, following a cyclone in Asia, one agency received AID funding to provide emergency housing. The program began within a few days of the disaster, even before many of the victims had returned to the area and before the bodies had been removed. In order to expedite construction, the agency purchased materials in a neighboring state and brought in laborers from outside the affected area to build the houses. When it was pointed out to the agency that the shelters were being built on land whose ownership was not clear and that the victims who desperately needed jobs were not being included in the program, the agency requested that the program be extended in order to revise it. The revisions were rejected, however, because AID had to expend its funds within a ninety-day period.

Other key organizations derive their influence more from experience than from resources. OXFAM plays a dual role in disasters as it is both an operational agency and a funding agency, depending on the country and its prior commitments. OXFAM was founded as a famine relief organization and has evolved into a development organization over the years. It has long been noted as one of the best disaster response organizations, and its programs have been regarded as innovative and relatively successful. Like any organization, it is only as good as its people on the scene, but the field directors have been granted a good measure of autonomy and as a result programs tailored to the needs of people, with extensive participation by the victims, have usually resulted. OXFAM has also been a leader in research in disaster-related technology. In the field of sanitation it is well known for the OXFAM sanitation unit, an innovative, though controversial, system for collecting and storing excreta in refugee camp situations, which was a major innovation for its time. While not all of its investments have proven sound (for example, the OXFAM polyurethane emergency shelters), it has taken the lead in disaster-related research.

2. For a discussion of the U.S. Government contribution to agencies, see John G. Sommer, *Beyond Charity* (1977), especially his table 4 in the appendix.

Save the Children is an amalgamation of the various Save the Children organizations in Europe and the United States. Each organization has its own field staff, but following disasters in certain areas it is supplemented by staff or volunteers sent by other members of the alliance. Following the earthquake in Guatemala, for example, the alliance sent an American and British team to conduct a disaster assessment and to determine an area for a project. This team was then supplemented by Norwegian, Danish, Swedish, and other American and British team members.
bers.

The SCF Alliance is best known for its work with children and for its medical and feeding teams, though it is not restricted to these sectors.

Terre des Hommes is a European organization with affiliates in Holland, Austria, Germany, and Belgium. It normally provides aid in the fields of medicine, public health, and services to mothers and children. A key organization not so much from performance as resources, it nonetheless has a growing program and a significant impact wherever it operates.

World Vision Relief Organization is the relief arm of World Vision International, a U.S.-based, worldwide Christian organization that provides humanitarian assistance in support of the evangelical movement. The organization and its affiliates are one of the largest relief organizations and can marshal vast resources. In the past, the organization has been criticized for allowing its evangelical activities to cross over into its relief work, more so than many of the other church-related organizations. In the early 1980s, World Vision appointed regional disaster officers and began comprehensive disaster preparedness planning for both natural and man-made disasters.

Disaster Research

There is a final key group: the disaster research institutions and disaster specialists who provide much of the research and technical assistance that guides the others. Among the research organizations are the Disaster Research Center at Ohio State University, the Natural Hazards Research and Applications Information Center at the University of Colorado in Boulder, and the Centre for Research on the Epidemiology of Disasters at the Catholic University of Louvain in Brussels. Ohio State has pioneered sociological and behavioral investigations into disasters, the Natural Hazards Workshop has led the field in research on the relationship of natural hazards to the human environment, and the Catholic University of Louvain group, headed by Dr. Michel Lechat, has been the forerunner in disaster epidemiology.

The International Disaster Institute (IDI) is an organization formed by the merger of the defunct Disaster Research Unit at Bradford University (U.K.) and the London Technical Group, a small nonprofit organization specializing in medical and health aspects of disasters. The IDI is striving to become the professional voice of the disaster profession. It publishes *Disasters: The International Journal of Disaster Studies and Practice*, the major publication dealing with disasters, and provides a forum for the few people who are interested in disasters on a full-time basis.

Mention should also be made of the private consulting firms that specialize in research and technical assistance to governments, and voluntary organizations operational in disasters. They have had a significant impact on disasters by mediating between the research institutions and the operational organizations. Most prominent are the engineering firms that have developed new approaches to building earthquake- and cyclone-resistant structures and organizations such as INTERTECT that provide on-site management and planning assistance.

THE PERSONNEL AT DIFFERENT LEVELS OF THE SYSTEM

Perhaps the most important factor in an agency's response to disaster is the quality and level of training of the field staff. An organization's percentage of career and professional staff often depends on its size and its programs in the Third World. Normally, however, the career staff are not the people who actually conduct the relief operation. The career staff are the managers, the specialists at moving aid through diplomatic channels, at planning the overall operation and managing the budgets. The people who actually do the work are rarely full-time members of the organization and almost never professional disaster specialists.

When disaster occurs, a responding organization will normally staff-up in one of two ways. First, if the organization already has a development program or a skeleton disaster staff, it will recruit additional persons or seek volunteers to carry out the program. If the organization has no prior experience in the area, it must send a representative there, not only to determine the program, but also to recruit the staff. Generally, fewer than 5 percent of the people involved in disaster relief have ever been involved in such work previously. Even at the managerial level, few program directors or key staff personnel have had prior disaster experience.

In the initial stages, a large portion of the work is carried out by the victims themselves with assistance from volunteers. As a program becomes established, the relief agency will contract a number of persons on a short-term basis to implement the long-term aspects of the program. As each program comes to a close, these volunteers and part-time staff are laid off, and it is highly unlikely that any will ever again be involved in a disaster. As we shall see later, this means that the organization loses its collective memory, which, in turn, affects its ability to learn the lessons of the disaster and incorporate these lessons into its response to the next disaster.

Who, then, are the so-called disaster experts? Generally, they are the upper-managerial level officials and representatives of agencies who go to the disaster scene and initiate a program. However, few of these people started off as volunteers to come up "through the ranks," learning about the operational constraints on a disaster relief program.

Among the few major agencies that do have a professional development program, promotion tends to take them away from the field. Once people do well in the field, they are rewarded by being promoted to a headquarters job. As people are promoted, they move farther and farther from responsibilities in the field. If the relief and development profession is to improve, we need to reverse this trend.

PROBLEMS WITHIN THE RELIEF SYSTEM

There are a number of major problems common to the relief system and the agencies and organizations within it. As with the influences on the relief system, many are unique and many are a result of the system itself.

Decision Making and Authority

The rules and procedures that govern the fieldwork of relief agencies often hinder or complicate response to disasters.

Decision making at the headquarters level. When agencies respond to disasters in the developing countries, the distances, communications, and transportation difficulties, as well as cultural obstacles, often inhibit effective humanitarian assistance. To be effective in this environment, choices must be made at the field level, and the people making these choices need a supportive, not restrictive, framework of rules, procedures, and policies to assist in this process.

Unfortunately, most organizations attempt to keep a good deal of the decision making at the headquarters level. The first move is usually to try to improve headquarters-field communications. Direct telex links are established; better telephone systems, even radio communications are installed. Next, procedures are revised to try to speed decisions through the headquarters. Stockpiling of supplies, maintaining of computer lists of experts on standby, and many other methods have been (and are being) tried. Yet the results still fall short of the desired response. The basic problem is that revising procedures and improving technology at headquarters does not necessarily improve the field response.

Several organizations working in disasters are seeking alternative approaches. The concepts being explored fall into three categories. The first is called a *limited authority* approach. The headquarters and local representatives review previous responses and draw up a list of activities that can be handled without consultation with headquarters or that require immediate, on-the-spot decisions that cannot wait for consultation with headquarters. In the first case, the authority to deal with such activities is delegated outright; in the second, policies are developed to provide a framework to guide representatives in making their choices. (This approach is in use today by organizations such as OXFAM and CARE.)

The second approach is called *dispatched authority*. When an emergency occurs, instead of the representative sending information to the headquarters for action, the headquarters sends a team of specialists to the field with authority to make (most) decisions on the spot. In some cases the team operates under special rules or emergency procedures, but it has been found that with this system few substantial rule changes are required. The ability to make decisions in the field is improved, and response is facilitated. (This approach is used largely by the disaster agencies of governments and by several large volags.)

The third concept is called *devolution*. Of all the approaches it is the most difficult to put into practice as it requires a fundamental rethinking of the structures necessary to provide relevant management in a Third World environment. Yet this appears to be the most effective structure, and many humanitarian organizations are moving toward this approach. Devolution is the structuring of an organization so that most of the decision making takes place in the affected country. This is accomplished in two ways. First, the headquarters' role is changed from that of decision making to policy making and coordination; and second, the organization is structured so that senior personnel with authority to act, within the policy framework and according to the rules of the organization, are placed in offices near the areas where response is required. Among those agencies where this approach has been used (for example, CWS), few changes in the rules were necessary.

This is the background against which decision making should be examined. While procedures can be changed to simplify and speed emergency response within headquarters, overall performance in the field will not be significantly altered as a result.

Donor constraints on gifts. The conflict of authority between donor and agency can be shown in this example: a major donor gives a relief agency funds to conduct a post-disaster medical program. The relief agency asks a medical university to provide volunteers for the assignment. The university agrees, provided that the staff will not be absent for more than sixty days. At the same time, an intergovernmental agency offers to provide additional support and material if the team will work with the staff of one of its existing programs in the affected area. Thus by the time the medical team arrives in the country, virtually all decisions relating to its mission have already been made, and there is little for a field director to do other than to design a program around those decisions. In practice, it is very difficult to reverse these decisions once they have been made, as relief agencies are extremely reluctant to return to donors and ask them to change or modify the conditions placed on their contributions. The problem, however, can be dealt with. Several agencies have realized that the time to influence donors' decisions is prior to the outbreak of a disaster. An agency prepares a guide for donors, outlining the qualifications and policies under which gifts will be received. Donor education is one of the most important aspects to be addressed in improving the performance of the relief system and eliminating the problem of prior constraints.

Accountability

It has been pointed out that disaster relief programs, while designed to help the victim, tend in fact to reflect the needs of the donors. This is the result of attempts by agencies to please their donors, as well as the lack of accountability of agencies and donors to the victims.

Two examples can illustrate lack of accountability. In the first, a relief agency establishes a food program in the immediate aftermath of a disaster. Due to language difficulties and lack of familiarity with the local community, the staff fails to ascertain what resources are available there. The relief effort inadvertently drives up the prices in the local markets, undercuts local shopkeepers by distributing massive amounts of free commodities, and reduces the ability of local farmers to market the crops they have salvaged. While many victims have received food aid, many others have been affected adversely. Yet what recourse do they have? Few have access to legal means and, in practice, few agencies provide an opportunity for those adversely affected to voice their concerns or influence program decisions.

The second example concerns storm shelters in hurricane-prone areas. It is common practice for many agencies to urge that schools, churches, or other large buildings be used as shelters. However, few of these buildings can withstand hurricane forces. They collapse, killing those who have sought refuge. Who then is accountable? The owner of the building, or the relief agency that urged that the shelters be designated without first studying the performance of large buildings in high winds?

For our purposes, accountability is defined as the establishing of both formal and informal ways in which beneficiaries can influence the content and direction of the program, with reasonable expectations that those in authority will comply with their decisions.[3]

There are several reasons why accountability does not exist today to any large extent. On one level, many agencies have a very unsophisticated view of relief operations, and many feel that because they are trying to do good work, the impact cannot be negative. In most cases, this is the most restricting factor: failure of the agencies to look beyond what appears to be self-evident and to explore in-depth the impact of their programs.

Other reasons are more profound and relate to the very nature of the relief system. With decision making often far removed from the scene of events, it becomes difficult to attach responsibility for actions in the field. Locally, as well as internationally, there are no recognized standards against which to measure performance of relief agencies and their programs, and governments are usually reluctant to enforce uniform policies or standards for fear of alienating the relief agencies and losing the aid they are providing. Governments assume that the relief agencies know what they are doing, and that they are experienced and professional, the experts that their public relations offices portray them as being.

Even if an agency makes major mistakes, there are no precedents for making it accountable to the people in the community. There are no precedents in international law, and as happens with the so-called good Samaritan clauses in medical law, private agencies would probably be exempted from most civil actions in any case. Where church-related organizations are involved, governments anxious to keep religion and politics apart are not likely to criticize or hold liable errant relief programs.

Given the obstacles that exist, how can agencies be held accountable and made more responsive to the needs of the people? Aid organizations must redefine their role in disasters and come to understand that they are participants in a process rather than the manager of that process (Ressler 1978). The agencies must be committed to an understanding of the long-range effects of aid, and their programs must have built-in flexibility and be based on time frames, technology, and materials appropriate to the victims.

Accountability requires that decision-making mechanisms be restructured and decentralized to the local level. The programs must be built upon extensive participation by the disaster victims at all levels of project planning and execution. The concept of accountability is rooted in the

3. Inter-American Foundation (1977), *They Know How . . .* , p.88.

philosophical assumption that people have the right to determine their own lives, cultures, traditions, values, and lifestyles.

Three indicators of program accountability are:

1. Beneficiaries can articulate their demands before the project activities begin.
2. Beneficiaries can, on a regular basis, take the initiative and make their desires known to the managers of the project.
3. Beneficiaries participate extensively in control and management of the project. Complete control is transferred early from the relief agency to the beneficiaries (Inter-American Foundation 1977).

Ian Davis (1975) has made clear the relation between accountability and a relief orientation: "Practice has shown that the more an organization is strictly relief-oriented, the less accountable it becomes. An agency that is looking simply to giving away material goods already collected and delivered is not likely to be overly concerned with developing a program with full and meaningful participation. Short-term relief agencies can enter a community, dump the aid and withdraw within a matter of weeks, never taking the time to assess the quality of its aid nor the impact."

Unless mechanisms are developed to hold intervenors accountable to the victims, post-disaster programs will continue to have only limited and mostly negative impact. This is not to say that agencies do not have responsibilities to their donors. Donors do have a right to know how their funds are being spent, and agencies are responsible for seeing that the aid is used quickly and constructively, but the ultimate accountability must be to the disaster victims, and the final test for evaluating a program must be "Does it meet the needs of the victims?"

Overloading Local Organizations

The organizations in the field that carry out actual relief activities are subjected to constant demands by donors and parent organizations. Development groups in particular are often called upon to expand their scope of activities into many areas outside their normal range of work. The result of trying to meet all the demands placed on them, by both the donors and the victims themselves, is "overloading." Two forms of overloading are obvious. First, the organization can be asked to take on too many projects with too much diversity, overtaxing its staff and diluting its effectiveness. Second, the organization may expand after receiving funds far beyond its capacity to control or dispense widely. Funding of local organizations must be handled very carefully. Many an effective development group has been destroyed because the amount of funds it received led to an overextension of its programs, staff, or capabilities and the resulting poorly executed program precipitated a chain of events that led to the organization's downfall.

In disaster situations, overloading is a particular problem for the more effective development groups operating in a country. Not only do their parent organizations wish to channel funds received as a result of the disaster through them, but often other organizations (governmental, inter-governmental, and even other private agencies) wish to capitalize on the experience and expertise of an agency by providing funding or asking it to expand its activities into areas of concern to the other intervenors.

Competition

At all levels of the relief system, competition is an inherent feature and a common practice. In the upper levels of the system, agencies find them-selves competing for funds, public awareness, and recognition from the same sources. At the middle and lower levels, competition for success is added to the list. Competition for recognition and influence can often be found in some donor governments.

For organizations in the field, competition for success and recognition of their achievements can become an all-consuming motivation. In some agencies, success is measured by the number of victims reached, the number of houses constructed, the number of tents distributed, or the tonnages involved. Many agencies are "rated" in the public eye by the amount of material they can deliver in the shortest period of time. There are mechanisms within the relief system that inadvertently encourage this attitude and competition. Examples are the donor lists maintained by various organizations.

The result of this competition is that attention is diverted away from real needs so that some agencies can get an edge over the others. In a recent study (Cuny and colleagues 1977) on the provision of emergency shelter and post-disaster housing, the authors found that "intervenors consistently set higher priority on the number of housing units produced, rather than on the contribution made to the building process." The number of houses is seen as the end product or result of the program. Success is measured in terms of the donor and not of the victims. As a result of the competition and the emphasis on numbers, the only contribution to the society is an artifact and few, if any, contributions are made to the social, economic, and construction aspects of building within the community.

Beyond a distortion of objectives, there are other negative consequences. Competition normally results in inequitable distribution of relief materials.

Nor do all victims receive equal attention. Each program wants to develop its own package and, even within the same communities, the level and extent of service offered by competing relief agencies can vary substantially.

A third result of competition is that it discourages cooperation between agencies in post-disaster situations, where the lack of technical information and expertise is often very marked. Lack of cooperation can mean that disaster victims are denied full access to major resources.

Finally, competition always results in redundancy and waste. During the early days of Programa Kuchuba'l, a large agency operating in the same communities decided that it should have its own housing education materials produced by its own artists. This resulted not only in duplication of effort to the same audience, but also (in the attempt to be different) the program director suggested a bracing method different from that suggested in the booklets produced by Programa Kuchuba'l. This method proved difficult to build and, if not constructed properly, to have no strength whatsoever.

Competition, of course, is not always bad, and many innovative programs and approaches have resulted. On the whole, however, competition is more destructive than constructive, and should be restricted and discouraged. The governments of the affected countries have ultimate responsibility for controlling the competition so that victims receive equal treatment by all intervenors. The methods that can be used are the development of uniform relief and reconstruction policies, the setting of basic standards for relief, and the development of model program approaches for providing aid. The time to adopt these methods, however, is long before a disaster strikes. Trying to sort through the competing and conflicting values and goals of the relief agencies during the actual conduct of post-disaster operations is virtually impossible.

Lack of Coordination

Coordination efforts normally go through several stages. In the immediate aftermath of a disaster, there is high interest in coordination among the relief agencies, and there are usually several attempts to establish effective cooperation. After about six weeks this interest falls off. This is because most agencies have already established their programs and are much more interested in fieldwork. Coordination then becomes a more local or regional activity, with the sharing of information and resources by agencies working in nearby communities. During this period, coordination tends to become sector-oriented; for example, agencies working in housing tend to coordinate activities among themselves.

In the final stage, which occurs well into the operation, usually in the reconstruction period, broader interagency cooperation at the executive level is established. Agencies that intend to conduct programs for more than several months find that coordination is helpful for dealing with the local government and vice versa. Furthermore, many agencies will branch out into other sectors, and more formal cooperating arrangements are seen as beneficial. At this point it is not unusual to see the formation of a new organization to serve as an information clearinghouse and to provide a forum for interagency meetings.

Coordination, however, could be a lot more effective, especially in the emergency period. The actions normally taken to establish coordination often serve to add further confusion to the situation. For example, organizations without operational experience in the country are often assigned the role of coordinator. Competition among agencies, not only for resources but also for publicity, works against cooperation. And many groups, convinced (often with an evangelistic fervor) that their way of operating is *the* only way, refuse to cooperate with any group that does not adhere to their methods.

Another obstacle to coordination among the international agencies, especially the volags, is the need many agencies feel to have a separate, identifiable program that they can show their donors. Alan Taylor (1978) has written that "individual programs are regularly fashioned with an eye to their publicity value, rather than according to whether they will fit in with a coordinated, effective and efficient response by all agencies."

To improve coordination, a certain amount of planning must be done prior to the onset of a disaster. Preparedness plans that will promote cooperation should be drawn up and agencies operating in the country should be designated to serve as coordinator should the need arise. However, the most effective cooperation in the world is no substitute for pre-disaster planning. The time to decide what to do is when there is time to consider all the options thoughtfully, not amidst the confusion and pressure of the emergency.

Obstacles to Change

Change has been slow in coming to the relief system for many reasons. The very nature of the system and the way it is organized is the primary obstacle. Contributing factors include the following:

LACK OF COLLECTIVE MEMORY

Relief organizations are often slow to change because they have not internalized lessons learned in the field. Most relief organizations are structured so that in a disaster they can increase in size from a small skeleton staff to a large operating group in a very short period of time. This model relies heavily on volunteers or short-term employees who have particular specialties. In general, these persons will not be familiar with disaster issues, nor have a long-term commitment to the organization. Most short-term staff see their role only as workers, not as evaluators or critics of the system. Only a few will be motivated to write about their experiences, and few have a base of experience from which to draw. Thus their reports are usually disregarded by the agencies.

There is a high turnover in professional staff of the relief organizations, particularly at the field level. Few agencies can afford to maintain a large relief staff during nondisaster periods, and thus the accrued experience is lost.

Many intervenors are active only in the emergency phase. Few of these agencies leave a residual team in the country for any period of time after the disaster, or monitor the results of their relief program. Therefore they never have a chance to see the long-term results of their actions or to incorporate these "lessons" into future programs.

FAILURE TO EVALUATE DISASTER PROGRAMS

Until recently, there were few good evaluations of disaster-aid programs. Only a handful of longitudinal studies have been carried out, and even information on the major program approaches used by voluntary agencies and governments is meager. The Presidential Commission on World Hunger, trying to obtain information on the impact of food aid programs carried out under the PL-480 provisions in 1978, could find only audits and logistics studies of food aid, but no evaluations of their effectiveness or impact. This despite the fact that these programs have been in operation since the 1950s. (A number of studies of the impact of PL-480 programs have since been initiated.)

The reasons why evaluations have not been conducted are varied. For the most part, agencies have not seen the need to evaluate their actions or their impact; that is, evaluations are not a priority activity. For many, evaluations are viewed as costly and time-consuming.

Evaluations also pose a threat to agencies, especially those dependent upon public support. If an evaluation is negative and this information made public, agencies fear a disruption in their funding.

Evaluations are often difficult to carry out, even when they are desired, because of the nature of the system and the high staff turnover. Furthermore, evaluation techniques, until recently, were not particularly well developed. Evaluations often centered on the agency and the donors' concerns, not on the victims' concerns or the impact of the aid program.

Typical evaluations were more concerned with the accounting procedures and the logistics of the program and completely ignored the social aspects.

The result of the failure to evaluate programs is that mistakes are repeated again and again and the base of information from which change evolves is not developed.

FAILURE TO APPLY RESEARCH

A major constraint on changes in the relief system is lack of research to facilitate change. Research in the disaster field to date has been segmented, with concentration on the technical aspects (such as earthquake engineering, hurricane monitoring, and weather modification) and to some degree the behavioral aspects (such as the reaction of a community to evacuation warnings and the response of a society to a disaster). Very little of this research has been concerned with the problems of disasters in the Third World. Russell Dynes, formerly the head of the Disaster Research Center, estimates that over 90 percent of all disaster research has concentrated on problems and needs of the industrialized societies and has little bearing on problems of the Third World (National Academy of Sciences 1978). The major research gap, however, is in the exploration of program approaches and strategies for intervenors. Unfortunately, there is little financial support for such research, because the agencies have not recognized the problem.

Another difficulty with the research that has been conducted is that of translating the results into useful applications. The problem is one of communication between research institutions and the relief agencies. In general, relief agencies (especially the volags) do not have the capability to interpret research results and to develop applications from them. To some extent, a small number of technical consultants familiar with field operations have partially filled this void, but many agencies still are reluctant to hire consultants and will not make the commitment to establish links with the research community.

The lack of cooperation between the research community and relief agencies is nowhere more evident than in the field of earthquake engineering. Tremendous advances have been made in this field. Universities and engineering firms have participated in international efforts to explore the nature of earthquakes and the way they affect structures. Significant strides are made each year. Unfortunately, voluntary agencies and other relief groups do not participate in these endeavors. A survey of voluntary agencies in Guatemala in 1976–77 showed that none of the agencies had contact with any of the major earthquake engineering institutions, nor (with only one or two exceptions) were the institutions consulted during the course of the reconstruction efforts. The earthquake engineering institutions, for their part, completely ignored the program implementors. Several international earthquake engineering organizations sent survey teams to Guatemala to study the collapse of buildings, bridges, and other structures, but made virtually no contact with those organizations involved in reconstruction programs.

Within the earthquake research groups, little effort has been directed toward addressing the problems of the people most at risk from earthquakes—those of low-income living in self-built earthen housing—even though this group accounts for the vast majority of deaths occurring from earthquakes each year. If the results of the research are to have any impact on reducing vulnerability to disasters, both the research community and the relief agencies must establish closer ties.

RELIANCE ON VOLUNTEERS

One obstacle to change that must be confronted by the voluntary agencies is the continuing use of volunteers in relief and reconstruction programs. As long as agencies continue to rely on volunteers, especially those who have no prior training and little information about the society and the role of volunteers in disasters, the performance of volags will continue to be hindered.

The use of volunteers, of course, is a very complex issue, and for many agencies will require addressing some of their most fundamental beliefs. Volunteerism is deeply rooted in Western culture and revolves around fundamental beliefs that people should rise to help one another and not profit from the exchange. Doubtless there is also an element of noblesse oblige of the industrial nations toward the Third World, and for some institutions, a still-lingering feeling of carrying "the white man's burden." But there are practical reasons, also, why volunteers are employed. Volunteers are cheap labor and are almost always available. In a disaster role, they are particularly compatible with emergency needs, as volunteers rarely want to work for long periods of time and thus fit well with the voluntary agency's concepts of the time phases of disaster.

Because few agencies have a sophisticated approach to disasters, they do not seek qualified or skilled people, and again the ready supply of volunteers fits well into their relief system. But as our understanding of disasters becomes more sophisticated, the role of volunteers will have to be redefined and de-emphasized in order for these agencies to improve their performance.

Reliance on volunteers creates two primary obstacles. The first is that the use of volunteers contributes to the problem of lost experience and the lack of a collective memory within an organization. In many organizations, volunteers make up the majority of the work force at the field level, and many eventually fill decision-making positions during the emergency and reconstruction periods. To lose this experience after every disaster practically guarantees that mistakes will be repeated frequently.

The second problem is that most volunteers are untrained and unskilled in the subtleties of disaster work. Because these people will be with the agency only for a short time, the organizations are normally reluctant to commit precious funds for staff development. Thus, untrained and, in many cases, unskilled workers are placed in positions where they will confront a host of sophisticated problems. The result is that programs designed to help the victims are simplistic and unsophisticated, and again, common mistakes are repeated.

A final difficulty is that many agencies recruit volunteers from their home countries for short-term disaster service. These volunteers take jobs that could easily be given to local people. Foreigners are used because they speak the same language as the agency field staff. For reasons of communication, they are given leadership positions over local workers. It makes little sense, either from an economic or a public relations stance, to hire a foreigner to do work that a local person could do (and probably do better), and the resentment that is caused can affect the outcome of the program.

This is not to say that there is not a role for volunteers in the relief system. Yet agencies that wish to continue to employ volunteers must re-examine the nature of their involvement and balance volunteers with trained professional staff. If the volags are serious about improving their relief (and development) skills and performance, reliance on volunteers must be reduced.

LACK OF TRAINING

At all levels of the relief system, there is a lack of training for personnel who must deal with disasters. Typically, an agency provides orientation to its new staff members on the organization itself, descriptions of its projects, and project management systems. But rarely is training provided on disaster management, especially detailed information on strategies, approaches, and problems to expect. The lack of training is particularly a problem within development organizations. Even in those groups that have staff training programs, the amount of time spent on disaster orientation is usually minimal. Especially lacking is even minimal training about the connection between disasters and development.

Some agencies have recently developed disaster handbooks or added a section on disasters to their field directors' handbooks. Beyond this, little additional information is provided.

A review of the disaster manuals of a number of these agencies unveils additional problems. Most treat disasters as logistics problems and recommend approaches and procedures that are coming under increased criticism by disaster experts. For field personnel who have received no training, these manuals may tend to reinforce stereotypes and inhibit the development of effective programs. (Notable exceptions are the *OXFAM Field Director's Handbook* and the UNHCR *Handbook for Emergencies*.)

One cause of the problem is the scarcity of training programs on disaster management and of instructors with field experience. Few courses exist, though some schools permit individual studies and research on disaster management topics, but only in certain technical fields (such as earthquake engineering, epidemiology, geology, and meteorology) are disasters studied systematically.

Recent developments are encouraging, however. A number of short courses on disasters have been organized (most notably, the Regional Disaster Preparedness Seminars of AID's Office of U.S. Foreign Disaster Assistance, the University of Louvain's Disaster Epidemiology Course, the London School of Hygiene and Tropical Medicine's training program for potential volunteers, and the East-West Center's disaster management training program for government ministries). Much more is needed, though, and it is hoped that additional formal training programs will be initiated, such as the disaster management diploma program of the University of Wisconsin-Extension.

8
Influences on Disaster Response

CULTURAL INFLUENCES AND BARRIERS

Cross-cultural influences on disaster response and the problems they create are easy to identify. They stem from the intervenor's lack of familiarity with with the victims' culture, with the resources available to the victims, and with the native language. Differing cultural values often pose major obstacles to effective relief aid, as even the cultural differences within a society can be vast. It is often difficult for relief agencies to determine in advance the primary cultural constraints with which they must deal, but failure to do so severely impedes their programs' progress.

One set of cross-cultural problems relates to decision making. The likelihood that mistakes will be made because of cross-cultural problems usually increases when decisions are made far from the affected area or by organizations new to the area. Many relief and development workers feel that if a relief program is to be successful, the intervening organization must have strong roots within the society in order to deal with the cross-cultural problems; and indeed, several organizations refuse to become involved in disasters unless they have had prior experience in that country. For agencies involved in actual fieldwork, prior experience is extremely important. For agencies whose primary interest is providing support to the host governments or to organizations in the field, the cross-cultural obstacles mentioned above can often be reduced through careful planning. But there is no substitute for involvement of knowledgeable people from within the society in the decision-making process.

TECHNOLOGICAL CAPABILITIES

Technology influences disaster aid in two ways: First, it enables agencies to devise quick, although not necessarily appropriate, solutions to needs.

Second, it influences the way in which needs are perceived and thus indirectly shapes many approaches. In other words, needs are seen in terms of solutions. Take, for example, the issue of emergency shelter. Technology makes it possible to build the shelters and to move them from one country to another very quickly.

If it were not possible to deliver these shelters immediately, intervenors would probably emphasize developing approaches that would complement local initiatives. Agencies would choose approaches that would support processes occurring naturally after disasters. The following list takes this a step further. The column on the left shows the priorities of the relief agencies (Agnew and Patterson 1976), the column on the right that of the victims.

Agencies' Perceptions of Shelter Needs	*Victims' Perceptions of Shelter Needs*
Temporary structure	Permanent housing
Low cost	Low cost
Rapid construction	Labor-intensive or self-help
Air-transportable	Traditional appearance
Lightweight, movable	Place to store animals
Low maintenance	Replicable by local craftsmen
Small construction crew	Conformity to traditional living patterns (that is, segregation by sex within the structure)

Technological solutions may also ignore contributing factors, especially the social or political needs of the disaster victims. Again turning to the housing sector, technological solutions may ignore or fail to address adequately such issues as land tenure or economic problems related to housing construction.

Other examples where technological capability has influenced response are the provision of mass innoculations for suspected diseases following natural disasters; the extensive use of aircraft in all phases of logistics and search-and-rescue; the supply of high-protein "synthetic" foods such as CSM, WSB, and K-Mix II; and the practice of importing relief matériel instead of purchasing it locally. Such actions have become commonplace, facilitated by technology available to the intervenors. But the question remains: Does the technological capacity to do these things obscure other needs in the affected community?

INFORMATION SOURCES

Another factor that can limit the effectiveness of the relief system is the sources from which intervenors obtain information about the society in which they propose to operate. Organizations operating in the field need information sources within the community. Cultural and language differences, however, often distort the picture received by the organization. The more removed the information is from the field, the greater the distortion. Outside the country, most agencies must rely on translated reports. Furthermore, events significant in the culture of the affected society may have no significance to someone living several thousand miles away.

PERCEPTIONS OF DISASTER

Agencies' Perceptions

There is a long-standing debate as to how to define a disaster. What concerns us here is a working definition and how it is defined by the intervenors and other participants, for the definitions used can provide clues to the perceptions governing their actions.

First, let us look at some of the common definitions provided by voluntary aid organizations:

"Disasters are unforeseen events that cause widespread loss of life and require immediate large-scale relief from outside resources."

"Disasters are unusual, widespread events that disrupt the social order and that require help from outside the affected community in order to restore normalcy."

"Disasters are disruptive events that destroy property, threaten lives and health, and that are of such a scale as to require outside assistance."

In each of these definitions lies a key to understanding the relief agencies' basic perception of disasters, and thus the basis on which they formulate their disaster programs. The idea common to each—that outside assistance is required—indicates what is perhaps the most prevalent perception. Within this phrase lies an imperative to act—for disasters by definition *require* intervention in the form of either materials or organizational assistance. It is implied that intervention can resolve or ameliorate unusual problems, and that material aid is one of the primary tools for problem solving.

How do these definitions shape the response of an organization? To begin with, the assumed need for outside aid colors the agency's disaster assessment. Scores of assessments are conducted each year to estimate the material losses caused by a disaster; then orders are placed immediately with suppliers or donors, and arrangements are made to ship the materials into the disaster area. Rarely, however, are thorough surveys conducted to determine whether the materials requested are available or can be resupplied through the normal market system within a reasonable period of time (or whether the survivors can obtain them without outside assistance), because the fundamental assumption is that they cannot.

If an agency believes that disasters are relief problems to be resolved by material aid, then disasters become logistics exercises. The structure of its relief system will be designed to move the aid as expeditiously as possible from point A to point B and thence to points C through Z with as little loss from pilferage, spoilage, and breakage as is feasible. Its programs will be measured by how quickly the people receive the goods. But questions linger. Should speed be the prime criterion? And more importantly, are disasters simply "relief" problems?

Another telling perception is identified by the term "unforeseen events." The fact is that most agencies regard disasters as caused primarily by natural phenomena and fail to establish the real root of the problem: vulnerability derived from poverty. Disasters are in fact neither unforeseen nor unpredictable; but as long as agencies continue to place emphasis on immediate relief rather than on mitigation, and fail to include disaster preparedness and disaster prevention as part of ongoing development schemes, the "unexpected" event will continue to capture their attention.

The final perception expressed in these definitions and articulated by many agencies is the assumption that, because of the magnitude or severity of the disaster, the affected community cannot cope. This belief (often fueled by media reports of looting, the breakdown of civil order, or of people traumatized by the event) leads to the belief that intervention from outside will serve the re-establishment of order and will "hold things together" until the people can get back on their feet. As we will see later, there is little evidence to support this belief. In fact, the people hit hardest by disasters are, in the words of Ian Davis, "coping experts"—people who are extremely self-reliant and, although poor, are quite capable of rapid recovery if adequate resources are made available. The questions to consider then are:

1. What type of assistance is most necessary: assistance in restarting and improving the existing ways in which people cope, or assistance in the form of rapidly delivered material aid?
2. Where is an agency likely to place its emphasis if it defines disasters as situations where people cannot cope?

Governments' Perceptions

More progressive governments usually define disasters in the same terms as do relief agencies, but the definition is expanded to include a much broader social and economic range of consequences. This can be noted in the following definitions:

"Disasters are sudden events that force the reallocation of already scarce resources to meet basic survival needs."

"Disasters are sudden and unforeseen events that disrupt normal activities and slow or retard progress toward economic and social development."

Government is concerned not only with helping the disaster victims recover; it is also concerned that the disaster not retard the social and economic progress being sought. There is concern that disasters will require a disproportionate amount of attention, diverting personnel and money away from more important, longer-term projects and into welfare and reconstruction activities. There are also fears that disasters will affect the gross national product, especially the production of those materials or crops that are needed for export in order to bring in valuable foreign exchange.

For governments that see disasters in this light, a primary objective is to obtain as much foreign assistance and aid as is possible, so that existing resources within the country will not have to be diverted. For governments choosing this course of action, foreign relief appears to be a godsend.

The perception of disasters as primarily a relief problem to be met with material aid is almost identical with the definitions of the relief agencies. There is no awareness that actions taken during a disaster and the reconstruction period have a bearing on the development process; rather, the disaster is seen as an event apart from development and one that serves only as a break, or retardant, in the development process.

An alternate set of views is often held by governments that are controlled by an oligarchy, where maintenance of the social and economic status quo is a prime objective. The origins of disaster are defined in the same terms, but the consequences are seen in a different light. While there are no public advocates of the following points of view, if actions were authors, the following would be quotes:

"Disasters are large-scale events that create a breakdown of law and order."

"Disasters are events that point to the social and economic inequities within the society and threaten the established order."

"Disasters are large-scale events that underscore a government's impotence and inability to act."

Governments who act upon such beliefs are trapped. If they appeal for and accept massive outside aid, might not the population realize just how weak the government is, thereby sowing the seeds of change? On the other hand, how can the government fail to accept outside assistance if it really is not capable itself of handling the disaster? This too could lead to large-scale popular unrest. Ironically, the more repressive and ineffective governments often see most clearly the developmental aspects and consequences of relief actions, although they themselves probably view foreign relief organizations more in terms of their logistics capabilities than as instigators of social change. To these governments, disasters are situations that must be controlled. Intervenors that provide aid must be alert to the possibility of becoming pawns in a game where the rules are never spelled out.

There is a third governmental definition that we will explore briefly here before returning to it in a later chapter. Here the possibilities presented by a disaster are recognized.

"Disasters provide an opportunity to rebuild a better society."

It does not question that aid is necessary. But now disaster is viewed as an opportunity, not as a set-back only. Among the perceived opportunities are a chance to rebuild a safer, healthier environment and to use a variety of resources that would not otherwise be available to assist the affected community in making a substantial leap forward on the road to "progress." To the government with this perception, there are never enough aid resources, and plans and programs are thrown together rapidly in order to take advantage of the new resources while they are available. In this view, three things are required: sufficient cash for the government to operate effectively; coordination of incoming aid; and reordering of priorities that will give the disaster area a larger share of the government's attention. A government with these objectives sees the immediate material aid provided by relief agencies as either an intermediate or stopgap measure, or as woefully inadequate to meet the greater needs. What a government wants most of all are the financial and material resources to carry out the greater plan.

Victims' Perceptions

It is difficult for the poor in developing countries to conceptualize a disaster. Life is always a struggle and the potential for the survival of the members of any family is only marginal. Early death is not an unusual event; in countries with low nutritional status and a high infant mortality rate, deaths within a family occur at rather regular intervals. Furthermore, the perceptions as to what the disaster means change as time from the actual disaster event increases. At first, disasters are perceived in terms of human loss and injuries, then material loss, and finally economic consequences. While a relief agency may see destruction of crops or homes as either an agricultural loss or a materials requirement, the victims see the loss in economic terms, namely, in income lost or income that must be diverted from income-generating activities to meet basic survival or comfort needs.

The sense of economic loss, or of economic opportunities lost, is the one perception that is common to all victims. It is also the common concern of each economic stratum among all the victims.

INFLUENCES WITHIN THE RELIEF SYSTEM

The operations of the relief system are often influenced by pressures unique either to disasters or to the disaster relief system. This is due, in part, to a misunderstanding of what actually happens in disasters, as well as to a real attempt to react quickly to human suffering and trauma. These pressures may have negative results.

The first of these pressures are time constraints in the form of deadlines to be met for most disaster programs. These time constraints are usually artificial and quite often arbitrary dates the agency sets as a means of hurrying along emergency and reconstruction programs. They are often related to what the donor perceives as a particular phase of a disaster or tied to some seasonal event, such as the onset of a rainy season or the winter. In very few cases do these deadlines have any meaning except to the agency that sets them and, for the people in the field who find their programs constrained and forced into unnecessary haste, they can be downright maddening.

A second constraint is the disaster-funding process. Because disasters are traumatic events, they can generate a tremendous amount of funds in a short period of time. In the early stages of a disaster, the availability of funds is phenomenal, but within a few months donations stop. Agencies know this and concentrate tremendous efforts on fund-raising immediately after the disaster has occurred. But early availability of large amounts of funds (which must be attracted by gaining the public's attention) brings with it a pressure to spend the funds as quickly as possible. Thus many agencies attempt to carry out their programs in a very short period of time while the funds are available and the disaster is in the public consciousness. The funding process contributes to the problem of time constraints. Often donors with the best of intentions set deadlines for expenditures of funds, the objective being to insure that disaster victims receive aid promptly. Unfortunately, haste and deadlines often result in programs that are poorly conceived, do not sufficiently involve disaster victims, and operate on information obtained at the height of confusion.

The next constraint is that of linkages between different levels of the system. Most organizations have clearly defined relationships during normal times. Following a disaster, organizations correctly feel that they must support those groups with which they have a prior relationship. The relationship must be re-examined, however, when an organization is forced to step out of its normal spheres of activity. A donor wishing to contribute funds for housing should look for an organization with housing experience. If the group with which the organization has a standing relationship is not in the housing field, it should either find a group that is in the field or change its priority.

Another problem unique to the system is the multiplicity of top-down pressures. In a system where donors donate to other donors who pass the money to other institutions that, in turn, fund other institutions doing the work in the field, the pressures for action and response multiply at each level. Following a disaster, urgency is heightened and the pressures added at each level of the system often result in excessive time being devoted to trying to meet each donor's perceived needs or requirements.

One aspect of this problem is the practice of *earmarking;* that is, the placing of constraints on how donated funds may be used. In the best of cases, funds are earmarked for certain types of programs. The donor may wish to contribute to housing reconstruction, medical aid, or social programs and, for the most part, this type of earmarking causes only mild inconvenience as long as the agency has the capability of carrying out the program designated by the donor.

Other constraints are also controversial and problematic in formulating a balanced relief or reconstruction program. Among the most common prior constraints are:

1. the requirement that all or a majority of the materials purchased be used within the donor's own country;
2. the requirement that donated goods be shipped on the carriers of the donor's own country;
3. the requirement that all materials shipped be granted duty-free status.

Immediately following the 1979 hurricane that struck the Dominican Republic, a large intergovernmental organization in Europe created a fund for housing reconstruction. It notified several private agencies working in the Dominican Republic that it would accept proposals. The New York headquarters of one agency, which had economic and agricultural development programs in the country, submitted a brief proposal, which was accepted on the day it was received.

Nine days after the disaster, the agency's field director in the Dominican Republic received a cable from his headquarters informing him that several hundred thousand dollars had been appropriated for a housing reconstruction program. It also informed the director that the program must be executed within sixty days. The director, who had no prior experience in housing, cabled his headquarters for authority to extend the deadline in order to determine how best to use the funds and to determine whether the organization should become involved. The headquarters, fearing loss of the money, instead began looking around for a housing consultant to assist the field director in setting up a program. When the consultant arrived, he determined that housing was a low priority in relation to other immediate post-disaster needs and that housing reconstruction should not take precedence over other matters. Headquarters, not pleased with this assessment, demanded that the field office decide quickly on a program and get it underway. After examining various options, the field staff decided that the only way that so large an amount of money could be spent at one time was to order vast quantities of building materials. A hasty survey of homeowners' preferences determined what building materials were the most desired and a large order was placed for them.

In the attempt to get the housing program moving, the agency met with several local housing groups. One in particular suggested an approach that the agency chose to work with (which had not had prior experience in headquarters with this proposal, which was to train housing construction workers and neighborhood people in how to use the materials being imported in a self-help housing program. Headquarters cabled back that it would prefer to support a group with which it was already working and instructed the director to operate through that group.

The result? A local group involved in housing was denied resources and funds that would have enabled it to increase its effectiveness, and the group the agency chose to work with (which had not had prior experience in housing) ended up conducting a slipshod materials distribution program that had little lasting impact on improving the housing stock.

INFLUENCES AND PRESSURES OF THE PRESS

The role and influence of the press in disasters is a hotly debated topic and a definitive work has not yet been written. The press has been praised for bringing the true stories of disasters to the public and for its humanitarian efforts in stimulating public response to the human needs and suffering caused by disasters. On the other hand, it has been condemned for presenting sensationalist views of that suffering and for distorting the public's perception of disaster recovery efforts. Whatever the position taken, it cannot be denied that the press has enormous influence on the workings of the relief system at all levels. Extensive press coverage of a disaster can create tremendous pressure on agencies and governments to become involved. It can also create tremendous pressure to react quickly and massively to alleviate the suffering portrayed by the media.

Not surprisingly, the media end up distorting the picture of what happens in disasters. They do this by concentrating on the suffering of the victims and by showing the unusual events that occur in a disaster situation. Confusion is often depicted as ineptitude, and cautious, deliberate planning is often viewed as foot-dragging incompetence or failure to react rapidly. Stories filed by news media are those that will be of interest to the unaffected (outside viewers) and will be colored by the perceptions of the correspondents, who are often constrained by many of the same cross-cultural influences as the relief agencies. Stories can create an impression of vast destruction by focusing on the damage of a few buildings when, in fact, damage may be relatively moderate. Especially harmful is the fact that most news stories reinforce the stereotypes that people have about disaster victims and the processes at play.

Although the media can motivate the public and generate a tremendous response that will swell the coffers of humanitarian agencies, they can "turn off" the public the next day with a series of negative stories on how the disaster is being handled or a portrayal of the inequities that inevitably occur in these situations. Many agencies reported that donations were extremely high in the first few days following the earthquake in Nicaragua in 1972, but that donations fell off rapidly when news media reported on the corruption of the Somoza government in distributing relief supplies. In reality, the Somoza government was responsible for only a portion of the relief supplies, and private agencies were relatively free from these problems. Yet their donations were severely curtailed as a result of these stories.

Agencies must play to the press for public support, and this creates problems. The types of assistance that can be easily portrayed on film or television are very attractive because they "show" the agency in action. Scenes of food, clothes, and blankets being distributed, medical staff at work, and houses under construction all serve the public relations needs of the agencies. Pre-disaster planning, vulnerability analysis, preparedness activities, community organization, psychological counseling, and other important activities that cannot be photographed are neglected. The result is that photographic images reinforce misconceptions and perpetuate myths, which inhibit change in emergency response.

9
Post-Disaster Programs

Programs are the vehicles by which agencies fulfill their reason for existing—relief for the victim and reconstruction of a functioning society. Programs are the link between concept and action; they embody everything discussed so far.

Yet program structure and management is neither taught nor studied. Of all the elements making up the relief system, programs are the most important and receive the least attention. It is not surprising that there is a tremendous breakdown between idealistic expectations of what the agency should be accomplishing and what actually results. This chapter explores the influences and problems of program structure and management and ends with some typical program models.

FACTORS THAT INFLUENCE
THE ESTABLISHMENT OF A PROGRAM

Even before a field program is established, there are many factors that will shape it. Many of these are extensions of the forces within the relief system itself, and others have to do with the nature of intervention. Let us briefly review five of the most important sets of constraints on a program.

Motives

Motives for intervention are:

1. *Humanitarian Concern.* The prime motive for intervention.
2. *A Presence on the Scene.* Many agencies become involved in disasters simply because they are already working in the affected country when the disaster strikes. It would be practically impossible for an agency

already involved in economic or humanitarian work to avoid becoming involved in a nearby disaster.

3. *Opportunity.* Many agencies see a disaster as a chance to establish a presence in a community for a longer-term involvement.

4. *Furtherance of Primary Goals.* Many agencies see relief work as a chance to further their primary goals. This is especially true of church organizations, which sometimes feel that by responding to a disaster they can introduce and establish themselves in order to further their missionary and charitable work.

5. *Demonstration of Concern or Friendship.* Many intervenors provide relief to demonstrate a concern for the society or to promote kinship. In most cases, this is an extension of humanitarian concern, but for governmental agencies, it can be an attempt to gain influence or to support a friendly government.

These motives subtly shape a relief program. For example, an organization wanting to establish a presence for long-term involvement is more likely to develop programs with strong community-based participation and be much more responsive to meeting initiatives developed by the community. An agency with programs in-country prior to the disaster will usually operate through its existing organization and simply expand the staff or scope of work to meet the perceived relief needs. Relief experts can normally look at an agency's motive for intervention and make an accurate prediction of the structure, staffing patterns, and, in many cases, the spheres of activity that an agency will adopt in a post-disaster situation.

Resources Available

The available resources, especially funds and matériel, determine both the nature and the scope of a relief program. It has been said that many relief programs are a reflection of what the agencies' donors will provide. For example, agencies that work closely with AID can usually be expected to become heavily involved in food programs. Agencies supported by small organizations, such as churches, or that rely on individual donations are likely to provide varied material assistance, such as blankets, clothing, tents, and canned goods.

Resources also affect the period of involvement. Agencies with limited resources normally work only in the immediate post-disaster period. Agencies with access to more funds will become involved in reconstruction.

Another resource that can affect the nature of a program is the type of expertise available to the agency. An agency with links to a medical institution can be expected to provide medical assistance. If engineers are available, water purification or sanitation programs may be added to the program portfolio. The availability of expertise should not be overlooked. A survey by INTERTECT in 1977 of the relief and reconstruction programs in Guatemala showed that most agencies fit expertise into their program, rather than seek expertise to meet certain program objectives (Ressler 1977).

Time-Frame

Time constraints are usually dictated by funding pressures, by donors, and by perceived seasonal obstacles. Short time-frames are the bane of good project planning, especially when pre-disaster planning has been neglected. A program operating under artificial time constraints can rarely be effective. Short time-frames affect staffing patterns, limit community involvement, and inhibit project planning.

Forte of the Agency

The normal activities of a relief organization will often determine the type of activities it undertakes in the post-disaster situation. An agency working in housing is likely to continue working in that sector following a disaster. An organization with medical experience can be expected to offer these services or to expand them. (It should be noted, however, that the lack of experience in a particular field has never been a perceived obstacle to intervention, and many organizations have plunged into various relief activities without the slightest expertise or experience.) This is especially a problem in housing reconstruction programs and in feeding and nutrition programs in drought relief.

Earmarked Funds

The types of activities chosen are often determined by donors. If an agency receives funds earmarked for housing reconstruction following an earth-quake, the agency must carry out such a program whether or not it has any expertise in the field. Earmarking is a growing problem for agencies. Once the money has been received, it is too late to bargain about the conditions. Donor education and the development of guidelines for donors must be a part of an agency's disaster preparedness.

An Agency's Mandate

Many relief agencies have been established to meet specific disaster relief objectives. But unless the agency's founders thoroughly understand the link between disasters and development, the terms on which the agency is based often prevent it from being completely effective.

UNDRO's problems are fundamental to the way it was originally organized. They are a manifestation of how a failure to link disasters and development can affect the performance of a relief agency. At the time UNDRO was established, disasters were treated in isolation from development. The founders felt that disaster aid required a separate office. Thus UNDRO was given autonomous status within the UN system (much like that of the UN High Commissioner for Refugees) and was not placed under the auspices of the UN Development Programme (UNDP). When the office began to undertake disaster mitigation activities, the staff found that most of the measures they advocated were surrounded by development issues and could be addressed only in those terms. By not being a part of the UNDP, the UNDRO representatives were not always "in tune" with local development needs and problems and thus missed many opportunities to link mitigation and vulnerability reduction to development programs. Furthermore, several of the measures they suggested were simply unrealistic in the local political and economic context.

The establishment of UNDRO also demonstrates how failure to understand the disaster processes and how the system works when an organization's mandate is written can affect the agency's performance. UNDRO's primary mandate is to serve as coordinator for international disaster assistance. Because the agency sees disasters primarily as emergencies, it focuses on trying to coordinate *emergency* response. Typically, UNDRO dispatches a coordinator to the affected country for the emergency period and asks that foreign donors coordinate their assistance through Geneva.

In practical terms, this is not very effective. Outsiders unfamiliar with the latest developments or the local politics should not try to coordinate—a local group should. While preparedness activities and establishment of links to the government prior to the disaster can help, an outside coordinator, especially one who stays only for the emergency period, can never be truly effective and in many cases has only added to the confusion and delays.

FACTORS THAT INFLUENCE THE SUCCESS OF A PROGRAM

Once a program has been established, there are three factors that affect the outcome and determine, to a great extent, whether or not the program will make an effective contribution to the relief or reconstruction effort. Because these factors influence program implementation, they must be thoroughly understood by anyone contemplating a post-disaster project.

Attitude of the Agency

The attitude that an agency takes in a community toward the victims and the behavior of its staff are a major influence on implementation. This has to do with factors mentioned earlier, namely, the agencies' perceptions of victims and victims' behavior after a disaster. If an agency and the program it formulates reflect a paternalistic attitude, success will be limited. Alternatively, if an organization takes the attitude that its role is to help victims help themselves, rather than to step into the breach, to take over, and make decisions until the people can get back on their feet, the first obstacle has been overcome.

Relationship to the Community

An extension of an agency's attitude toward the disaster victims is its view of its role generally. Does it see itself as an agent of the relief process, or as a participant in community processes striving to meet community goals? The more an agency can become an integral part of the community, the more effective its relief programs will become.

Decision Making

The way in which an organization makes decisions is the most important factor influencing the relative success or failure of a program. Even if an organization is close to the community and is prepared to respond to initiatives from the victims, rather than initiate "solutions" itself, overall effectiveness will be limited and in many cases nonexistent, unless the organization places decision making at the community level. Many programs are steeped in democratic traditions and intentions, yet the final authority in all decision making resides with program staff, not with community leaders. Even with the most progressive intentions, a program cannot be effective unless decision making is shared. A post-disaster program can be nothing more than charity unless authority is shared with the community.

Assumptions about where ultimate power should rest are often reflected in the management model chosen by a program. An organization striving for effective community participation often finds that the management model selected inhibits, and in some cases prohibits, the very participation it is seeking. The tables of organization most often used are a reflection of industrial practice. These are designed to facilitate decision making from the top down, not from the bottom up. (So restrictive are these models that in many cases, the title of "field marshall" would be more appropriate than that of "field director.") If a program is to include community participation, staff must develop an organization that stresses participatory management and decision making at all levels.

COMMON PROBLEMS IN POST-DISASTER PROGRAMS

Program planning in many agencies can best be characterized as planning by default. Take, for example, the usual way a housing program is established. First, an agency requests an area or is assigned one by the government. The agency then estimates how many houses are required, determines the amount of money available, and divides the funds by the number of houses required. It then seeks a building system that enables it to build the required number of houses at that cost. Usually a standard design is adopted and mass construction begins. When the required number of houses has been built or when funds run out, the program ends.

The agency then measures its success by determining the number of units produced, whether they were produced within a certain time limit, and whether the project was completed within the budget. The houses are seen as the end product. Success is measured in terms of the donor and not the victim. Nothing has been left in the community other than an artifact—no contributions to the building process and no new skills. Often the newly constructed building cannot be repaired or maintained.

The following is a list of problems that are common to relief and reconstruction programs. They are divided into two parts, planning and execution.

Common Problems in Project Planning

An analysis of program planning carried out by intervenors in a number of recent relief operations reveals twelve common errors. This group, sometimes referred to as "the dirty dozen," consists of the following:

1. *Poor conceptualization of the project.* Not enough can be said about this topic. The vast majority of relief and reconstruction programs are conducted without the establishment of formal goals or objectives. Often there are vague pronouncements or statements such as "To help the victim" or "To reconstruct houses." Until a staff has established where it is going, it will be difficult to determine how to get there.

2. *Failure to establish policies to shape program planning.* Policies provide the framework by which staff makes choices throughout the program planning process. The failure to establish policies at an early date leaves a program without any guiding principles and with no firm basis upon which to make decisions.

3. *Failure to involve fully the local people in the planning process.* Enough said.

4. *Failure to examine the complete range of options.* Too often, an agency selects the first approach to solving a particular problem that it thinks of. Usually this is a matter of not taking enough time to explore the choices, or unfamiliarity with the alternatives.

5. *Selection of only one strategy or approach to problem solving.* Often an organization will "fixate" on a particular methodology and will develop a whole program around one standard approach. In essence, the agency is putting all of its eggs into one basket and if anything goes wrong, or if the approach meets with only limited success, the entire program may have to be restructured. Furthermore, the selection of only one approach does not easily accommodate variances in the affected community.

6. *Failure to balance the program.* A balanced program is one that meets a variety of related needs. For example: a housing reconstruction program that provides training in improved construction techniques, job opportunities for local builders and craftsmen, employment opportunities so that local people can gain the funds necessary to participate in the program, and supplementary projects designed to improve the sites and services (such as sanitation) would be considered a balanced program. One that simply provides a replacement for a damaged house would not.

7. *Overextension.* Programs become overextended by (1) trying to meet too many needs, (2) trying to meet the needs of too many people, or (3) trying to meet the needs in too broad an area. A good example of overextension occurred in Guatemala when a small relief agency with a staff of seven offered to provide housing reconstruction services to a geographic area of over 1500 square kilometers that had not only a rural population, but also a number of large towns. The total number of people in the area approached 75,000. When the program made a commitment to the government to provide services in this area, it had already received a total of $25,000 for reconstruction. During the course of the agency's efforts, it received an additional $25,000 and some roofing material as an in-kind contribution from a foreign government. The total monetary resources of the agency were approximately $80,000. From this was subtracted the cost of the staff, transportation and vehicles, and other overhead items. Had the agency been able to use the entire amount, the total contribution to the area would have been only slightly more than $1 per person. Even if the funds

A monument to waste: temporary housing unused and abandoned.

could have been used creatively, the number of people effectively served could not have been more than approximately 10 percent of those in the project area.

8. *Failure to examine cause-and-effect relationships.* Failure to look ahead is often a result of inexperience. Yet by thinking through many of the program options and trying to gauge the outcome, agencies could avoid many mistakes. In his paper on accountability (1978), Everett Ressler argues that as a part of the formal planning process, agencies should prepare a program-impact assessment similar to the environmental impact statements that are required of many construction projects.

9. *Failure to select a management model that fits the objectives of the project.* As mentioned earlier, the choice of management model and table of organization are crucial to successful project implementation.

10. *Failure to develop a management plan.* An examination of most relief or reconstruction programs will reveal a failure in this area. Good program management requires proper sequencing of activities, assignment of resources and personnel, establishment of milestones by which a program can gauge its performance, and the pairing of resources and personnel. Rarely do relief or reconstruction plans contain even the most rudimentary flow charts of activities. Without management plans, resources cannot be used efficiently. Agencies should emphasize the basics of program planning

in their training of program administrators, and model plans should be developed for disaster projects.

11. *Failure to budget a project properly.* Budget estimates are one of the most difficult exercises in project planning. Not only must a budget be prepared in an inflationary environment, but the amount of funds and their date of transfer to the program are often unknown. Thus incremental budget planning is required, and a certain amount of flexibility must be built in.

12. *Failure to obtain proper technical inputs.* This is largely a result of failure by the agencies to expand their horizons, and an attempt to oversimplify their humanitarian work. In most cases, agencies are simply not aware of all the related issues nor the technical expertise that is available.

Another aspect of the problem is the use of inappropriate technical inputs. For example, following many disasters, agencies send medical teams with the latest technical equipment and medicines. In most cases, however, what is needed is not high-tech curative medicine, but low-technology, community-based preventive health measures, such as sanitation and hygiene.

The use of technology and selection of the appropriate technology is always a problem for agencies with no prior experience in a community and little knowledge of the society in which the disaster has occurred. The time to determine the appropriate technology, therefore, is before a disaster has occurred.

Common Problems in Program Execution

The following problems are commonly found in the execution of relief programs.

1. *Overloading* the location organization with too much work or money.

2. *Concentration on the product, not the process.* Many agencies concentrate on the attainment of measurable goals, such as the number of people fed, sheltered, and clothed, and ways to measure their performance in these terms. Using these criteria, the agencies often neglect the process by which the goals are attained. In most cases, however, the process is at least as important as the product.

3. *Failure to support local coping mechanisms.* This was discussed earlier, but it cannot be overemphasized. Agencies must be extremely careful to support the local coping mechanisms as much as possible, or at the very least not to undermine their effectiveness.

4. *Failure to concentrate resources where the agency is most effective.*

5. *Staying in relief too long.* Many agencies fail to note the rapidly changing circumstances in the post-disaster environment. The time for emergency

relief and charitable programs passes quickly and other approaches are required in the transition to longer-term reconstruction activities. An agency that continues to provide relief during the reconstruction period will not only be providing aid inappropriate for the period, but will hamper the reconstruction efforts of other agencies and even delay the recovery.

6. *Failure to use local resources.* Many agencies find that it is easier to import the materials, supplies, and expertise than to acquire them in the affected community. Often imported supplies are cheaper, even with the added transport costs; because of the disrupted market structure following a disaster, they can often be obtained more quickly. Importing of resources, however, reduces participation by the local community, and bypasses an opportunity to provide a stimulus to recovery.

7. *Failure to prevent the recurrence of a disaster.* This is one of the hidden, yet most prevalent, faults of reconstruction programs. There are two aspects to mitigation: physical vulnerability and the socioeconomic. For example, houses can be made safer and communities can be relocated to less vulnerable sites. If disasters are a result of long-term socioeconomic problems in a society, agencies cannot address the vulnerability problem without undertaking a wider look at overall development aspects of the problem. The challenge is to formulate plans that are more development-oriented than disaster-oriented, but that include disaster mitigation as an integral part.

8. *Failure to develop local capabilities.* Opportunities to develop local capabilities are often missed. A relief program offers many opportunities for training or enhancing the skills of local people. Program management, accounting, construction techniques, materials handling, and vehicle maintenance are but a few of the skills that can be developed. Most important are the skills for planning and carrying out projects, which can be imparted to local leaders so that they in turn can formulate and carry out programs of their own. Helping others to develop skills can be time-consuming and more expensive, but is an added contribution to the community.

CRITERIA FOR ASSESSING A PROGRAM

There are various ways to assess a program, and each type of program has its own criteria. There are, however, several general criteria that can be applied to ascertain overall benefit. These are based on the *contributions* the program makes to the community. Contributions are divided into two sets: short-term, or immediate, contribution, and long-term, or developmental.

The immediate contribution is measured in three ways. First, the alleviation of suffering or the burdens caused by the disaster. This is the humanitarian contribution. Second, the contribution to or support of local coping mechanisms. This is determined by whether the program works through or enhances the capabilities of the mechanisms within the society that normally deal with disaster. The third measurement is whether a program shortens the length of time between emergency and full recovery.

The developmental contributions that a program makes are more difficult to judge, as well as extremely important, especially for assessing recovery and reconstruction programs. Actions are measured first by their contribution toward long-term development of the society, which is determined by the extent to which the program helped to develop local leadership and contributed to institution building and to the improvement of skills within the society.

The second developmental measurements are the spin-off benefits. For example, did the post-disaster program contribute to developmental goals or set in motion activities that would help attain these broader objectives?

Finally, the developmental contribution should be measured by the degree of increased safety of the community. A post-disaster program that simply returns a society to the same state of vulnerability that it had prior to the disaster would obviously fail this test.

SOME COMMON PROGRAM MODELS

Now that we have examined some of the common problems, as well as the assessment criteria, let's take a look at some of the more common program models and the styles of aid giving employed in disasters.

Program Styles

The manner in which an agency dispenses aid is referred to as the style. The four characteristic styles usually reflect the attitudes and objectives of the agencies (and are described here in the informal terms often used by field staff).

1. *Quick and Dirty.* This style can be identified by a quick response with massive material aid. The usual objective is to saturate an area as quickly as possible with relief items and to create as much visibility with as little entanglement as possible. The prime criterion is speed, especially speed of delivery. Quick and dirty programs are usually carried out in the emergency phase. The emphasis on delivery of relief materials is based on the assumption that material aid can solve many of the needs. (This is often called the "logistics approach" to disaster aid.)

Many of the agencies that use the quick and dirty style are well organized and highly efficient. Victim needs that recur in every disaster are identified and materials are sought (or drawn from stockpiles) to meet these needs. By standardizing the materials, the agency can substantially reduce the time required for acquisition, stockpiling, and shipment. But this can create other problems.

Because the basic decisions are made by the donor, with little opportunity for victim participation, they often result in delivery of inappropriate aid. Overall, quick and dirty programs have very little real impact on solving problems, and in those programs where the logistic systems have not been developed properly, the sorting of arriving materials can delay other higher priority deliveries and tie other distribution systems into knots.

2. *Firefighting.* The style is characterized by an ad hoc response to problems or needs. There is no prior planning or setting of objectives until the requests are received.

Found in all phases of the post-disaster period, this style of program is considered a notch above the quick and dirty style because it does relate to needs of or demands from the community. Problems arise, however, because it may be difficult to determine real priorities in the confusion after a disaster, and the requests, or nature of the requests, often depend on who is doing the asking. In terms of execution, it is difficult to tie the program together and make best use of resources because the program is responding to many diverse needs.

3. *Development through Disaster.* The objective here is to use the process of rehabilitation and reconstruction to achieve development goals. These programs concentrate on accomplishing all their goals during the transition phase. (In more practical terms, they may be trying to do everything before the money runs out.)

While a step in the right direction, this style of program is often frustrated by the fact that the priorities of the victims are not always the same as those of the agency, and that the potential for change during the transition phase is not as high as generally believed.

4. *Planting the Seed.* This style reflects an awareness that development is a slow process and that disasters offer certain *limited* opportunities for change. The emphasis is on setting up an environment and the infrastructure necessary to continue development activities after the disaster program is terminated. Intervention may occur at any point, though it is usually in the rehabilitation or reconstruction phase. Agencies stress the development of community leaders and organizations and a high degree of participation by the victims. These programs emphasize processes, not products, and material aid is secondary in the overall program.

Program Approaches

The way in which an agency provides aid determines both the shape of its programs and the degree of input and sophistication required to manage and complete them. In general, there are three discernible program approaches.

1. *The Shotgun Approach.* The objective of the shotgun approach is to provide aid in as many different sectors (e.g., health, housing) as possible. It is different from other approaches in that the activities are not tied together and thus do not complement or supplement each other. Critics of the approach note that it represents the "action end" of the premise that a little aid is better than none.

The shotgun approach is used more by relief than development agencies and by the newer, less experienced groups. If an agency has enough resources and good staff, the programs can have modest success, though management of many diverse, unconnected programs can be difficult. For an agency with limited resources, the shotgun approach soon puts it out of business, as resources are quickly dispersed. Furthermore, overhead costs of running many diverse programs can be relatively high.

A variation of the shotgun approach is sometimes used by large agencies without experience in an affected area. Initially, they set up projects in different sectors on a trial basis. When circumstances permit, the agencies evaluate the projects, phasing out the less promising ones and directing the resources to the more successful. Unless the projects are integrated, however, or are in the same sector, the diversity of the problems encountered by the staff remains little changed, though the actual number of problems may be reduced.

2. *The Single Sector Approach.* In this approach, an agency focuses all of its efforts and resources in one sector, for example, housing. It may, however, conduct a variety of projects and use a number of different methods to attain its goals. A typical housing reconstruction program might include provision of building materials, training of home builders, and making housing loans and grants available. Usually, the various activities are complementary and may be designed so that each contributes to the overall goals. Single-sector programs allow an agency to concentrate resources and reduce the need to diversify technical inputs. (For example, technicians in the housing fields are generally familiar with all the related aspects from construction to financing. Similarly, health personnel know the related activities peripheral to their work.)

The single sector approach can be used by an agency of any size during any phase of a disaster. If an agency undertakes a variety of activities, it needs a degree of sophistication to integrate them into a balanced program successfully. Single sector programs are considered more effective than shotgun programs and can be used in both urban and rural areas.

3. *The Integrated Recovery Program.* An IRP is a balanced program that responds to a variety of needs in a stricken community. The objective is to help the whole community to recover by addressing the needs in the key sectors. IRPs use, and are similar in concept to, the holistic approach found in integrated rural development programs (IRDPs). A variety of projects and activities may be conducted in different sectors, but they are planned, balanced, and integrated in such a way that each is complementary to and builds upon the other activities. If conducted properly, IRPs afford an agency the best vehicle to introduce change and to have a long-term impact upon a community.

A typical IRP might include the following activities. First, work schemes to repair community facilities would be started to enable people to obtain cash to buy replacement goods and materials lost in the disaster. The injection of cash would stimulate local markets and help speed their recovery. To facilitate this activity further, the program would provide aid to the small business sector, possibly with loans or grants, or help to provide the materials to be sold. By addressing needs in all the major sectors, the agency can help the entire community to recover uniformly, resulting in a shorter, less turbulent recovery period.

An IRP is characterized by: (1) stimulation of activity in various sectors, (2) the sequencing of activities at appropriate times, and (3) the use of a combination of direct and indirect methods to achieve objectives. IRPs work best in small communities and are rarely successful in urban areas, even those with clearly defined or identifiable neighborhoods.

With an IRP, there are four prerequisites for success: a thorough understanding of disasters and the processes at work; a high degree of sophistication in planning and execution; a good sense of timing; and the ability to recognize the transition from one phase to another.

Nonprogram Approaches

Up to this point, we have focused on how agencies formulate *programs* to meet disaster needs. The common practice is to develop a program for every major need or set of needs identified. Yet programs have very definite limitations. Funding is for a fixed period. An organizational framework must be established and various types of administrative machinery must be set up. When funds end, the program ends.

The "program approach" to problem solving will, of course, continue to be the major way agencies respond to disasters, but there are other nonprogram options and intervention strategies. As an example, let's take the situation in Guatemala in 1976. All the major organizations set up programs to provide metal roofing sheets, locally known as *lamina*, to the disaster victims at low cost. Altogether, the agencies' investment in *lamina* amounted to over $10 million. But was there another option? What would have happened if the relief organizations had made a decision to guarantee low-interest loans through existing loan institutions for everyone in the disaster-affected area, and to help small businesses or the government to develop a surplus of the building material? The distribution of *lamina* might have been handled without having to develop elaborate programs and without tying up such a large amount of cash.

An example of a nonprogram approach on a smaller scale was found in Jamaica in 1979. Heavy rains in the western part of the country produced large lakes, which stood for several months and through the normal cropping season. Several hundred farmers were displaced. Instead of developing a welfare program for the displaced farmers, a number of churches offered temporary use of church lands for farming. Money they had collected for the flood victims was placed on deposit at local lending institutions to guarantee loans to the farmers for seed and farm tools. Thus the farmers were able to continue their normal work with minimal disruption, and once the loans were repaid at the end of the harvest, the deposits were withdrawn and used as grants to those returning families still in need after the sale of their crops.

Most disaster programs, especially those of volags, are designed to help the poor. Unfortunately, in the Third World, the poor, affected disproportionately by disasters, usually outnumber the resources available. Innovative, nonprogram strategies can be used in concert with traditional program approaches to extend those resources.

10
Programa Kuchuba'l: A Case Study of a Reconstruction Program

Program planning, management, and execution, as well as the various factors that influence a program, are best seen in a case study. A good example is Programa Kuchuba'l.

Programa Kuchuba'l was chosen because it had a wide-ranging effect on many of the other programs conducted in Guatemala. It was a highly sophisticated program, one which pioneered the development of new methods and strategies for dealing with disasters, and it presented an alternative to the traditional methods used in post-disaster aid.

HISTORY AND DEVELOPMENT OF THE PROGRAM

Background

The earthquakes of February 4, 1976, covered a wide area of Guatemala. Destruction was greatest in the upper highlands of central Guatemala. In the center of this area lay the *municipios* (municipal districts) of San Martín Jilotepeque, Santa Apolonia, Chimaltenango, Tecpán, and San José Poaquil. Here approximately 90% of the structures were either destroyed or substantially damaged.

The population is predominantly Cakchiquel-speaking Indians, who live in the towns (*pueblos*) or rural villages (*aldeas*). This region is one of the densest in all of Latin America.

The farmers in the area lead a marginal existence, with many families forced annually to go to the coast to help harvest coffee, cotton, sugar cane, and other major cash crops on the large estates (*fincas*) of the coastal plains. The main crops in the highlands are corn and wheat, and only recently have improvements in the agricultural system been introduced that have allowed the farmers to realize greater returns and a gradual improvement in the standard of living. Even with these changes, however, it is still a marginal

164

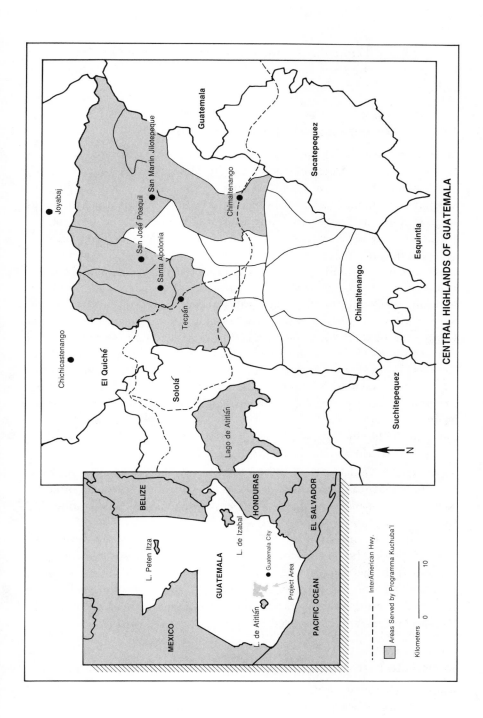

CENTRAL HIGHLANDS OF GUATEMALA

- - - - - InterAmerican Hwy.

[shaded] Areas Served by Programma Kuchuba'l

Kilometers 0 ———— 10

165

existence; and before the earthquake, a delicate balance between gradual economic improvement and possible economic disaster was only slowly tilting in favor of the former.

Principal Organizations and Their Relationships

Prior to the earthquake, there were several organizations working actively in this area, mainly in economic and agricultural development. One of these, World Neighbors, had been working for thirteen years, helping to strengthen cooperatives and training extensionists to work with farmers and their families in agriculture, nutrition, and health. At the time of the earthquake, World Neighbors was administering two development programs in the area. One covered the *municipio* of San Martín Jilotepeque (with thirteen paid staff and about fifty volunteer extensionists), and the other centered in Tecpán and covered the *municipios* of Tecpán, Santa Apolonia, and San José Poaquil (with six paid staff and twenty-five volunteer extension workers). World Neighbors was also assisting the El Quetzal Agricultural Co-op and the Kato-Ki Savings and Loan Co-op. The Kato-Ki had offices in most of the *pueblos* and members in almost all of the *aldeas* in the region. Recent improvements in agriculture enabled many of the members to begin small savings accounts with the co-op. The World Neighbors programs encouraged saving as a means of self-reliance and as "insurance" against possible economic disaster (such as crop failure or an illness or death in the family).

Some of World Neighbors' activities at the time of the earthquake were supported by OXFAM U.K., a British volag with independent affiliates in the United States, Belgium, Canada, and Australia. The field director, Reggie Norton, had served as a field representative in Managua following the 1972 earthquake.

The interrelationship of the organizations at the time of the earthquake was as follows: The Quetzal and the Kato-Ki Cooperatives were principally supported by the members of the co-ops themselves, with organizational, technical, and funding assistance from World Neighbors. World Neighbors was administering two integrated rural development projects, one of which, the San Martín Project, received its funding from OXFAM.

Immediate Post-Disaster Activities of OXFAM/World Neighbors

Immediately following the earthquake, the co-ops became the very first of the local organizations to respond to the people's needs. The members worked to help rescue other villagers, establish communications, and conduct damage surveys; and they met with as many people as possible to determine what the initial priorities were. These were transmitted to World Neighbors and OXFAM. Initially, the major activities of the first few days revolved around the need to set up a distribution system for blankets and medical aid, which were purchased locally. The initial success of the distribution program, which dispersed materials through the World Neighbors organization, demonstrated that it was possible to carry on large distribution schemes.

As the leaders of the cooperatives and World Neighbors programs met with people in the villages, they developed a list of priorities and presented it to the staff of OXFAM. After much discussion, three priority areas were delineated:

1. *Financial assistance to buy small silos to protect the grains that had been left exposed by the earthquake.* In Guatemala, farmers traditionally store their corn and wheat in one room of their house. Thus when the house was destroyed, they needed a new place to store and protect what could be salvaged.

2. *Re-establishment of the markets.* The farmers felt that there would not be enough aid for everyone, and it was important to have a market so they could sell their grains. They were also worried about the importing and free distribution of grains by some relief organizations, which they feared would flood the market and reduce the prices on their grains.

3. *Assistance in rebuilding housing.* The number one priority of the people here was clearly *lamina*. Before the earthquake, people with sufficient resources were buying *lamina*, and it had a high level of prestige and cultural acceptance. *Lamina* can be erected very quickly, does not use a great deal of wood for support compared with alternative materials, and is relatively safe. It can be used in a provisional shelter and then reused in the permanent house. People placed a high priority on roofing for two reasons:

> It was clear that the heavy tiles commonly used had killed many people when they fell off the roof during the quake. It was plain that the houses that had *lamina* had withstood the earthquake in greater numbers than those with tile;
>
> There were only two and one-half months until the beginning of the rainy season, and people wanted some sort of roofing material that would provide shelter quickly and could then be incorporated into a permanent structure.

Other roofing materials (such as straw and asbestos cement sheets) were explored but rejected for a variety of technical, cultural, and practical reasons. Thus a major purchasing and distribution plan for *lamina* was drawn up.

Several other important issues arose early. First was the determination of the people and area to be served. The co-ops wanted to distribute the *lamina* only to their own members. They felt that if they served everyone, there would be no incentive for people to join the co-op, and they wanted to use the program to help strengthen the co-op.

OXFAM and World Neighbors countered by saying that the co-op should serve the entire area, thereby demonstrating a commitment to helping everyone and demonstrating the value of the organization. This would increase popularity and thus membership. The agencies also pointed out that there would be ample resources to serve everyone. Co-op leaders were afraid that if they did not agree, the agencies would start an independent program that could eventually supersede the co-ops in importance, thereby reducing their effectiveness. The leaders therefore finally agreed to serve all the people in the area. Later, they further agreed to extend services to co-op members who resided outside the area.

Description of Housing before the Earthquake

An understanding of the housing before the earthquake helps us to understand the reasons why different elements of the reconstruction program came into being. First, housing in the area failed not because of the materials used, but because of the manner in which they were used. Houses had high walls, heavy roofs, load-bearing walls, and were un-balanced. An analysis of the damage showed that in only a very few cases did the adobe itself fail; rather, the houses came down because they were not built to resist earthquakes. If people undertook a self-help housing program, they would have to teach better construction methods.

In several of the villages, a type of construction known as *bajareque* was used. *Bajareque* closely resembles the wattle-and-daub method of construction. Bamboo poles or small sticks are placed in horizontal rows on either side of vertical poles and attached by special vines, wire, or nails. The *bajareque*-type structure is indigenous to the area and employs a method dating back to the pre-Colombian period. While it is not entirely earthquake-resistant, a house of *bajareque* construction with a lightweight roof of grass or *lamina* stood remarkably well.

In the project area, people traditionally built evolutionary structures; that is, the house starts with one or two rooms and gradually, over the years, more are added. By the time the structure attains its final form, it has undergone a number of changes, evolving from a small square structure into a longer, rectangular building and then, especially in the *pueblos*, into an L-shaped structure. With each addition, the balance of the house changes, and its ability to resist an earthquake is lessened.

Studies of housing in earthquake reconstruction programs have indicated that the houses built after disasters also follow this evolutionary process. Following an earthquake, people initially rebuild with lighter materials. As time passes, however, the earthquake is forgotten and the traditional materials again become prominent. Gradually, the housing is virtually identical to what was destroyed.

This underscored the need for construction of a strong, earthquake-resistant frame and for teaching better construction methods from the very outset of the reconstruction period.

Setting up Programa Kuchuba'l

A housing committee was set up consisting of one representative from OXFAM, one from World Neighbors, and a consultant from INTERTECT. The first step was establishing an overall policy for the program. The policy contained these provisions:

1. The program was to be controlled by the local people.
2. The program must use and be supportive of the local organizations, as well as the natural coping mechanisms of the society.
3. The structures to be built must use materials, skills, and techniques normally available.
4. The structures must be affordable for local people.
5. The choice of whether or not to build, or even to use the earthquake-resistant principles, must be left up to the individual.

There were many comments about the last policy because the OXFAM/World Neighbors program did not use its resources to build houses for people, or attempt to force people to incorporate earthquake-resistant building techniques into their houses. Other organizations built houses according to pre-set plans, developed without the participation of the people in the design process. There was also some resentment from the victims themselves because Programa Kuchuba'l would not build them houses as the others were doing. OXFAM and World Neighbors remained adamant, however, that the decision to build and the choice of materials and techniques should remain with the home owner.

Goals and Objectives

The next step was to develop a set of goals for the program and to develop a methodology for meeting them. The initial program evolved as follows:

1. The first component of the housing program was the *lamina* distribution program. Later, additional materials, such as wood preservatives,

A Guatemalan takes his *lamina* home. (Photo: Dave Collins/Save the Children)

nails, and other construction materials were provided through the materials distribution network.

Most of the items distributed through the network were provided at a subsidized price. Wood was sold at cost; everything else was sold at one-half of the wholesale price.

2. An extensive program would be undertaken to teach better construction methods. This program would consist of four parts:

Training the local builders;
Training new extensionists and *promotores* in the housing skills;
Training existing staff in the housing skills;
Training, as time permitted, other interested groups and voluntary
Training, as time permitted, other interested groups
and voluntary agencies working in the area.

The primary emphasis of the training program was on local *albañiles* (masons) and *carpinteros* (carpenters). These were the people already respected in the community as builders, who in the long run would be asked for advice and whose recommendations and actions would be followed. The advantage of concentrating on *albañiles* was that they already knew how to build; thus all they would need was training in how to use earthquake-resistant techniques. Also, by concentrating on the *albañiles*, the project would support the local building process, as it would be improving skills and supporting the builders. *Albañiles* were selected as instructors to teach the building techniques to others.

Secondary emphasis was placed on the training of extensionists. There were two groups of World Neighbors-trained agricultural extensionists, one in San Martín and one in Tecpán. They were to receive additional training

A local builder explains techniques for housing construction. (Photo: World Neighbors)

Local builders participate in building a safe house to learn better building techniques. (Photo: Mary McKay/World Neighbors)

so they could teach earthquake-resistant construction in addition to their other work. But because they were not builders, it was also necessary that they receive instruction in basic construction techniques.

3. A program of building model structures throughout the program area was undertaken to provide:

> On-the-job training for builders and extensionists;
> Model houses showing the earthquake-resistant principles
>   and demonstrating that local materials could be used safely;
> Limited housing for persons within the program area who were
>   unable to reconstruct their own dwellings, for example, widows and
>   the elderly;
> Housing for the program and co-op staff;
> Community buildings to provide meeting halls for villages.

The last two merit special attention. The question of staff housing became an issue early on. Some felt that it might appear as if the staff were taking advantage of the program to better their own interests. The program felt that because the staff were community leaders, their living in houses that used the new construction techniques would encourage others to follow suit. It was also felt that because they were working with the program, they did not have time to devote to their own housing, and therefore it would be a nice gesture to provide some help in rebuilding. It was stipulated, however, that they provide or pay for the materials, while the program would provide the labor.

The community centers were also debated. The consultants felt from their experience that all the demonstration structures should be houses. The other members of the committee, and the representatives of the communities, argued that community centers were needed in each of the villages to serve as a focal point for community organization, and that building them was an activity in which the whole village would participate. Furthermore, since they would be used frequently, a greater number of people would be exposed to the construction techniques.

4. A program of technical assistance would be provided to the villagers and *albañiles*. The objectives were:

> To work out problems with the new construction techniques arising from the use of local materials;
> To work out problems arising from the introduction of new building materials.

5. A program to advise local groups on proper salvage techniques and to demonstrate proper techniques of inspection, recovery, storage, and repair of materials salvaged from the ruins was instituted. Where possible, model salvage projects were to be carried out to demonstrate these techniques.

There were several factors that would assist the proposed housing program. First, local groups were functioning well, especially the co-op organizations supported by World Neighbors. Informal organizations, such as the extended families and ad hoc groups, were also beginning to get together to discuss reconstruction. Especially impressive was the way local leaders had responded to the emergency. The *lamina* distribution program just beginning was working smoothly, and it became obvious that many people not previously associated with the co-op had turned to it as a place where their ideas and needs would get a fair hearing.

Also on the plus side was the fact that local builders were anxious to learn how to build earthquake-resistant houses. Many of the builders had already discussed how they should confront the problem of rebuilding. They knew economics would force most people to rebuild with adobe, and they wanted to know how to build safe houses.

There was a wide range of literacy among the builders. Some could read or write Spanish fairly well and even interpret technical drawings, but others had no formal education and had learned their building skills through apprenticeship and on-the-job training. Thus the program had to develop new methods of communicating these skills to people at vastly different levels of literacy.

Initial Organization of the Program

While the program was being set up, several events occurred that influenced the organizational structure of the Programa Kuchuba'l.

Two weeks after the earthquake, volag representatives met with the new National Emergency Committee and outlined their future plans. The NEC suggested that each agency be given responsibility for defined areas, and two days later, OXFAM submitted a plan outlining the *lamina* sales program and the areas it proposed to cover. The plan was accepted by the NEC, and OXFAM was designated as the authority responsible for relief and reconstruction in the *aldeas* and rural areas of San Martín Jilotepeque, Tecpán, San José Poaquil, and the *pueblos, aldeas*, and rural areas of Santa Apolonia.

It was felt that the organization of the program should reflect each one of the areas. However, the Kato-Ki and El Quetzal Co-ops had been working in areas other than those covered by the agreement. Therefore, it was decided that a special branch of the program would be set up for these members.

During the emergency, there were essentially two staffs. One had headquarters in Guatemala City, where it maintained contact with the government and other volags, as well as procured materials. The second was the housing committee, which was located in Antigua. Generally, those in the city were OXFAM staff, those in Antigua, World Neighbors. Due to problems in communication and differences in ideas, each moved in different directions, and it became difficult to coordinate their activities and operations. By the end of the fourth week, it was necessary to establish a coordinating body to provide leadership and direction.

A month after the earthquake, a meeting of the key program people was held in Guatemala City. The new program—called Programa Kuchuba'l (Cakchiquel for "working together")— a joint effort of OXFAM and a union of World Neighbors programs and cooperatives, was officially established. A formal table of organization was adopted and a board, made up of the key project personnel plus representatives from the local people, was established. Many of the personnel in the pre-earthquake programs were incorporated into Programa Kuchuba'l and were expected to carry out dual roles, with the understanding that as reconstruction activities waned, they would return to their normal activities. Materials distribution was assigned to the cooperatives; the housing education program was to be carried out by a new housing office in charge of coordination, production of educational materials, and technical innovations; and the training of *albañiles* was under the supervision of World Neighbors.

The initial structure of Programa Kuchuba'l is shown on page 175.

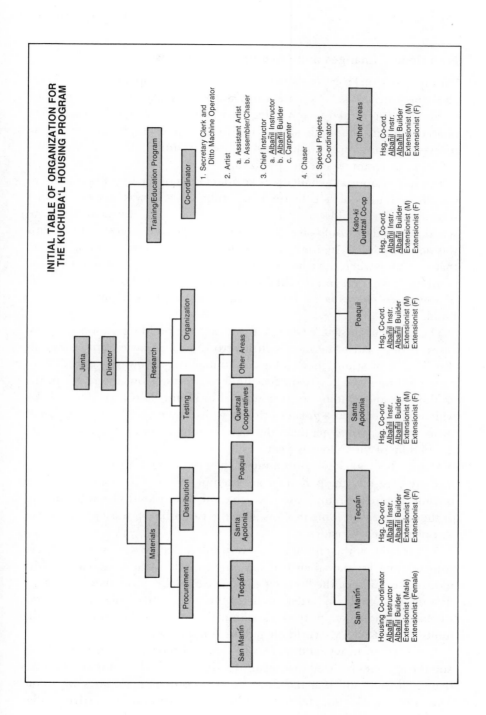

INITIAL TABLE OF ORGANIZATION FOR
THE KUCHUBA'L HOUSING PROGRAM

Evolutionary Changes and Operational Problems

Various parts of Programa Kuchuba'l continued to operate several years after the earthquake. As time from the earthquake increased and the communities returned to some degree of normalcy, various projects were phased out and emphasis shifted to others. For example, as the people recovered economically and markets were restored, the materials distribution program was de-emphasized.

The most important change was an adaptation of the overall program to the time frame of reconstruction. Originally, it was estimated that reconstruction would take two years, and most of the activities were scheduled so they would take place during this period. However, one factor was not considered. In every country, there is a traditional building season; that is, a time when the climate permits construction and people have the combination of time, money, and materials to devote to housing. If any one of the three elements is not present, then people will not be able to build.

The earthquake struck Guatemala during the building season. In most cases, people had some money (from crops) and because of the materials distribution program, they had access to materials. However, they did not have the time, for they spent that time recovering from the shock of the earthquake and tending to their normal economic and agricultural tasks, which they viewed as a greater priority. Most of the people built makeshift structures that would get them through the remainder of the year and into the middle of the following year.

Most relief agencies concentrated their housing activities in the immediate post-disaster period in an attempt to build as many houses as possible before the rainy season, which came three months later. By the end of the rainy season (nine months after the earthquake), most agencies had completed their activities.

A year later, at the end of the harvest, many people were ready to begin construction, for they then had the time as well as the materials and the money. But most of the housing assistance available immediately after the disaster was gone. In order to meet this increased demand, Programa Kuchuba'l had to adapt to work within the people's time frame, not the limits of the OXFAM/World Neighbors funding period.

This cycle of heavy (and increased) demand repeated itself a year later, and the agencies realized that reconstruction would take many years longer than estimated and that the funds for reconstruction would soon wane. Thus the agencies sought and emphasized self-supporting activities that would continue after funding ceased.

Most of the functional changes occurred in the housing education component. The most important of these concerned the method of teaching and the target group. Initially, the new building methods were conveyed in a different manner in each area. In Tecpán, Santa Apolonia, and Poaquil, classes were given for *albañiles* in each community, while in San Martín emphasis was on teaching the World Neighbors' extensionists, who would then try to teach the individual families. Both approaches had their drawbacks, so an alternative, more personal, method was tried. In July, a vocational school for *albañiles* was set up at central points in the project area. Emphasis was shifted from general classes on earthquake-resistant techniques to a more thorough curriculum covering all aspects of housing construction and the skills required. During this time, emphasis also changed from teaching the *maestros de obra* and families to turning out new *albañiles*.

Because the staff intended to place as much of the program as possible in the hands of the local people, World Neighbors appointed the chief instructor as director of the housing education project, replacing the World Neighbors' staff person (an American). A superb and highly respected *maestro de obra* who had quickly grasped the new concepts, he nevertheless was not prepared for the administrative aspects of the position, nor in practice could he continue both to teach and administrate. When this became obvious, World Neighbors felt obligated to step in and reassume control, causing a small crisis of confidence and briefly undermining the respect in which World Neighbors was held as a result of its stated goal of local management. Looking back, there is no doubt that the chief instructor could have taken over the directorate later had he been given a chance to acquire the skills, but the experience points out the need to balance idealism with common sense.

Another operational problem that continued to hamper the program was the lack of available Guatemalan technical expertise. Despite several efforts to recruit local engineers and architects to work with Kuchuba'l, none were found who were familiar with traditional construction. Thus the consultants (INTERTECT) were retained for a series of one-month visits at three-month intervals to check on progress. The result was that if a technical problem arose, a decision was delayed until the consultants returned. The lesson here is that either the agencies must develop their in-house capabilities or if local expertise cannot be found, should contract long-term consultancies.

A situation arose in the first year that affected all the agencies and the attitudes of the local people toward foreign assistance. The National Emergency Committee (NEC) encouraged each voluntary agency to undertake reconstruction in a designated area, instead of duplicating efforts throughout the affected region. The purpose of this policy was to avoid overlapping of resources, to help distribute aid to all regions, and to assist the voluntary agencies in raising money, as the policy would allow each organization to describe a defined area to its donors where they could see the results of their contributions.

Despite its intent, the assignment of areas had negative implications. First, not all the relief organizations were made subject to the same type of agreement. Some agencies received authorization to work in the entire country. This issue caused strain between groups working in the same area.

Second, the government made no effort to check out the ability of the organizations undertaking the commitment to rebuild various towns. For example, Chimaltenango, which is a major town of 35,000 people, was assigned to an organization based in California. It was not a volag, but a small group of businessmen who were involved in relief primarily for tax purposes, and were not capable of carrying out any type of reconstruction program, or even of raising a substantial amount of money for assistance. In fact, when these businessmen committed themselves to rebuild Chimaltenango, they did not even know where the city was located!

The assignment of areas might have had some benefits had NEC thought more about the division and assignment of agencies throughout the country. However, the policy created competition between agencies, generating more negative than positive results. The problem was that the policy created inequities in the distribution of relief and reconstruction aid. The level of assistance provided in each area was different, and many agencies distributed aid under differing requirements and policies. For example, some agencies sold *lamina* at subsidized prices, some gave it away free, and some instituted *lamina*-for-work programs. Thus local people resented certain programs. This was especially a problem when one agency sold materials while the agency in the adjacent area provided them free.

The letter of commitment between the government and each organization left the impression that the volag was given *sole* responsibility for reconstruction in the assigned area, and many agencies took this pledge quite literally. One organization, in fact, issued an order to its assigned village to stop all reconstruction activity until the agency could figure out what to do.

There is one way in which the system could have been improved. Had the NEC, and later the National Reconstruction Committee (NRC), established *uniform reconstruction policies* (for example, setting a standard policy for sales of *lamina*), this would have done away with many of the inequities of the system.

From the very beginning, the OXFAM staff in Guatemala City was active in trying to get the government to adopt a uniform policy for the distribution of *lamina*. OXFAM had already decided that it would subsidize its sales and felt that this policy should be adopted by the government or at least by all the foreign relief agencies. The government rejected the idea initially, for it felt that the victims should not have to pay for anything. After a number of discussions with the OXFAM staff, however, the government changed its mind and *requested* voluntary agencies to follow such a policy. Most refused to go along. Some pointed out that, in their advertising, they promised not to sell materials. In some cases materials had been donated under laws or agreements that expressly prohibited sales. Therefore, they were bound to donate the materials. This impasse caused problems for the organizations that were selling materials or teaching improved construction. Even those that had been working in Guatemala for a long time were severely criticized because they would not give away the materials or build complete houses as areas in neighboring agencies were doing. People even stayed away from Programa Kuchaba'l's educational efforts in the hope that it would get OXFAM and World Neighbors to change their policy (Froman et al. 1977).

THE UNIQUE ASPECTS OF PROGRAMA KUCHUBA'L

The three things that made Programa Kuchuba'l unique were the high degree of citizen participation and involvement at all levels of the program, the educational component, and the sophisticated strategies for utilizing project funds.

Involvement of the People and Reinforcement of Local Institutions

Programa Kuchuba'l had one of the highest degrees of participation of any program in Guatemala. From the very beginning, and at every level, OXFAM and World Neighbors stressed that the people were to be involved in planning and carrying out the program. Planning and management of the program were accomplished through the *junta directivo* (joint directorate), which was made up of representatives from each of the participating organizations (OXFAM, World Neighbors, the co-ops, and the World Neighbors–supported extension programs). The head of each of the projects (housing, block making, and road construction) usually attended, but could not vote. Decisions were made collectively, though the OXFAM director undoubtedly had a larger influence because OXFAM provided the majority of funds.

At the community level, participation by each *aldea* was a prerequisite for initiating program activities. The program staff visited each village and offered to hold a class on safe construction and to discuss the program. After the class, the community exchanged ideas on how the techniques could be disseminated and how they themselves would participate. The staff explained that the program would assist a village only if invited, and if the community would provide the site, most of the construction materials, and the labor. In turn, the program would provide any construction materials that had to be purchased outside the community.

Each village selected one *albañil* or other suitable candidate to receive training in how to build a safe structure. (While in training, each builder received a salary from the program, since no villager could afford to donate a month's work.) After training, the builder would return to the community and supervise a crew of volunteer builders in the construction of a demonstration building (usually a village meeting hall). All decisions concerning the meeting hall, plus the organization for supplying labor and materials, were the responsibility of the village. Since the community provided most of the materials, the villagers had to decide what size and shape of building they were willing to build. Also, the villagers had to discuss what building materials would be used by the majority of people in that community, and decide what type of wall construction they wanted (the majority of buildings were made of *adobe de canto*, a type of construction where the adobes are placed on their sides, or *bajareque*, a form of construction using mud and cane).

Thus at the community level, it is clear that the program not only stressed local decision making and involvement, but further reinforced the existing community structures (coping mechanisms) and supported the local builders, while at the same time improving and contributing to their skills.

At the grass roots level, the choice was up to each family whether or not to use the techniques prescribed, and whether or not to use one of the *albañiles* trained in the program. Thus the ultimate accountability for these decisions was in the hands of each family.

From the onset of the program, it was obvious that many of the rural families could not afford to hire a trained *albañil* to build their houses. To give those families who wished to use the methods an opportunity to do so, a strategy was worked out that would reduce the total cost of construction, yet still support the local builders. *Grupos Kuchuba'les*, or mutual aid groups, were set up. Each group consisted of five families who agreed to work together, first building one house, then another until all five families had a new house. Each agreed to follow as closely as possible the recom-

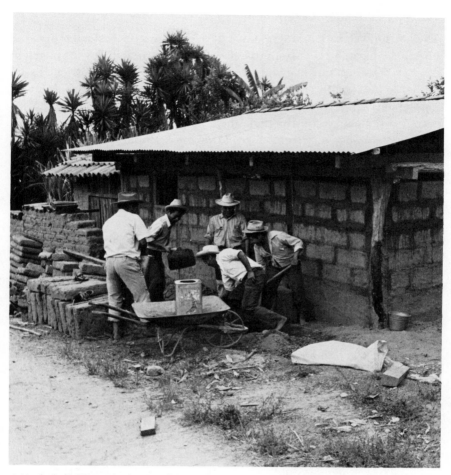

A Kuchuba'l Group works together to rebuild a house in a disaster area. (Photo: World Neighbors)

mendations for earthquake-resistant housing promoted by the program. A program-trained builder was assigned to each Kuchuba'l group to supervise the construction and teach each of the men the proper techniques.

By the end of the cycle, all five houses were relatively safe and all five new homeowners had become competent at this form of construction. Because no two houses were exactly alike, the builders were able to see ways in which different design and configuration problems were resolved. They also benefited from organizing and working in a mutual aid group at such a small scale. Thus at this level, the program was able to strengthen small-scale community organization further as well as help build self-reliance.

Housing Education Component

The housing education program that developed was the first attempt to use housing education as an approach to reconstruction following a major disaster. It was unique in giving priority to long-term objectives. The use of low-cost indigenous materials and support of the normal building "profession" and processes were also unique and key elements.

In earthquake reconstruction, there are three basic possibilities for housing assistance to victims. First, to provide people with the resources, money, or materials to rebuild; second, to provide a replacement house for the one destroyed; or third, to work within the usual system for building houses and teach better building methods.

Each of these approaches has its own advantages and disadvantages. If resources alone are provided, the programs are not complicated and overheads are low. As far as safety is concerned, however, people will probably rebuild the same types of houses as before and the long-term problem of vulnerability will not be resolved. If the second approach is chosen, the relief agency will either have to develop a large architectural and engineering staff to meet the design needs of different families, or select a few standardized buildings and mass-produce them, thereby eliminating each family's participation in the design process. Furthermore, construction of whole houses entails a much larger financial commitment to each house and substantially reduces the number of people served by the project.

OXFAM and World Neighbors chose the third approach. Their choice was based on the belief that there was a need to improve technical construction skills to enable local people to build effectively and safely in a country that is extremely prone to earthquakes. They wanted to ensure that the local, rural people could provide themselves with earthquake-resistant houses, not only during reconstruction, but long into the future.

In order for the housing education program to work, four steps were necessary. First, the technical solutions to the problems of vulnerability had to be worked out. At the time, there was not much literature available to the voluntary agencies. What was available was either too technical or suggested impractical solutions. There was no information available about the *bajareque* structures, approximately one-third of those in the rural areas. Within Guatemala, there were no professionals to whom the program could turn for advice. Even at the national universities, traditional structures and materials were not included in the curriculum of the engineering and architectural schools, even though 90 percent of the buildings, and those most vulnerable, were of these types. Thus, to obtain the technical

A relief agency worker illustrates safe construction sites. (Photo: World Neighbors)

information necessary and to have expert advice, the program was forced to hire housing consultants.

The consultants immediately set out to develop practical guidelines and techniques for modification of housing. The technical information available was reduced to simple principles, and several test structures were built to decide how these methods could be incorporated into practical construction. Based on these ideas, a number of simple, practical manuals were developed to illustrate these techniques. The manuals were prepared for the general public as well as for those who would do the actual construction.

The next step was to convince the public to accept the techniques. To do this, classes were given in each of the communities. The classes attempted to explain how earthquakes affect houses and how houses could be modified to withstand the forces. If people showed interest, a demonstration structure (described earlier) was erected. Throughout the program, efforts were made to convince the public to use these methods. Wall posters, leaflets, public meetings, and private talks with individual families building new houses were all a part of the promotion effort.

At the same time, it was necessary to teach the local builders the new techniques. By participating in the general classes given to the community, the builders' interest was aroused. Some were then selected to participate in the construction of the demonstration building and had a chance to learn first-hand the various techniques. The construction of only one building, however, proved to be inadequate, and soon it was obvious that a more detailed program would have to be set up to offer vocational training for local builders.

The training of the builders was the part of the program most emphasized over the years. At first, training was directed toward the experienced and established builders, especially those who had attained the status of *maestro de obra*. In the first few weeks after the earthquake, there was intense interest among these men and participation in the program was high. As reconstruction progressed, however, the demand for trained builders in all types of construction rose, as did the salaries offered, and many went to work on more sophisticated programs, or moved to Guatemala City where they could obtain a salary much higher than that in the rural areas.

Thus the training program began to focus its attention on vocational training for less-experienced tradesmen or new builders. By the end of the first year, vocational courses were established at centers in San Martín, Tecpán, and Poaquil. Over the months, the range of topics expanded from adobe and *bajareque* into some of the more contemporary types of construction, including brick and cement block.

The training program was able to combine theoretical classes with supervised practical experience. Each of the student builders had an opportunity to participate in construction in either the community buildings or houses built as part of the *Grupos Kuchuba'les*.

In the later stages of the program, a new element was added to the vocational training. The housing staff formed a construction company that would hire the graduates of the program, so that they could continue to work under the supervision of the chief instructors and hone their skills while continuing to help people rebuild their houses. Furthermore, some of the *albañiles* were able to participate in the management of the company, which further added to their capabilities. The construction company now operates without any assistance from Programa Kuchuba'l. Thus it has become a way of continuing the work without further input from the voluntary agencies.

Financial Strategies

The innovative financial strategies used centered on the materials distribution programs. The basic tenet of the OXFAM and World Neighbors staff was that free aid was not to be given out beyond the actual emergency period.

Thus the program had to establish a policy for distribution that would be both equitable and at the same time serve those who most needed the material.

Three alternatives were discussed:

1. *Gifts.* Some proposed that *lamina* be distributed as a gift to all families, regardless of their economic status.

The weaknesses of this approach were:

    a. If materials were provided free of charge, the program would end once they were distributed and funds ran out. Because *lamina* and other construction materials were expensive, and because funds were limited, the agencies' ability to cover a wide area would be restricted.

    b. A strong feeling existed among groups with experience working in Guatemala that giving things away was not harmonious with ongoing development programs in the area and that recipients would lose their sense of dignity as the result of a "charity" approach.

However, one of the strengths of the charity approach, theoretically, was the people who simply could not afford to buy *lamina*, such as widows, the elderly, and others left destitute by the disaster, would still receive roofing materials.

2. *Long-term loans.* Proponents of this approach argued that people did not have cash to spend on roofing materials right away, but could pay the full costs of the materials plus interest and administrative charges on a long-term basis.

The problems with this approach were:

    a. The staff estimated that the loans would cost about 30 percent to administer just in the first year.

    b. The repayment of loans under these circumstances was doubtful. By making unrealistic loans, the program could undermine the rural credit system that had been built up over the years.

c. It was felt that there were no existing rural credit facilities capable of providing this type of service on the large scale required.

d. The people did not like to borrow, because they believed that their land would be confiscated if they did not repay.

3. *Subsidized sales.* Under this approach, it was proposed that *lamina* be sold to people at a significantly reduced rate, about 50 percent of cost.

The advantages of this approach were:

a. *Lamina* could be supplied to twice the population covered under give-away plans, since the money paid could be reinvested in further *lamina* purchases.

b. The choice of whether or not to buy *lamina* (as opposed to other available roofing materials), as well as some choice regarding gauge, size, and quantity, was left to the consumer.

c. The method would turn over cash immediately.

d. It would be relatively simple to administer. Costs, complexity of administration, and problems of distribution would be minimal.

e. The consumer would be involved in a commercial transaction, not a charity scheme.

The most apparent weakness of this system was that there were people who could not afford to pay for *lamina* at any price.

After much discussion, the following plan was laid out:

1. To make *lamina* available at roughly a 50 percent subsidy price.

2. To undertake surveys at a later date, to ascertain which families were not able to acquire *lamina* through the subsidy system. For those who could not afford to purchase *lamina*, either:

a. A *lamina*-for work program would be set up for families who could work.

b. A gift of the *lamina* would be made to families who could not work.

After March 15, all distribution was taken over by the Kato-Ki Co-op. In return for its services, the cooperative received a per-sheet commission, which covered its expenses and overhead, and included a small profit. Each family was permitted to purchase ten sheets of *lamina* at the subsidized price.

Although the cooperative provided this service, sales were open to all (in the assigned area).

The decision to sell materials presented the program with two additional problems. The first was how to provide work, and of what type, so that people who wanted materials but truly could not afford to purchase them could earn the money needed. Second, the total amount of money being paid for the materials represented a sizable percentage of the cash available to the poor after the disaster. The staff was concerned about the consequences of taking such a substantial sum out of the community at this critical period, and therefore a method to return the cash had to be developed.

Once the initial distribution was completed, and most had purchased their first allotment of *lamina*, a number of people proposed that the money returned from the sales be placed back into the communities in a series of work programs. It was suggested that the reflow funds be turned over to the communities, based on the amount of *lamina* purchased, so that this money could be used to finance local or village projects of their own choosing.

Others felt that the money from the sales should continue to be reinvested in materials so that more would be available to each family. They noted that the initial allotment was only enough to build very small dwellings, and most people needed two to three times the amount currently being offered to rebuild a house of normal size. They felt that if other funds could be obtained for a work program, the reflow funds should continue to be designated for materials. When sales were completed, any money left over could be used by the cooperatives to help them develop further their services to members and the community.

Because other funds could be obtained in this case, it was decided that the reflow funds would continue to be reinvested in materials. OXFAM obtained another grant to initiate the work program.

The type of work program to offer also provoked a discussion. Some continued to push for letting each community decide how to spend the money. Others countered that if the money was made available to the communities, it would be used to finance projects normally carried out by the people voluntarily, thus destroying a tradition that was felt to be one of the most positive aspects of the rural social system.[1]

Finally, for practical as well as philosophical reasons, people decided to upgrade and improve rural roads. Most of the roads in the area are not hard-surfaced. If surfaced at all, they are covered with gravel. Few of the roads have provisions for adequate drainage, and many are virtually impassable during the rainy season. Also, many of the roads to the smaller *aldeas* are not wide enough for trucks or buses, and the people have to carry most of their crops into the towns in order to sell them. After consultations with the program staff, the co-op, and the *alcaldes* and their auxiliaries in each of the *municipios*, it was decided that Kuchuba'l would undertake a road improvement program to try to make the principal roads in the project

1. In actual practice, this concern was unfounded. Several other programs that sold materials, for example, the Save the Children programs in Joyabaj and Quiché, turned the money directly over to the communities to let them use as they wished for municipal projects. The projects they chose were innovative and not those normally carried out by volunteer labor.

By improving roads, Programma Kuchuba'l provided jobs and cash for reconstruction and made a contribution to the economic development of the rural areas. (Photo: World Neighbors)

area into all-weather roads capable of taking intermediate to large-size trucks.

The advantages of the plan were that several objectives could be attained in addition to returning the cash.

New, simple techniques for improving and maintaining rural roads were demonstrated, increased access to the region was provided, which would have a long-term beneficial economic impact, and bus service to many small communities could be extended. Thus long-term benefits (development objectives) could also be accrued.

REVIEW AND ANALYSIS OF PROGRAMA KUCHUBA'L

A method for analyzing programs can be found by working back through the criteria presented in the first part of the chapter. To complete our review of Programa Kuchuba'l, we will use these criteria as a "yardstick" for measuring the program.

Approach and Style

To begin with, OXFAM and World Neighbors chose a *program* approach to address the problems in the aftermath of the earthquake. It evolved as a single-sector program, concentrating on housing reconstruction. (Even though road building was included, its objective was to support activities in the housing sector.) Though the program is classified as a single-sector program, objectives in other sectors were attained as a result of project activities.

The style of the program changed as the program moved along. Originally, housing reconstruction was seen as a relatively short-term endeavor, and it was felt that all the objectives could be met during the initial funding period. When it became obvious that reconstruction would continue for a long period of time, more emphasis was placed on self-supporting activities that would help meet the objectives after the program officially terminated. Thus the style changed from "development through disaster" to "planting the seed."

Contributions

By evaluating the impact of the program, we can see the short- and long-term contributions. They indicate a program with a high, beneficial impact on the community. In the short-term, the program helped alleviate the burden of reconstruction by providing materials that reduced the overall cost of rebuilding. Throughout the course of the program, the staff and the project activities supported the local coping mechanisms. Programa Kuchuba'l worked through the cooperatives, the local, traditional governing bodies, and the committees established by the government following the earthquake. In terms of local processes, Kuchuba'l supported the local builders and enhanced their capabilities.

Because Programa Kuchuba'l chose to work at the same pace as the other reconstruction activities in the community, it was not able to reduce the time between the disaster and full recovery. Its activities, however, did not prolong the time.

The long-term contribution is also clear. Throughout the program, development objectives were stressed and, especially for those involved directly in the various project activities, permanent new opportunities were provided. Spin-off activities, such as the road improvement project, contributed to other development objectives, especially in the economic sector. Contracting the cooperatives as the agent for the materials distribution program helped to strengthen these institutions and enhance their standing in the community.

Finally, Programa Kuchuba'l has helped to reduce the vulnerability of the people to a future earthquake disaster by improving the housing stock and developing the capacity of the local builders to construct safer housing.

Program Planning

The staff of Programa Kuchuba'l addressed each problem and aspect of the program cautiously, discussing each option thoroughly, and thus avoiding many of the common pitfalls in program planning. The process was informal, but with guidance from the experienced OXFAM field director and advice from the consultant, the staff developed a structured program. The only weakness was poor conceptualization. Each staff member had his or her own perception of the objectives and despite numerous attempts to bring the diverse concepts into harmony and quantify the goals, the overall focus was not attained until several months after the program was underway. The other aspects of the planning process, however, more than made up for this deficiency. Policies to guide the program were set and generally adhered to. Involvement of the beneficiaries in all aspects and at all levels of the program was extensive. There were multiple strategies for achieving the overall objectives, and a fairly well-balanced program evolved. The scale of the program proved to be adequate and well suited to the size of the population. Technical inputs in both the housing construction and road improvement programs were both adequate and appropriate to the technological level of the people.

Concern about the possible impact of each of the activities was a constant element of project planning. People were especially concerned to avoid any type of project activity that would create a dependency. The first housing education program coordinator, Mary McKay, discussed this aspect in a paper presented at the Oxford Conference on Disasters and Small Dwellings in March of 1978:

> We were concerned about an attitude of dependency. It is generally accepted that those most affected by disasters are the poorest sectors of society. The typical poor victim's pre-disaster attitude and conditions of dependency are implied with his poverty and lack of power. Therefore, especially in a disaster situation, when the victims have been humiliated by the natural elements, they need to be helped to respond in ways that stress self-confidence, self-reliance and genuine ability and skill in dealing with the situation. This must be contrasted with an approach where victims are "taken care of" and decisions are made for them. To reinforce dependency is to reinforce the chronic problem! (McKay 1978)

Project Execution

Programa Kuchuba'l encountered one of the most basic problems common to reconstruction programs—overloading. In the immediate post-disaster situation, the cooperatives were busy with their own priorities and unable to undertake adequately all the tasks the agencies requested. Thus the World Neighbors staff had to step in to help until the cooperatives were able to take on wider responsibilities. The co-ops recovered quickly, however, and soon took over the *lamina* distribution. In later stages of the distribution program, it was necessary to provide funds for additional staff in order to smooth out some of the difficulties that arose, especially in accounting and warehousing.

An early reliance on the World Neighbors extensionists to carry out the housing education component in the San Martín area overburdened them, and was in many ways expecting too much of men who had not had prior experience as *albañiles*. The result was that the housing education component did not have the same impact as did others.[2] These problems were overcome when the vocational training school for *albañiles* was established.

The project overcame most of the other problems commonly encountered in the execution of relief programs. By stressing education and involvement, the program concentrated on process, not product. The use of local resources, in terms of people and skills, as well as materials, was stressed throughout the project. And finally, by immediately providing the highly sought-after building materials, the program quickly moved out of the emergency phase toward more permanent reconstruction.

Influences

It is interesting to review the influences that helped to shape the direction and content of Programa Kuchuba'l. The overriding motive for involvement was, of course, humanitarian concern, but the fact that World Neighbors and OXFAM were both on the scene when the disaster struck meant that they would become involved for much longer than either agency wished at the outset. Both organizations hoped to provide only the immediate emergency assistance and then return to their long-term development work. However, both the OXFAM and World Neighbors field directors reported that requests for reconstruction assistance were much

2. In all fairness to the World Neighbors extensionists, there were also other factors that contributed to the slow pace of reconstruction.

higher than they had anticipated, and they realized that most development work would cease until reconstruction needs had been met. Because of their prior involvement with the communities, they felt that they could not turn their backs and ignore the requests for assistance.

Another factor in the agencies' decision to become involved in reconstruction was a concern about things that were happening as a result of reconstruction activities.

Mary McKay reports:

World Neighbors and OXFAM faced the earthquake . . . from a perspective of twelve years development work in [Guatemala]. We were convinced that our response had to be consistent with our long-term development goals of self-reliance and human development which had been built into our programs of soil conservation, agriculture, health, nutrition and leadership training, but all around us relief activities started taking place that we felt were in direct opposition to our goals of self-confidence and self-reliance . . . in particular, outside agencies started building greatly subsidized houses for the survivors. The local people were recipients with no say in housing planning, design or the organization of [material] distribution. In short, many forces were at work creating a paternalistic dependence on material supplies from the outside, and a decision-making process originating outside the local community. (McKay 1978)

Thus there were three motives for intervention: humanitarian concern, a presence on the scene, and a felt need to defend and protect their concept of development in the reconstruction environment.

The resources available to the agency, as well as the resources available within the stricken community, shaped aspects of both the construction and distribution programs. Because the amount of money available to OXFAM was relatively limited (in terms of the number of beneficiaries), the subsidy scheme was seen as a practical method of extending the buying power and serving more people in the project area. The realization that relief agencies did not have the resources to build houses for everyone contributed to the decision to undertake a housing education program.

The approach of World Neighbors to rural development centered on the training and use of extensionists to introduce new items and methods. Experience with an education approach and the techniques of conveying information to rural people was their forte, and was undoubtedly a strong factor in steering the organization toward, and shaping the concept of, the housing education component.

Both organizations approached the affected community with an attitude of respect for the people, their institutions, and their traditions. Because of their pre-earthquake involvement, the agencies were able to participate as partners in reconstruction rather than as benefactors, and the people could approach the staff with problems and influence decisions. Because decision making was shared, the effectiveness of the program and the influence it had over the long term were greatly enhanced.

Epilogue

It would be nice to report that the program was still in progress, and that new and exciting contributions were being made. Unfortunately this is not so, for Kuchuba'l, like many of the other post-disaster programs, was forced to cease operation because of the political violence that increased steadily in the years following the earthquake. Many of the *promotores* and staff tried to keep a semblance of the program going amidst the turmoil and continued to offer technical assistance to families who were just starting to rebuild. But organizing the poor for collective action, even to rebuild their own houses, was an activity viewed with concern by many who wanted no change in the status quo. Several of the staff received anonymous threats and were warned to stop their work. In this environment, the staff met and decided quietly to end all formal activities. While Program Kuchuba'l is no longer in operation, the people who were trained and the ideas and the skills that were taught are still available and continue to be used. Thus the program will continue to make a contribution long into the future.

III
Alternatives and New Directions

11
Conceptualizing Disaster Recovery

A disaster may be defined as an event that causes a temporary break in the normal life of a community. The time between the disaster occurrence and the point at which normal activities are re-established is considered the recovery time. The goal of both governmental and nongovernmental agencies is to reduce this time.

Total recovery from a disaster is measured in four ways: (1) emotional recovery of the victims; (2) economic recovery, including replacement of the income lost, the restoration of jobs and/or the means of production, and restoration of the markets; (3) replacement of physical losses, which includes replacement of personal belongings, the home, and in some cases, the replacement of land; and (4) replacement of opportunity.

In order to develop appropriate responses to shorten recovery time, it is necessary to understand three things: the pre-disaster norm, what factors can affect time of recovery, and the different effect of different strategies.

THE PRE-DISASTER NORM

It is necessary to know what the community was like before the disaster before attempting to restore that norm. It is impossible, of course, for an intervenor to learn everything about a society, especially in the aftermath of a disaster. There are key elements, though, which all intervenors should strive to identify and understand. The basic family structure, economic patterns, governmental structure, religious affiliations, customs and practices, and power relationships are important.

Each program to be undertaken also requires the interviewer to understand the process through which activities are accomplished. A housing reconstruction program, for example, requires a broad understanding of housing, not simply in terms of the buildings, but as a *process*, consisting of a blend of labor, skills, capital, financing, settlement patterns, culture, status, environmental protection, and tradition. Even in the most unsophisticated societies, each process has many participants, and all play an intricate, balanced role in the society. Parts of each process, and possibly later programs as well, may be jeopardized by a disaster. By failing to understand the elements of each community activity and their interrelationships, an outsider may respond inappropriately and delay or prevent a return to normal.

THE FACTORS AFFECTING RECOVERY TIME

There are many factors that control the amount of time between the disaster and a return to normal. The following speed recovery:

1. *Risk of secondary disasters.* Many hazards are accompanied by second to structure the emergency response and to lay the groundwork for recovery. By planning each activity before a disaster, an agency can examine each thoroughly and make rational decisions without the added pressures of a disaster. While preparedness plans usually address immediate actions such as search and rescue or evacuation, plans can be expanded to provide guidance to structure activities in the transition and reconstruction phases. Plans for these phases should include development of broad objectives and provide a policy framework under which all agencies can operate.

2. *Clarity of policy and direction.* Leadership is obviously an important factor in the response to a disaster. One of the most important tasks for those in positions of authority is to provide a clear picture of goals and objectives, the means by which they are to be attained, and the "rules" that govern post-disaster actions. On the basis of these policies and standards, relief and reconstruction assistance can be provided in an equitable manner and delays resulting from indecision can be reduced. Such policies and directions are best developed *before* a disaster.

3. *Collective motivation.* The greatest resource following a disaster is the collective motivation of the people. This motivation can be translated into cooperative action and many opportunities for speeding recovery can be found.

4. *Good communications.* There is a need for good communications during all phases of a disaster. The emphasis, however, should not be on improving the *means* of communication (that is, radios and other electronic communications equipment), but on improving the flow of information and the type of information communicated. Good communication is the art of knowing what type of information to send; how to prepare it in such a

way that it is relevant to the needs of those receiving it; and communicating with the right people.

5. *Technical assistance.* In any post-disaster program, there are always questions that need to be answered by competent technical personnel. This information must be available and presented in such a way that it will be comprehensible to those who are working at each level of the program.

6. *Cash flow.* Post-disaster programs are dependent upon an adequate flow of cash. Because the costs of purchasing materials on a large scale will be fairly high, and financial institutions are themselves likely to be disrupted, agencies may experience difficulty arranging credit, and many items or services will have to be purchased with cash. Agencies can anticipate these problems and develop mechanisms to avoid lengthy delays.

7. *Reuse of salvaged materials.* The salvage and reuse of materials can provide the infrastructure for reconstruction. In many cases, the victims can completely rebuild with material salvaged from the debris. By encouraging salvaging and providing additional complementary materials, intervenors can speed recovery.

The following slow recovery.

1. *Risk of secondary disasters.* Many hazards are accompanied by second events. For example, an earthquake can be followed by a series of secondary tremors. These may last for only a few days or for as long as several months. Some tremors may even be stronger than the original earthquake. Survivors may be reluctant to begin reconstruction or even salvage materials from the rubble until the threat of a secondary disaster has passed.

2. *Uncertainty regarding possible relocation.* If the victims are uncertain as to whether or not they can safely remain at their previous homesite or at the place they had moved to after the disaster, they will hesitate to engage in long-term activities. Uncertainty about relocation can be caused both by a reluctance to occupy a site that was vulnerable in the disaster and by uncertainty about government intentions regarding relocation or re-settlement.

3. *Delayed materials.* The speed with which recovery begins depends on the availability of tools and materials. In almost every disaster, there are adequate resources for rebuilding either in the community or in the surrounding region. Access to these materials, however, may be reduced by official actions, such as evacuation or bulldozing. In those cases where materials are not available, reconstruction will be delayed pending arrival of

supplies. With adequate preparedness, however, intervenors can determine most needs before a disaster occurs and can work out contingency arrangements to supply the necessary materials.

4. *Conflicting expert advice.* One of the major problems following a disaster is deciding whose advice to follow. At all levels of the disaster-affected community—from the government's relief officials to the field directors of voluntary agencies, down to the local inhabitants themselves—people are constantly bombarded with information, much of it conflicting. Persons at all levels of the disaster relief system, and especially those with no previous disaster training or experience, are constantly faced with the dilemma of interpreting the information and deciding on its relevance to their situation.

This advice may not be suited to the local situation: it could be too highly technical; it may not be cost-effective; or it may not be culturally acceptable. Often the people offering the advice are not qualified to give it. Motivated but inexperienced volunteers provide most of the labor for relief operations. While the advice they give is often based on the best of intentions, it usually comes from preconceived ideas as to what a relief operation should be, not from training or experience. (When relief agencies send this personnel, they inadvertently legitimize their advice.) Thus conflicts of opinion are bound to arise.

The problem of conflicting expertise and advice can be overcome only through adequate pre-disaster planning and training of relief personnel at all decision-making levels within the relief structure.

5. *Inflation and market instability.* In situations where material is available, recovery time is influenced by its cost. If prices are not controlled and high inflation occurs, recovery time will increase. Similarly, an unstable market affected by speculation or hoarding will prolong reconstruction, as will excessive customs delays in cases where building materials must be imported.

To be effective, prices must be controlled in all parts of the market. In Guatemala, for example, the government failed to control the add-on transportation costs applied to *lamina* and cement. When distributing those commodities throughout the country, the cost of cement, which was two *quetzales* (U.S. $2.00) per bag at the factory, rose to as much as five *quetzales* a bag less than 100 kilometers from the point where it was produced.

6. *Land tenure problems.* Politically sensitive and among the most difficult factors to address are land ownership, land distribution, and legal land reform. After a disaster, these issues are often further complicated by such questions as: Should victims be assisted to rebuild on land that is not their own? Where should landless people be resettled? Who will provide the land

Unsorted and often useless aid creates headaches for volunteer relief workers. (Photo: Laffont/Sygma)

for resettlement? These issues can all prolong recovery time unless they are quickly and properly addressed.

7. *Public rejection of plans.* Often in the rush to provide assistance, agencies will undertake programs without considering their acceptability to the victims. There are numerous examples of victims rejecting aid offered by intervenors, both governmental and nongovernmental. The reason may be that the aid is culturally unacceptable or too costly. Whatever the reasons, time and effort, not to mention the expense, will be lost, and the intervenor will have to begin again. The time lost is an extension of recovery time.

8. *Surveys.* While surveys can be invaluable aids to planning emergency or reconstruction actions, unless they are properly planned and develop *relevant* information, they can delay reconstruction activities by tying up personnel and resources. In some cases, actions have been delayed until surveys are completed. The problem is not that surveys are not needed, but rather the type of data that is most appropriate and the method that should be used to obtain it (a topic to which I will return). The loss of this time can mean loss of resources and commitment that would be invaluable in reconstruction.

9. *Irrelevant aid.* The arrival of massive amounts of useless relief goods, untrained personnel and volunteers, and untrained officials all add

confusion to a disaster and delay recovery actions. Furthermore, the time and money spent sorting out and eliminating this unnecessary assistance cannot be recaptured.

10. *Bureaucracy.* Disaster response requires a streamlined decision-making process, flexible standard operating procedures, and good internal communications.

HOW RELIEF STRATEGIES RELATE TO TIME OF RECOVERY

In order to understand how different types of programs affect recovery time, it is helpful to theorize about assistance strategies. While most relief and reconstruction programs have certain objectives in mind, few agencies go beyond that point and conceptualize their intervention in terms of strategies. If pressed, most intervenors would explain their aid in terms of its humanitarian objectives, especially that of easing the burden on the victims. For purposes of discussion, we can broaden this to define the two most common strategies; that is, to provide aid to help victims *until* they recover, and to provide aid to *help* them recover. The underlying concept is that the assistance provided will free up the victims' own resources and reduce the cost (or burden). If an agency provides replacement goods, for example, the people can use their own money for higher priority items. Thus, if an agency reduces the burden on the victims, the recovery time should be shortened. In practice, these two strategies are usually equated to specific disaster phases, the first in the emergency phase, the second in transition and reconstruction phases.

Each of these strategies can affect recovery time. Generally speaking, simply helping victims until they can get going has little overall impact on reducing recovery time and, depending on how the aid is provided, may even prolong it. Programs following this strategy are usually classified as relief programs and are typified by such actions as distribution of food, clothing, household items, and tents. Helping people *to* recover, on the other hand, can demonstrably reduce recovery time. Such programs provide the resources needed and generally concentrate on longer-term objectives. For example, they may provide materials for reconstruction, cash or credit, and opportunities (such as work schemes) for people to acquire resources to balance out what assistance they receive. This strategy requires a bit more sophistication, but the programs are more beneficial and reduce the time to full recovery.

There is a third strategy that facilitates intervention in both the emergency as well as the subsequent transition and reconstruction phases. That strategy is to identify and provide those resources or actions that can *accelerate* recovery. This does not require any more sophistication than the second strategy, but it does require an understanding of disasters. Typical actions are provision of building materials for use in temporary shelters that can later be incorporated into permanent housing; stimulation of markets or the normal economic systems; and setting up work programs for victims that not only provide resources but also accomplish reconstruction objectives. In short, to accelerate the recovery process, agencies provide or restore the infrastructures of a community, provide the materials required, and make opportunities for the victims.

12
Mitigation and Preparedness

INTRODUCTION

Up until this point, we have discussed disasters in terms of reaction, both by the affected societies and the relief agencies. An underlying theme, however, has been that disasters are not unforeseen events and that the technology now exists to identify the hazards that threaten a community and to estimate the areas and the settlements that will be affected. One can then prepare for the disaster and substantially reduce, or mitigate, its impact. These two actions are known as pre-disaster planning.

Frederick Krimgold pioneered the early conceptualization of pre-disaster planning, which he describes as follows:

> Planning may be defined as the process of preparing a set of decisions for action in the future directed at achieving goals by optimal means.
> The stated goals of disaster relief are the reduction of human suffering, the improvement of material well-being, and the increase of personal security. It goes without saying that these goals are best served if disaster, in the first place, can be avoided or reduced. Thus, the primary goal of pre-disaster planning may be seen as the prevention or mitigation of disaster. If we refer to the definition of disaster in terms of the need for "outside" help, we may describe the goal of pre-disaster planning as the creation of self-sufficiency in dealing with natural phenomena. In those cases where prevention is not possible, the goal must be to plan for the effective application of aid. . . . (1974)

Pre-disaster planning is the term used to describe the comprehensive range of efforts made to reduce the destruction and disruption of a disaster before it occurs. The term is intended to denote action and accurately describes the most important part of the activity–*planning*. This is distinctly different from post-disaster activities, which involve operations.

Pre-disaster planning consists of three types of activities: disaster prevention, disaster mitigation, and disaster preparedness. *Disaster prevention* focuses on the hazard that causes the disaster and tries to eliminate or drastically reduce its direct effects. The best example of disaster prevention is the construction of dams or levies to prevent flooding. As a general rule, prevention is expensive and the results are often far less than hoped.

Disaster mitigation focuses on measures that can be taken to minimize the destruction and disruptive effects of a hazard and thus lessen the magnitude of a disaster. Mitigation efforts offer by far the best and most cost-effective method for dealing with disasters. With good planning, most mitigation measures can be integrated with normal development activities at very little, sometimes no, additional cost. Some examples are: strengthening buildings so that they are hurricane- or earthquake-resistant; the planting of crops that are less affected by disasters; changing crop cycles so that crops mature and are harvested before the peak of a hurricane or rainstorm season; adoption of land-use controls to restrict development in high-risk areas; and development of diversified economies so that losses in one sector can be absorbed by others.

The underlying assumption of *disaster preparedness* is that disasters are no time to be trying to decide what to do. Preparedness focuses on developing plans to respond to a disaster once it threatens or has occurred. At its simplest, preparedness is an estimation of emergency needs and the identification of resources to meet those needs. A more sophisticated definition is that preparedness is the development of plans to structure the entire post-disaster response, to ensure that emergency aid is managed so that each activity lays the foundation for the next, and to plan the response so that each sector contributes in some way to the others. The first objective of preparedness is to get the absolute maximum benefit out of relief and to swiftly complete the transition from emergency assistance to rehabilitation and reconstruction. The second is to insure that disaster assistance makes the greatest possible contribution to ongoing development. Finally, preparedness should guide reconstruction so that it reduces vulnerability and mitigates a recurrence of the disaster.

People have much more experience in preparedness than in other pre-disaster planning activities. The best known are the development of warning and evacuation plans; stockpiling of supplies; developing emergency plans for hospitals; improving infrastructure to support or facilitate emergency services; establishing emergency command, control, and communications systems; training in search and rescue and first aid. Other measures less known but equally important include developing disaster assessment plans; establishing relief and reconstruction standards and policies; developing stand-by plans for economic assistance to victims; developing crop salvage and marketing plans for economic assistance to victims; developing crop salvage and marketing plans for small farmers; adopting legislation defining emergency powers; and establishing prior inter-governmental and/or multilateral agreements for disaster assistance to support the planned response.

In recent years there has been some debate among the experts about which activity to emphasize. In the 1950s, most of the emphasis was on preparedness, much of which was an unsophisticated spin-off from Cold War civil defense activities. In the 1960s, there was intense interest in prevention, fueled by the public's enchantment with the space age and everything technological. In the 1970s, there was a shift toward mitigation, sparked by Krimgold's writings. The pendulum seems to be moving back toward preparedness, though on a much more sophisticated level.

The reasons for this swing are not difficult to understand. Prevention, once seen as the ultimate answer to disasters, has come under growing criticism. While such actions as weather modification and earthquake control were formerly thought desirable, the more we learn about the purpose of these events in nature, the more likely we are to challenge the wisdom of preventing their occurrence on environmental and ecological grounds. Even such long-touted measures as flood control are now seen to have adverse effects, and while research continues, the emphasis has shifted more to mitigation and to finding ecologically suitable alternatives.

Mitigation itself is proving to be more difficult to accomplish in the Third World than was originally foreseen. Mitigation is a complex process, and many of its parts cannot be dealt with in terms of a disaster only, for they are also related to development.

As we have seen, disasters can be a primary cause of underdevelopment, as well as intertwined with a country's progress toward development. Similarly, many mitigation activities either require a certain level of development or are themselves development activities. Third World countries are so affected by disaster in part because of their inability or failure to address the root causes of poverty and underdevelopment. Thus it is difficult to carry out mitigation activities successfully. For example, many of the most vulnerable areas are urban squatter settlements that have sprung up due to lack of opportunity in rural areas. They are often situated on hazardous sites because governments have failed to provide suitable alternatives due to incapacity, neglect, or failure to seek land reform. For people living there, two of the traditional tools of mitigation, zoning and building regulations, simply will not work. Thus prevention and mitigation can work only in situations where all these problems are addressed. In summary, progress toward development is required in order to mitigate, and mitigation is required in order to develop.

Preparedness, on the other hand, offers something that governments and agencies can do now, at low cost, and that can have positive results in any situation.

Disaster preparedness measures can be undertaken with the skills that are available within the country, with the technological resources that are available, and usually with little outside assistance. The most vulnerable areas can be identified; contingency plans can be developed; where necessary, supplies or materials can be stockpiled; and plans can be drawn, outlining the actions to be taken by all concerned.

Preparedness is at best an interim measure. Monies spent on preparedness are considered nonrecoverable and they will not contribute to development. But while the benefits of preparedness are short-term, this investment can save lives, and money spent on preparedness will help to reduce the incidence of suffering following the disaster and can shorten recovery time.

MITIGATION

The objective of disaster mitigation is, obviously, to lessen the impact of a disaster. Traditionally, mitigation has concentrated on human settlements and man-made buildings and structures, with the focus on development of land use regulations, settlement planning, the development of techniques for strengthening buildings and structures, and the development of building codes to encourage or enforce use of these building techniques.

A broader and more progressive view of mitigation has evolved in the last decade. For example, efforts can be taken to diversify economies and to balance and place job- and income-producing resources strategically so as to reduce the likelihood that all would be affected in a disaster. Economic buffers such as insurance have received new emphasis. In the agricultural sector, there have been conscious moves to reduce the vulnerability of one-crop societies by diversifying the staples and introducing new cropping methods.

Concepts in Mitigation

Mitigation activities can be classified as passive or active. Passive mitigation is the development or application of measures such as building codes, land use, zoning, and urban or regional planning techniques to reduce vulnerability. Active mitigation encompasses those activities that require direct contact with the people. When using active approaches, the implementing body assumes the role of an activist in helping to guide balanced growth and reduce vulnerability. Activities include public education, the introduction of modification techniques, the initiation of housing improvement programs, the promotion of land swaps or relocation of people from vulnerable to suitable and safe sites, and economic diversification of those sectors most vulnerable to disasters. Passive mitigation measures cannot work without active measures to follow them up. But active mitigation can be independent of passive activities.

In practice, passive activities have had little impact on reducing vulnerability in the Third World. For the most part, zoning and building codes are unenforceable. This is in part due to the fact that the codes adopted are often based on those developed in the industrialized countries for engineered structures. In the few countries where people have attempted to develop applicable codes for nonengineered structures, the types that most Third World people live in, the methods chosen to reinforce the buildings have proved too costly or too complicated for local craftsmen to understand and implement. Several innovations, however, have been introduced, including the use of building guidelines that describe the options for increasing the resistance of a building through simple and low-cost methods, and the use of performance standards in lieu of the more restrictive zoning and land use regulations.[1] Zoning and building regulations are usually considered restrictive. Active mitigation is considered more "permissive" and usually allows for more variations based on local needs.

Steps in Mitigation

Reducing the harmful effects of natural disasters requires actions on three fronts: reducing vulnerability of the physical settlements and houses; reducing vulnerability of the economy; and the strengthening of the social structure of a community, so that coping mechanisms can help absorb the shock of a disaster and promote rapid recovery.

REDUCING PHYSICAL VULNERABILITY

Vulnerability reduction for communities and human settlements has been emphasized more than any other activity to date, and the methodology employed has been thoroughly tested. The first step is to identify the high-risk areas. This is done by relating a hazard, such as an earthquake, to the terrain and to the probability that such an event will occur. This activity is

---

1. For further information on the use of building guidelines, see the Save the Children Fund "Report on the Joyabaj Reconstruction Program," Report #2, August 1976.

known as risk mapping and the results of the analyses are usually presented in the form of "risk maps," which show the type and degree of hazard represented by a particular natural phenomenon on a given geographic location. Earthquake risk mapping, for example, identifies faults and the underlying geological conditions of the locality. Flood plain mapping indicates the areas likely to be covered by water during floods of given magnitudes (Krimgold 1974).

A further refinement of risk mapping is known as microzonation, which is simply risk mapping at a very small scale. For example, within any particular area there are numerous geological variations that can dampen or reduce the forces of earthquakes. Thus, even within a high risk zone, some areas will be safer than others. Microzonation delineates each of these areas so that communities can select the safest possible sites for development, or the location of critical facilities.

Risk mapping requires technical skills and the application of various scientific disciplines; thus it is said to be a function of the technical services. Risk mapping is usually assigned to organizations at the government level and can be a joint effort of such groups as geological departments, meteorological services, and water resource management departments. The disciplines involved could include geology, meteorology, hydrology, engineering, geophysics, geography, agriculture, forestry, physics, cartography, and remote sensing.

This is not to say that high-risk areas cannot be identified by nontechnical means. Certainly, historic patterns of disaster and the recurrence of disaster hazards can provide a practical guide in determining whether or not a community is at risk from certain phenomena. (People have explored many resources in an attempt to gather historical information about disasters. In Latin America, it is not uncommon to review old church records for information about earthquakes. In Jamaica, researchers trying to determine the occurrence of storm surges turned to accounts of shipwrecked Spanish gold fleets and pirates' log books for information on the date and location of the events. And the attempt to recover stolen Maya artifacts known as stelae from Central American archeological sites received new impetus when it was learned that many of the stelae recorded significant events such as severe storms and earthquakes.)

The second step in vulnerability reduction is to identify those communities that are particularly susceptible to damage or destruction. This is done by relating risk to human settlements and their structures. One determines whether a community is situated on a site within a high-risk area, and if this is the case, the specific areas that are the most vulnerable, based on the microzonation data. At the same time, the buildings and structures (such as dams and hydroelectric facilities) are evaluated to determine if they can withstand the forces in nature to which they may be subjected.

Vulnerability analysis is said to be both a technical and planning function. Many of the disciplines involved in risk mapping are also involved here, but emphasis clearly shifts to engineering, architecture, and planning.

The third step is the selection of the vulnerability reduction strategy. This requires two sets of actions. First is the determination of the site strategy. Options may include construction of protective works, such as embankments, to protect from flooding; zoning to control development of the site; restricted development (to ensure that any development meets certain standards that take into consideration the threat to the site), and land swaps, which would provide alternatives to development of the site.

The second set of actions determines the *structural strategies* for reducing vulnerability. These include the imposition of design criteria or building standards to govern construction; the modification of existing structures; and the replacement of existing structures with newer buildings more resistant to disasters.

The selection of vulnerability reduction strategies is again considered both an engineering and a planning function, but a new dimension—the political one—is added at this point, for in the end, the strategies selected will be the result of political decisions, based as much on a government's capabilities as on its perception of the possibilities, potential, and value of mitigation.

Peru provides a good example for examining the physical vulnerability reduction process. It is one of the most seismically active countries in the world; between 1970 and 1980, several minor and two major earthquakes struck the country.

Peru is situated on the South American Plate, close to a major fault, where the South American Plate abuts the Nazca Plate (see page 211). At this juncture, there is a subduction zone, which means, in effect, that the faster-moving South American Plate is attempting to pass over the slower-moving Nazca Plate. It is this relative movement that causes the earthquakes that periodically affect the country.

While earthquakes can occur anywhere along this subduction zone, as a general rule the earthquakes will be stronger the closer they occur to the earth's surface. This means that the coastal region and western-most portions of the mountains will experience more ground motion than the eastern portions of the country.

Major fault systems exist throughout the mountains, however, and any earthquake that occurs in the western-most regions can trigger movement along a parallel fault farther inland. One example is the earthquake that

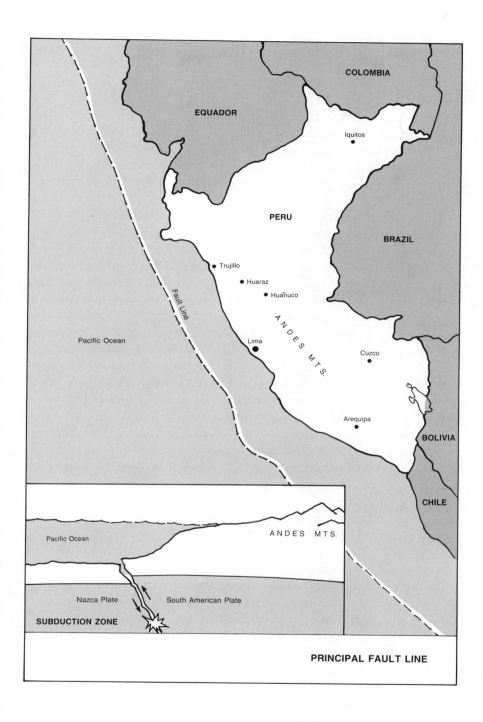

COLOMBIA

EQUADOR

Iquitos

PERU

BRAZIL

Trujillo

Huaraz

Huánuco

A N D E S   M T S.

Pacific Ocean

Lima

Cuzco

Arequipa

Fault Line

BOLIVIA

CHILE

Pacific Ocean

A N D E S   M T S.

Nazca Plate

South American Plate

SUBDUCTION ZONE

PRINCIPAL FAULT LINE

occurred near Chimbote in 1970. The epicenter was located in the ocean west of Chimbote, but its effect was felt in the mountain regions near the city of Huaraz, which is located on one of the major parallel fault systems in the mountains.

By locating the major fault systems and recording the movement of the faults, as well as examining the history of earthquakes throughout the country, it is possible to assemble maps showing where the greatest seismic activity occurs and to identify the relative potential for recurrence of seismic activity in each of the zones. This information is presented in the map on page 213.

The casualties and widespread damage in each earthquake have under-scored the vulnerability of the population and shown that the housing stock of the vast majority of the people cannot withstand the forces of the earthquakes. Making the houses safe requires one of two approaches: either provision of stronger building systems, or re-engineering the building materials now used. Both approaches are possible, but they require resources not widely available to the majority of the population, namely, money, materials, and technical skills. Almost 80 percent of the people in Peru live in nonengineered structures. Even within the larger cities (for example, Lima, Arequipa, Ica, Trujillo), engineering and architectural input into housing construction is minimal. In Lima alone, over three million people live in nonengineered buildings that do not meet basic criteria for earthquake-resistant construction.

The map on page 214 shows the predominant housing type for different areas of Peru. To the side of each type is a number representing its potential for collapse in an earthquake. This map shows that the most vulnerable structures are located along the coast and in the mountainous regions. By comparing the map on p. 214 with the maps on pages 213 and 215 (showing population distribution), we can identify the most vulnerable regions of Peru. These are illustrated on page 216.

REDUCING ECONOMIC VULNERABILITY

Reducing economic vulnerability follows much the same pattern as does reducing physical vulnerability. Step one, for example, is virtually the same, namely, identifying those areas where there is a high probability that a disaster event could occur. The second step is to identify the sectors of the economy that are vulnerable in disasters. This is done by relating risk to economic activities or means of production. First, the key elements of the economy and those that are particularly vulnerable to a disaster are identified. Often this is not difficult, especially for countries that have one-crop economies, or only a few industries, or are earners of foreign currency. Every economic activity should be examined, however, to determine

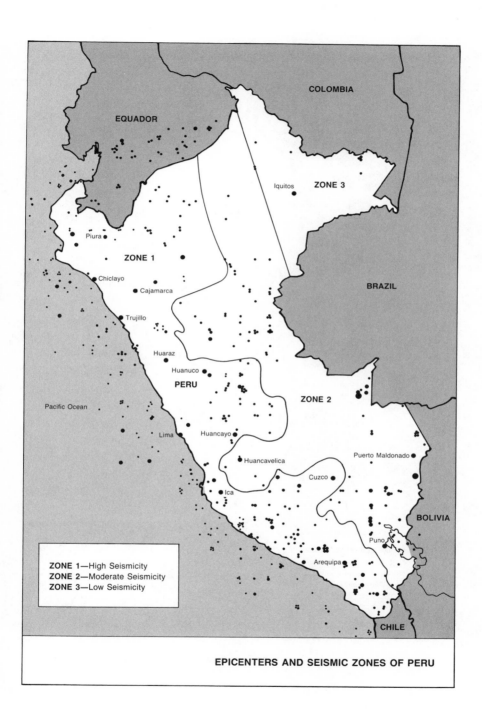

EPICENTERS AND SEISMIC ZONES OF PERU

ZONE 1—High Seismicity
ZONE 2—Moderate Seismicity
ZONE 3—Low Seismicity

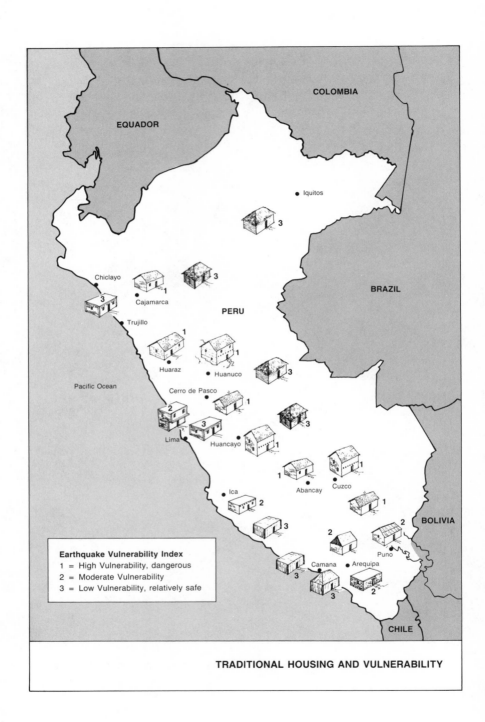

COLOMBIA

EQUADOR

• Iquitos

3

Chiclayo
1
Cajamarca

3

• Trujillo

3

PERU

BRAZIL

1

Huaraz

1

Huanuco

3

Pacific Ocean

Cerro de Pasco

1

2

3

Lima

Huancayo

1

3

1

Abancay

Cuzco

1

1

Ica

2

3

2

2

Puno

2

BOLIVIA

Camana

Arequipa

3

3

2

CHILE

Earthquake Vulnerability Index
1 = High Vulnerability, dangerous
2 = Moderate Vulnerability
3 = Low Vulnerability, relatively safe

TRADITIONAL HOUSING AND VULNERABILITY

214

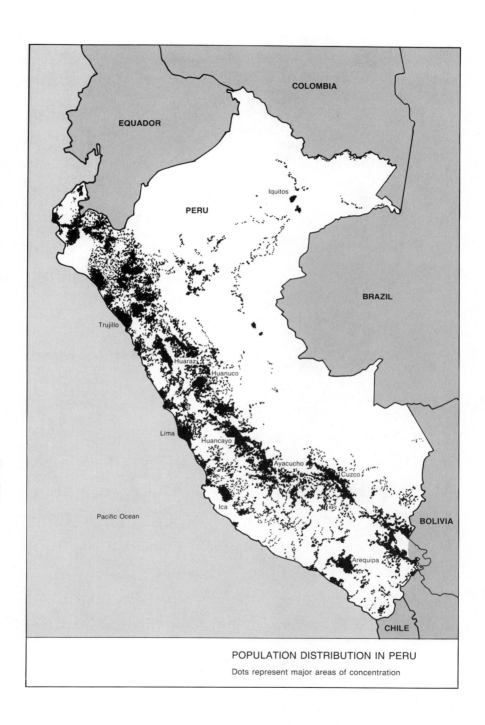

POPULATION DISTRIBUTION IN PERU

Dots represent major areas of concentration

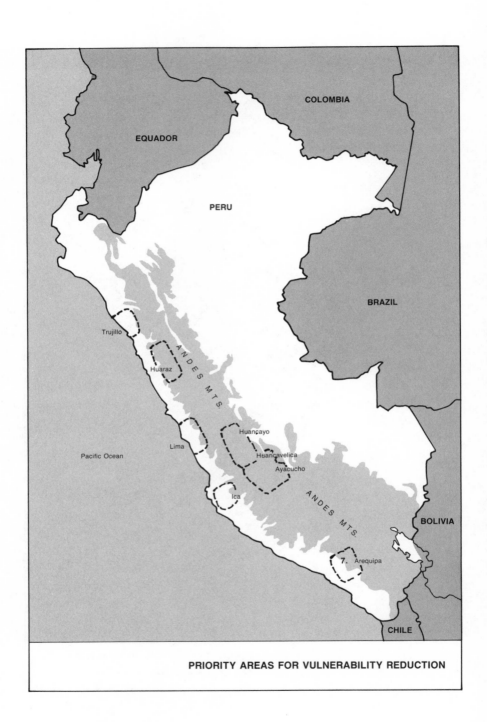

PRIORITY AREAS FOR VULNERABILITY REDUCTION

COLOMBIA

EQUADOR

PERU

BRAZIL

Trujillo

ANDES MTS.

Huaraz

Huancayo

Lima

Pacific Ocean

Huancavelica

Ayacucho

Ica

ANDES MTS.

BOLIVIA

7. Arequipa

CHILE

216

whether each type of threatening event could affect a significant portion of that activity. This type of analysis should be conducted both at the macro and micro levels. While a flood may not have a significant economic impact on a country as a whole, it may have a major impact on a community or region.

In determining economic vulnerability, there are other critical activities and installations that should be considered. Energy facilities and systems are of prime concern, as are transportation networks and road systems, in addition to financial institutions. Vulnerability studies in Jamaica revealed that the main power generating station, the fuel-oil storage depot, the principal wharves, the largest airport, the central bank, and the government's central data processing center, as well as the major financial institutions, were all located in areas subject to damage from earthquakes, hurricanes, flash floods, and land subsidence in earthquakes, not to mention fire or explosion from a nearby refinery.

The third step is the selection of a vulnerability reduction strategy. Economic protection can be provided in three ways: diversification, insurance, and the establishment of reserves. Diversification spreads the risk, so that if a disaster occurs, the total losses in any one area or sector are acceptable. For many countries, diversification can be a difficult choice. Small nations that are dependent upon one or two crops for their livelihood may find it politically difficult to justify diversification simply on grounds of disaster mitigation. Once again, long-term development choices come into play, and ultimately the decision may rest more on political or economic factors than on disaster-mitigation strategies.

The role of insurance in disaster mitigation will be discussed later, but suffice it to say now that insurance is another method for spreading the risk and providing adequate capital and resources for reconstruction.

Reserves can be established at all levels. Governments can establish cash and food reserves that can be released following a disaster. Families can also be encouraged to establish savings upon which they can rely in lieu of insurance. Many innovative methods have been tried. Recent efforts to protect against famine include development of food banks and an international food reserve system. In Peru, where wood is in short supply, the government has established forest preserves with fast-growing eucalyptus trees, which can be used by communities in times of disaster for rebuilding houses.

Other simple measures can also be effective. In hurricane areas where crops are harvested just before the hurricane season, small farmers can be encouraged to build ferro cement or other strong grain silos to help protect harvests until they are sold. Agencies should help communities to identify small-scale community-based measures to reduce vulnerability.

REDUCING VULNERABILITY TO THE SOCIAL STRUCTURE OF A COMMUNITY

Reducing the vulnerability of a community social structure is the most difficult of the mitigation measures. For the most part, this can best be accomplished through extending normal development work in one of three ways. The first is institution building. Local organizations that serve as coping mechanisms can be identified and strengthened. A conscious effort can be made to increase their capacities and skills, thus enhancing their ability to deal with a crisis.

The second activity is to increase the number of coping mechanisms within a community. By developing formal institutions and linking these groups to outside resources, one establishes a vehicle for intervention and the provision of assistance.

The third activity is to broaden the contacts of local groups and to encourage whatever promotes cooperation among different elements or groups within the society. Such cooperation can reduce the social impact of a disaster.

In their development activities, agencies should be careful to avoid those that will further increase or institutionalize a society's vulnerability. It is especially important to identify dependency relationships, particularly those that are threatened in disaster, and work to eliminate them.

By increasing self-sufficiency and reliance on internal resources, agencies improve the ability of local people to cope with disaster. This can be a mitigating factor and can help to speed recovery.

Participation in Mitigation

Disaster mitigation is the responsibility of all organizations working in a threatened area. There has often been a tendency to leave mitigation measures to governments or to intergovernmental organizations. Voluntary agencies, however, have an important role to play, especially in reducing economic and social structure vulnerability. By recognizing the threat of disaster, organizations can include remedial measures in many of their normal development activities. It has been said that almost any good development program can have a positive effect on mitigating disasters. In fact, many of the activities carried out under the normal development programs have done so. The introduction of wheat, for example, to India in the 1960s and 1970s, not only improved the nutritional balance, but also helped diversify the agriculture and reduce the possibility of widespread famine due to rice crop failure or insect infestation. In Guatemala, the establishment of savings and loan programs by the cooperative movement mitigated the economic impact of disasters and gave those suffering losses in the earthquake a reserve of money that could be committed for reconstruction. Without this cash reserve and its instant availability after the disaster, recovery time would have been prolonged.

Thus hazard reduction measures should be taken into account in the administration of general development aid (Krimgold 1974). One can take leadership in mitigation in housing, agriculture, economic development, urban and regional development, village planning, and community organization. It should be remembered, however, that mitigation activities included in normal programs cost relatively little, but retroactive mitigation, especially in settlements and buildings, is very costly.

Common Mistakes in Mitigation

The following are some of the more common mistakes agencies make when dealing with mitigation.

1. *Placing responsibility for certain mitigation activities in the wrong type of organization.* For example, some countries have assigned physical mitigation responsibilities to social service agencies. It is important to determine the particular function of the mitigation activity and to assign it to an agency with appropriate responsibilities, interests, and capabilities.

2. *Overreliance on passive rather than active mitigation.* Many countries have attempted to follow the model of the industrial societies and pass strict legislation in the hope that these measures would encourage mitigation. For developing countries, active measures should be emphasized.

3. *Failure to determine the complete range of options.* Mitigation is a complex undertaking, and many options exist. Agencies should be careful to examine the complete range and select a mix of strategies for dealing with vulnerability reduction, not being content with the selection of only one approach.

4. *Failure to identify all the disaster threats.* Most communities are threatened by more than just one type of disaster. In areas such as the Caribbean, where hurricanes are considered an annual threat, it is easy to forget that earthquakes, volcanoes, and regionalized flooding also pose hazards. Countries must be sure to determine all the potential threats and design their mitigation programs accordingly.

5. *Failure to relate vulnerability reduction to normal development plans and activities.* As stressed earlier, vulnerability reduction will have little impact unless it is conducted in concert with normal development activities. Only

if one stresses the development aspects will mitigation be feasible in many developing countries.

DISASTER PREPAREDNESS

In disaster management, opportunities arise where you make them, and the best way to make opportunities is through disaster preparedness. For many years, preparedness was viewed only in terms of emergency response; that is, the reaction to a pending emergency and the activities that would take place in the immediate aftermath. Thus preparedness concentrated on developing warning and evacuation procedures and on limited steps, such as stockpiling, that would speed material aid. A more sophisticated approach is now being taken, and typical preparedness activities include predetermination of effective strategies and appropriate modes of involvement, development of tools needed by the emergency staff, development of plans for the actual response, and training for crisis operations. Generally, people are beginning to exploit the opportunities for improving the whole range of response, in all phases of a disaster and at all levels of the relief system.

Concisely stated, the objectives of preparedness are to protect lives and property from an immediate threat, to promote rapid reaction in the immediate aftermath of a disaster, and to structure the response to both the emergency and longer-term recovery operations. Modern disaster preparedness is based on the realization that disasters are no time to be trying to figure out what to do, and that the most rational course of action can be determined ahead of time.

Preparedness is concerned with activities that occur immediately before a disaster, such as warning and evacuation; during the disaster, such as maintaining communications and protecting critical facilities and lifelines; and immediately following the disaster, including search and rescue, disaster assessment, evacuation and treatment of injured persons, security in the disaster-affected area, restoration of lifelines and critical facilities that have been damaged, and further evacuation of areas threatened by secondary disasters.

Preparedness is normally seen as an activity of the planning and engineering disciplines as well as medical, social, and security services. Practical experience has shown that the best organizations to assume responsibility for preparedness are operational agencies. For governments, this means ministries that have their own communications and transport, as well as administrative facilities (for this reason, preparedness is often left to the military or paramilitary organizations such as civil defense agencies).

Appropriate ministries are public works departments, housing ministries, or other "operational" agencies.

Concepts in Preparedness

As in mitigation, preparedness activities can be divided into passive and active categories. The more traditional activities that are usually associated with preparedness, including the preparation of disaster manuals, stockpiling of relief goods, and the development of computer lists of resources and personnel, are usually considered as passive in nature. Active measures include development of comprehensive response plans, the monitoring of threatening hazards (such as hurricane tracking or stream level monitoring), training of emergency personnel, and development of the tools and methods of emergency response.

Disaster warning and evacuation measures are usually categorized as active preparedness measures, though, in fact, they can also be classified as an initial *response* to a disaster threat.

Elements of Preparedness Planning

Preparedness planning borrows from both mitigation and relief program planning procedures. First the risk areas are determined and mapped and then the vulnerable settlements are identified. Next the responses that would be possible in the event of a disaster are examined. Then the resources necessary before one can react are estimated and the deficiencies are listed.

Once this information has been gathered, a preparedness plan is developed. This includes six steps. First is the prior determination of the objectives to be met in each affected sector. Second, the strategies and approaches necessary to accomplish these objectives and plug any gaps that have been identified are determined.

The third step is the development of an implementing instrument. This is usually in the form of a disaster preparedness plan, a formal document that sets out the sequence of activities and the responsibilities of each participant.

The purpose of the plan is to place all activities in a comprehensive framework, so that they can be executed in an orderly and sequential manner. Normally, activities are divided into parts, so that resources can be marshaled at each critical place and stage, and disaster managers can concentrate on the most critical activities at the appropriate time.

Plans for a small agency or community may be no more than a brief checklist and description of activities with the assignment of responsibilities noted on the margins, while a national preparedness plan may include a series of documents, including network diagrams and flow charts of activities, subplans (known as emergency action plans) for each sector, department, and/or agency, scores of checklists and emergency procedures to be followed, along with a statement of policies. Whatever form a plan follows, it is important that it be written down, both to serve as a reference and to ensure that no activities are forgotten in the haste of the disaster.

To be successful as an implementing instrument, an emergency preparedness plan must meet the following requirements:

1. It must present the sequence of activities in a logical and clear manner.
2. It must be comprehensive and balanced.
3. It must assign specific tasks and responsibility for each.
4. It must link appropriate organizations and establish mechanisms to bring people and organizations together at the critical points.
5. It must reflect the policies of the implementing agencies or the national government in a disaster.

The fourth step in preparedness is the development of the tools necessary to respond and implement the plan. Tools include the establishment of communications networks; transport capabilities; action plans, procedures, and checklists for specific areas; the establishment of evacuation routes; and the acquisition and strategic placement of search and rescue equipment.

The fifth step is the strategic placement of resources *to be used* in the response. For most agencies, this means stockpiling or working out relationships with suppliers to enable rapid acquisition and delivery of needed relief materials. Other activities may include drawing up lists of materials, personnel, and other resources, and the establishment of contingency funds. For the international relief agencies, stockpiling has become a much debated topic, with many critics pointing out that it is of only limited benefit unless carried out in-country. (See "Issues in Preparedness" later in this chapter.)

Generally, if a resource is of real value, then stockpiling should be encouraged in or close to a threatened community.

The final step in preparedness is training and drill. A preparedness plan and the tools of preparedness are of little value unless people know how to use them effectively. Performance is enhanced first by training, which means acquainting personnel with the plan and the sequence of activities, as well as with the tools and resources, and instruction on how to use each effectively. Drill includes practice designed to make each activity routine and thereby help reduce time of response, and to help identify the bottlenecks and "debug" the system. Disasters, fortunately, occur infrequently. But between disasters, people and institutions change, and it is easy for gaps to develop and for people to forget what has been set out in the plan. Periodic review and drill is the only practical way of keeping the preparedness activities fresh in everyone's mind and adapting the plan to changing organizational structures and to changing needs. (An innovative method of keeping the preparedness plan up-to-date has been formulated in Sri Lanka. Each year at the beginning of the cyclone season, the government holds a "Cyclone Awareness Day." On that day, each government department and nongovernmental institution with a disaster assignment is required to review and update its plan and send a notice of any changes to the central disaster coordinating office.) In many countries, it is normal practice for critical facilities, such as hospitals and power generating facilities, to conduct periodic disaster drills, which are analyzed to determine what changes need to be made in the disaster plan.

Without constant drill and training, disaster preparedness efforts will come to naught. Recently, a small island nation that had been struck by heavy flooding decided to establish a preparedness plan. After several months of painstaking activities, the new plan was prepared and submitted to the government. Only after it was adopted was it learned that a similar plan had been prepared twenty-five years earlier in response to flooding in the same location. Because there had been no provision for drill or updating, it had been forgotten over the years.

Common Problems in Preparedness

A review of preparedness planning and an assessment of activities carried out under a preparedness plan has indicated a number of common problems. These are:

1. Overcentralization of authority and failure to delegate authority to local levels;
2. Failure to sequence post-disaster activities;
3. Failure to structure the emergency response and actions in the transition phase;
4. Overreliance on electronic communications, especially telephones;
5. Failure to plan adequate and appropriate disaster assessment measures;
6. Failure to build in flexibility and an ability to respond to changing situations;
7. Overemphasis on speed of delivery of material aid rather than on the process of determining actual needs and priorities;

8. Failure to determine appropriate mechanisms for delivering aid at the appropriate periods;
9. Failure to establish methods for terminating or diverting inappropriate aid;
10. Failure to plan adequate protection of critical facilities;
11. Placing responsibility for preparedness planning in the wrong ministry;
12. Overemphasis on relief activities (as opposed to search and rescue, protection of critical facilities, etc.)

While implementing preparedness plans, agencies often fail to involve local people fully and to take coping mechanisms into account in the preparedness planning and training.

Issues in Preparedness

1. *Stockpiling.* Critics point to the fact that distribution of relief supplies rests more on human than technological factors, and that the ability to move materials rapidly from Europe or North America to the developing countries is of little consequence if they cannot be distributed rapidly once they arrive. Another issue is the appropriateness of the aid that is stockpiled. While there is no doubt that some equipment, tools, and resources are helpful in disasters, much of the aid that is traditionally stockpiled is of little real value to the disaster victims (despite the fact that they may stand in line for hours to receive it).

Other critics point out that for stockpiling to be effective, it must be carried out in or very close to the area where it will be used.

Arguments often focus on tents and other emergency shelter items. As an alternative to tents, some relief strategists have proposed that stockpiles of building materials, especially roofing sheets, be placed near threatened communities. Others argue that if the agency has the capability to stockpile materials in this manner, it makes little sense to withhold them until a disaster strikes, especially when they could be useful in improving the safety of the existing buildings. They argue that money is better spent on vulnerability reduction than stockpiling.

The answer to the stockpiling question probably lies somewhere in between the arguments. Stockpiling can be effective, especially if it is carried out in the country, and there are certainly some materials and resources required in every disaster that a poor country cannot justify buying. Medical supplies, especially, are costly and often have a short shelf life. Thus it probably makes sense for these to be stockpiled and provided by the international relief system. Donors should be careful, however, to ensure that the aid provided is appropriate and that the ability to stockpile does not result in the stockpiling of inappropriate aid, or the transfer of these materials at inappropriate times, or in such a way as to clog up the pipeline needed for more critical items.

2. *Community Shelters.* A preparedness issue that often arises is the question of providing large shelters for persons living in areas threatened by cyclonic storms. Much of the traditional preparedness literature advises officials to designate churches, schools, or other large buildings as shelters. Proponents often point to similar practices in the United States. While this practice has been fairly successful here, there are two serious drawbacks to using this approach in developing countries. In the United States, the buildings designated as shelters were especially designed or reinforced to withstand hurricane-force winds. The designation of similar large-scale buildings in developing countries is practical only if they meet the same design criteria and standards—which few do. In fact, many are less stable in high winds than the surrounding houses. The record of these buildings when used as shelters is alarming. In Andhra Pradesh, following the cyclone in 1977, three buildings (churches and schools) failed, with a total loss of over 400 lives. In Dominica, some experts attribute the relatively low loss of life in Hurricane David (1979) to the fact that there was no warning and people were not able to get to the churches designated as hurricane shelters. Of the six main churches, four were totally destroyed.

The second question is that of designating any building in a low-lying or flood-prone area as a shelter. Hurricanes can propel storm surges dozens of kilometers inland with awesome force that no building is safe against. Even if the building does survive the pounding of the wave action, the water may rise as high as 10 meters, entirely covering one- and two-story buildings. Every building used as a community shelter in the coastal area of Andra Pradesh during the 1977 cyclone was submerged by the surge. In fourteen of the buildings to which people had fled for protection, there were no survivors.

Thus even if buildings are specially designed or reinforced as shelters, there would still be a danger.

There are other practical issues involved in the question of coastal storm shelters. In rural areas, it would be difficult and cost-prohibitive to build and maintain a single structure large enough to house all the people in a particular region, and it is unlikely that shelters could be distributed widely enough to be close to all threatened families. Furthermore, the success of shelters would still be dependent upon adequate warning and evacuation systems. Unless an adequate early warning system was developed, people in riverine environments or on islands would be unable to get to the shelters in the first place.

What then is the alternative? Most experts concur that the best measure is adequate warning and evacuation of the threatened area. They argue that in areas along the coast, especially those where storm surges could occur, people should not be encouraged to remain. Since the technology is now available to track cyclonic storms, more emphasis should be placed on public information and awareness of the need to evacuate. This should be accompanied by construction of evacuation routes and hurricane-resistant reception centers for evacuees.

3. *Centralization versus Decentralization.* One of the management issues in disaster preparedness is the question of how much centralization of authority is required for the effective administration of preparedness and emergency response activities. When emergency preparedness was a new topic, little was known about a society's response to a disaster, and it was assumed that people confronted by disaster would panic and behave in unusual ways. It was believed that a strong central office with ultimate authority and power would be the most effective way of controlling the situation and keeping the social fabric together. Krimgold has written, "An emergency is often used to justify changes in the ordinary procedure for making decisions. It provides an excuse which allows national authorities to decide local questions or in turn an excuse for international authorities to decide national questions. In the name of emergency, property can be confiscated, people can be forced to leave their homes and democratic processes can be circumvented" (1974).

The other danger is that in order for a highly centralized bureaucratic system to work, it must have a pyramidal and hierarchical administrative framework. In such systems, there is a loss of information at each level of the organization each time a communication is sent, and the final message received may be different from the original transmitted. Furthermore, such a system is dependent on the functioning of the central office. If that is damaged or communications are severed, the whole system will break down.

Our increased understanding of disaster response by societies indicates an alternative approach to management and argues the case for decentralization. If disaster assistance is to be compatible and "in phase" with actions that are occurring within the community (which as we have seen are usually quite logical and rational), preparedness activities and decisions should also be community-based. It would be difficult for a national or even regional disaster plan to take into account all the local variations found at the community level. Decentralization is important because it allows for local variations in culture, community, and need. Thus "the shortest possible distance between the people who make decisions and the people who are subject to the result of those decisions should be maintained" (Krimgold 1974).

This is not to say that there is no need for a central coordinating body for preparedness activities, which should be endowed with a degree of authority, for such an organization can assure that there is minimal overlap in provision of services and that all assistance is provided on an equitable basis (if given the proper working tools, such as uniform assistance policies). The role of the central office is to coordinate resources outside the community and help meet the needs identified by the local plan.

4. *Use of the Military and Civil Defense.* In many countries, responsibility for civil disaster preparedness is placed in the hands of agencies that are either a formal part of the defense ministry or rely heavily on military organizations. This reflects common practices in the United States and Europe during the 1950s and 60s. During the Cold War, many of the industrialized nations built extensive civil defense networks to respond to civilian needs in the event of a nuclear attack. Responsibility for coordinating activities was normally placed in the hands of military or paramilitary organizations.

As tensions lessened in the 1960s, it was decided to expand these organizations to include a response to civil disasters and to integrate the resources, which include warning devices, shelters, food supplies, and search and rescue equipment, into municipal and state preparedness activities. (In the United States, the change from a strictly military to an expanded civil portfolio is reflected in the progressive name changes from Civil Defense to Civil Defense Preparedness Agency, now integrated in the Federal Emergency Management Agency.) The reasons were not always humanitarian. Some defense planners saw natural disasters as a working laboratory for nuclear war preparations.

There are a number of advantages to using the military in a civil disaster. Usually, the military has an excellent and highly mobile communications system. Units of soldiers can operate self-sufficiently for several days at a time, and they have access to vehicles and heavy equipment useful in many disaster roles. Furthermore, the military is trained to act in an orderly and disciplined manner, which can have major psychological advantages in a chaotic situation.

On the other hand, there are a number of problems associated with the military. First, military units are not suited to long-term disaster roles. Very few commanders are willing to allow their troops or key personnel to devote

A tent city goes unoccupied because people were reluctant to leave their homes and belongings for tents in a stark, unimaginative camp. (Photo UNDRO)

extensive time to non-defense-related activities. Thus organizations that are dependent upon the military in key sectors must by necessity limit their involvement to the emergency period.

A second problem is that any organization or activity tends to mold its method of operation around the key participants. If the military assumes a major role in disaster response, activities will be molded to military capabilities. A subtle example of this is the emphasis on the use of tents as emergency shelter. Because military organizations already have the units and can quickly erect them, few alternatives are sought.

Another example is the way in which tent camps for evacuees are set up. Military engineers will naturally use their own base planning procedures and lay the camps out along military lines. These plans are designed to be orderly, compact, and to achieve a high density. While suitable for military needs, the plans neglect the basic requirements of adequate space for families, and the needs of special groups among the disaster victims. Furthermore, a high density may encourage the spread of disease and the development of undesirable social conditions within a camp, all of which can have a negative long-term effect on the inhabitants.

The third problem is precisely that which makes the military so efficient in the first place, that is, its highly centralized control system. The military hierarchy is designed to facilitate control and to centralize authority. But in a disaster, people need to get together and develop collective responses. A military hierarchy of decision making can discourage and inhibit this process.

Another common problem is that many civil defense agencies are dominated by senior military officers. This may result in the agency being subtly reformed into an operational arm of the military or becoming a shadow command designed to "take over" in a disaster.

In many countries the military represents the power of a repressive government, and local people, far from welcoming the arrival of the military after a disaster, are often fearful of any increased presence of the armed forces. Unfortunately, many preparedness experts from the international relief agencies routinely encourage developing countries to pattern their preparedness plans and organizations after Western civil defense models and thus inadvertently encourage a higher degree of military presence than is really desirable.

The best answer to these dilemmas is to integrate the military's capacities under civilian control. The resources that are needed in a disaster and that the military can easily provide should be identified, including communications, medical services, and transport. Plans should be made to place *small* units under the temporary authority of civil officials for specific tasks. It will then be easier for nonmilitary authorities to manage these resources, and local leaders will not feel overwhelmed or threatened by the presence of soldiers in their community.

An effective, and nonthreatening, way of integrating military and civil functions is to assign only officers with a technical background to civil defense agencies, and at the local level, to place command of military units under the authority of senior noncommissioned officers.

5. *Technical Assistance.* Much of the increased interest in disaster preparedness in the developing countries has been stimulated by the assistance agencies of the industrialized countries and some of the international consortia of nongovernment agencies. The two most influential organizations currently involved are the AID office of U.S. Foreign Disaster Assistance (OFDA) and the League of Red Cross Societies. OFDA has taken strong and valuable steps in aiding the development of national disaster plans. Beginning in the early 1970s, OFDA (then titled "Foreign Disaster Relief Coordinator") began a series of annual seminars for representatives from relief and development organizations in Third World countries. Participants heard lectures from noted disaster specialists and visited state and national civil defense agencies in the U.S.

In the latter part of the decade, OFDA changed its approach and began holding seminars that were more closely attuned to the needs in each region. Participants were encouraged to outline and describe their own needs, which OFDA and other organizations could later help them try to meet. The most successful of these seminars was held in 1979 on St. Lucia and resulted in a variety of regional Caribbean disaster preparedness activities.

The work of the League has been influential too, not only in establishing preparedness activities as a function of local Red Cross societies, but also as an example to other nongovernmental agencies as to what can be accomplished through preparedness. The League has also promoted national pre-disaster planning by asking national societies to encourage their governments to develop national disaster plans. "In this activity, functioning as a humanitarian pressure group, the Red Cross has been responsible for a significant part of the pre-disaster planning which has taken place . . . in the developing countries" (Krimgold 1974).

Other nongovernmental organizations are beginning to take note of pre-disaster planning possibilities. This is especially true among international volag coordinating bodies. For example, the World Council of Churches has recently undertaken preparedness activities and is encouraging its member churches to do likewise. The World Vision con- has also begun to take steps along these lines. Very promising attempts at preparedness at the local level are being made by CADEC (Christian Action for Development in the Caribbean), under a special Disasters Emergency Relief and Welfare Committee supported by technical assistance from Church World Service, OXFAM, and Catholic Relief Services.

There are a number of recurring problems associated with providing technical assistance in the development of emergency preparedness plans. First is the problem of selecting an appropriate model for the plan. Often a standard model or models based on systems used in industrialized countries are suggested as a base for local derivatives. Relying heavily on highly technical or capital-intensive equipment and resources, such plans are usually inappropriate for developing countries.

Although in any preparedness plan there will be recurring organizational, operational, and staffing patterns, it is clear that each country or organization requires a unique combination of these elements. Models developed by each country should present the best plan for meeting local needs and capabilities and reflect the material and human resources available. "Constructing models based on the characteristics of the most wealthy and technologically advanced nations must be avoided. The danger of such models is that they lead less developed societies to overlook their own indigenous resources in developing incremental improvements in their disaster preparations, thereby becoming more dependent on outside assistance" (Fritz 1971).

A second set of problems involves emphasis. More often than not, technical aid has concentrated only on relief, especially that provided by the international donor community. In fact, in certain cases preparedness assistance has seemed to be focused more on facilitating aid by international donors than on the response capabilities of the disaster-affected community. To be effective, technical assistance should concentrate on the full range of preparedness needs and activities.

The best means of overcoming many of these problems is by making a subtle shift in emphasis. Instead of concentrating on the adoption of specific models or plans, technical assistance should be aimed at providing a conceptual framework within which an organization can review the options and develop its own approach and structure. While it is not possible to design a preparedness model or disaster plan that can be adapted to all situations and environments, it is possible to develop satisfactory measures that will be adequate for most situations. Technical assistance can support local efforts by providing access to resources and information that will facilitate the preparedness and response activities. By bringing people together to discuss common issues, problems, and experiences, measures such as the AID Disaster Preparedness Seminars can benefit preparedness activities.

6. *Planning the Political Elements.* One of the most frequently overlooked aspects of pre-disaster planning is the political element. When a major disaster occurs, the prime minister or president of the nation will naturally want to demonstrate concern by taking personal steps to assist. In many countries, a personal representative is designated to be in charge of relief or reconstruction and reports directly to the chief of state. In some cases, this has led to the formation of entirely new disaster response teams and the circumvention of the networks established through disaster preparedness.

In nongovernmental agencies, the phenomenon also exists. If a disaster is of an immense magnitude, the head of the organization often feels compelled to visit the scene and "check on how things are going." Many field directors have seen their carefully developed programs squashed before they got off the ground by one of these "state visits," where the chief of the organization demanded quick action or key changes based on his or her assumption of what is necessary in a disaster.

It is quite logical, and indeed proper, that chief executives insist on some degree of personal involvement. The problem, however, is that such intervention by persons who are not a part of the pre-disaster planning process can slow, complicate, or even erase painstaking preparedness and mitigation efforts.

Yet there are some measures one can take to prevent such intervention from being too disruptive. For governments, a supervisory committee can be established to oversee preparedness and response actions. The position of presiding officer, as well as several other positions on the committee, can be left vacant until a disaster strikes, at which point the chief of state can select a personal representative to head the organization or can even take command personally. The other members of the committee would be professionals, or persons who have a continuing interest in disaster planning and coordination, and who are familiar with the plans that have already been established. These people would constitute a majority of the committee, and during nondisaster periods, it would have a temporary presiding officer.

For the international nongovernmental agencies, there is no such easy remedy. The best solution is to try to instill an awareness of the organization's disaster plans and approaches so that a visiting executive will not feel inclined to interfere. This is especially important for groups whose presiding officers are chosen from outside the organization, not from those who have "come up from the ranks."

The Role of Volags and Small Groups in Pre-disaster Planning

Too often, groups such as volags, churches, or small community organizations are omitted from pre-disaster planning activities. Many small groups feel that preparedness or mitigation activities are beyond their capabilities, or feel that it is not their place to become involved. As we have seen, however, small groups are among the most effective of the coping mechanisms and play a key role in disaster recovery. Thus they should be encouraged to participate to the fullest extent possible.

There are many roles that small groups can fulfill and activities they can undertake, especially in preparedness. At the most basic level, small groups can promote public awareness of natural hazards and promote public action to mitigate or prepare for a pending disaster. Second, agencies can work together with community groups to develop an organizational framework for meeting people's needs in a disaster and assign responsibilities for certain tasks to appropriate groups. This step, the development of an organizational framework for coping, is the most important action that can be taken at the local level.

Actions to reduce losses at the local level are called "community-based disaster preparedness" activities. Volags and small groups can be very effective in helping to organize and implement these measures. For example, in some cyclone-prone rice-producing areas, two ways of reducing crop losses could be introduced. If the weather cycle permits, crops could be planted several weeks earlier so that they could be harvested before the peak of the hurricane season. The introduction of improved storage for harvested rice, such as small-scale ferro-cement silos, would reduce losses should a cyclone strike after the harvest.

Social service agencies, especially churches and their affiliates, should learn more about their role in psychological recovery. One of the most valuable roles played by these organizations is helping families and individuals overcome the emotional stresses of a disaster. It is surprising how few groups are adequately trained or prepared to help individuals and families deal with widespread traumatic events, such as mass casualties, family reunification, and the loss of possessions.

Organizations with access to resources for longer-term recovery should develop policies to guide their recovery programs. It should be remembered that in a region-wide disaster, the social services available at the local level will be minimal, and organizations should determine in advance what affected groups to serve and the best means for maximizing the resources available. The possible gaps in the delivery of social services can be readily identified or estimated, and steps should be taken to plan appropriate action to plug these gaps.

A simplified pre-disaster planning process for small groups is as follows:

Step 1: Identify the key sectors and areas likely to be affected in each community.

Step 2: Determine what types of assistance people will need and estimate the types and levels of assistance they could reasonably expect to receive from within the community and from outside resources. From this list, identify the gaps that will exist.

Step 3: Determine what services the organization can provide, giving priority to the gaps identified in step 2.

Step 4: Determine how each one of the gaps can be met and develop a plan for providing these services when needed.

Step 5: Review the plan and determine if the organization needs any additional services or assistance to implement the plan, and if so, make arrangements to obtain these services when appropriate.

It should be remembered that any preparedness activity, no matter how small, can have significant results. Recently in Bolivia, a small group of farmers established a new settlement in the Amazonian jungle. The farmers knew the best land was along the edge of a river, but also knew that it would flood periodically. Of immediate concern was the realization that in the floods poisonous snakes from the jungle would seek refuge in farm houses. Because medical help was hours away, the community decided that certain measures would be necessary to safeguard people. A church-sponsored organization was asked to help establish a nearby clinic on high ground, and to install a battery-operated refrigerator to store antisnakebite serum. This precaution paid off several years later when a flood did strike and a fourteen-year-old girl was bitten. She was subsequently saved by the serum that had been stored.

The Role of Insurance

Insurance is a mitigation measure often overlooked in disaster studies. In the industrialized societies, insurance is a major factor in individual, corporate, and community recovery. Furthermore, insurance is often used as an incentive to mitigation. For example, insurance companies can agree to lower the annual cost of the insurance if a family or company in a disaster-prone area takes certain measures to strengthen its buildings or to protect the property. Insurance companies have been quite creative in developing mitigation incentives for businesses and industrial facilities, not only in the United States and Europe, but also in the Third World. For families, however, insurance companies have not risen to the challenge of developing programs for those of moderate and low income.

To understand the importance of insurance, it is necessary to understand the role it plays in a disaster. For families, insurance can eliminate or reduce the possibility of complete financial ruin. For families and small businesses, it can provide access to funding not otherwise available. It is doubtful, for example, that poor people would be able to borrow substantial sums after a disaster in order to rebuild. Insurance is a cheap way to make sure that they have access to these funds.

Other factors such as the impact of insurance following a disaster should not be overlooked. First, insurance proceeds are a means of injecting unfettered capital into a post-disaster situation. All other funding sources after disasters have certain constraints. Loans may be provided to disaster victims, but they will normally be given only for a specific purpose, for example, reconstruction of housing or rehabilitation of businesses. In many cases, the borrower will never actually see the money, or will have little say over how it can be spent. Insurance, on the other hand, pays money directly to policy holders, who can use the money as they see fit. More often than not, the individual will reinvest the money to replace the loss, but the choice is left up to the individual.

Second is the effect that a rapid payoff can have on a community. It normally takes two to six weeks for insurance companies to assess damages and pay out their claims. Some researchers have noted that quick and substantial settlements can have a major impact on lessening the emergency period and beginning a transition into rehabilitation and reconstruction. In Dominica in 1979, the beginning of reconstruction was marked by the settlement of insurance claims. This injection of capital, even on a small scale, has not only a psychological benefit, but can also stimulate rehiring and the restart of markets. As a rule, the larger the payoffs or the greater the percentage of people covered by insurance, the more quickly recovery will begin and the shorter the recovery period.

Third is the role that insurance plays in reducing the burden on financial institutions in the afflicted community. If businesses and industries, especially, are not insured, the money for their reconstruction will have to be provided by the financial houses within the community, or from nearby regions. This reduces the capital available for reconstruction of small businesses and for use by families and individuals.

Thus insurance can have a major impact on mitigating the effects of a disaster. Unfortunately, there are few creative programs or companies that are willing to extend these benefits directly to the poor. There are, however, some indirect means of providing these benefits. For example, the institutions to which poor people belong may be insurable when the individuals and families are not. This is especially true in the case of cooperatives. Dominica again provides a good example. The Dominican economy is based on two crops. Approximately 60 percent of the farmers produce either bananas or coconuts. Most of the farmers work small plots of land, averaging less than twenty acres. All the farmers belong to a producers' cooperative and sell their produce through the cooperative to one authorized buyer (in the case of bananas, to WINDBAN, the Windward Islands Banana Company).

Because most of the farms are marginal, it would be impossible for the farmers to obtain insurance on an individual basis. WINDBAN, however, as a corporation and major exporter, can buy insurance and did so prior to the hurricane. After the disaster, WINDBAN received a settlement of several million dollars. WINDBAN, in turn, divided this among the farmers based on a fixed amount per acre. Farmers received only slightly less than the amount that they would have received from sales of their crops during that year. With this influx of capital, farmers were able to clear their land and purchase the new plants and seedlings needed to reestablish their groves. This had other positive benefits. The people purchased their replacement supplies through the normal markets, and thus were able to help stimulate recovery in that sector.

Volags and other development groups can play a significant role by working with their counterparts, especially cooperatives and other community-based institutions, to develop innovative insurance schemes to extend the benefits of insurance to the poor.

13
Program Planning and Management

The delivery of relief and reconstruction aid can be improved substantially by detailed program planning and through sound program management. Program planning is the more important, for if all aspects of the program are thoroughly considered, if objectives are clearly defined, and tasks are properly sequenced, many of the management problems that often develop can be avoided. Program planning is not complicated and does not take a lot of time. The following is a description of some of the key considerations and steps in post-disaster program planning and management.

DETERMINING HOW AND WHERE TO INTERVENE

The first step in intervention is deciding how and where the agency can be most helpful. As already mentioned, one of the earliest activities following a disaster is disaster assessment. It was also mentioned that there are two types of assessments, namely, damage assessment and needs assessment. For most relief and reconstruction programs, needs assessment is the more important. Needs can best be determined by visiting representative areas and talking to selected groups in the affected communities. Emergency needs are usually obvious; long-term needs may be more difficult to ascertain. Furthermore, needs change from day to day. What is important is identifying the needs at the times they must be met.

Once the basic needs have been identified, they should be quantified. Agencies should be careful not to become too involved in surveying, but should attempt to estimate percentages of families requiring different types of assistance. "A count needs to be taken of the reserves of food, medicine, clothing and building materials existing within the community, and of the capacity of the victims to help themselves and each other. Rarely will everyone in the area be stricken, and of those who are, not all will take advantage of the relief offered" (Taylor 1979a).

The next step is to determine what gaps exist in the overall delivery of assistance. Agencies should remember that other relief organizations will also provide aid, and their plans should be taken into account before the agency decides which activities it will undertake in any particular area.

INITIAL STEPS IN PROGRAM PLANNING

Once an agency has decided on a certain course of action, the next step is to define precisely what the program hopes to attain and to establish a framework for guiding the decisions that will be required in subsequent activities. To do this, an agency first sets its policies, establishes goals and objectives, and finally selects the strategies and approaches by which to attain the objectives. The process sounds simple and, in fact, it is. Yet it is surprising how many agencies fail to use these practices and flounder because no one is sure precisely what the goals of the program are.

Setting Policies

Policies are used to shape the response. They provide a framework, or standard, by which choices are measured. Setting policies is one of the easiest of all the program planning steps, but unfortunately is the one that is the most often neglected. Ideally, an agency that frequently responds to disasters sets its policies as part of its preparedness activities, and thus, when a disaster breaks, those involved in the initial program have some guidance in structuring their decision making.

The following policies, which were derived by the CRS staff in the Dominican Republic to guide its housing reconstruction program following Hurricanes Frederick and David in 1979, demonstrate how simple a policy framework can be:

To support and expand local actions or groups;
To conduct all activities in such a way as to meet development goals;
To maximize all expenditures through recapture of funds, extension of buying power, multiple objective planning;
To give priority to people who are not eligible for any other form of assistance (or to those one step up);
To rely on appropriate technology;
To spend majority of funds within the project areas;
To give priority to [a particular] area or sector.

Every time an organization then needs to make important choices, it can first review them against the policies it has set to determine whether or not the choices "fit."

Objectives

Identifying the objectives of the program is the next step in planning. Again, the setting of objectives does not need to be overly complicated. Each objective can be put in a narrative form and should describe what the agency hopes to obtain by each action or set of actions in each program or sector of activity. Once again, an example of objectives from the CRS program in the Dominican Republic:

To upgrade the standard of housing within the project area;
To provide increased job opportunities;
To improve or diversify local skills;
To provide alternate income to people whose economic livelihood has
     been hurt by the storm;
To restore or develop new equitable marketing systems within the project.

During the discussion of objectives, staff should also discuss how programs in different sectors can be tied together to attain broader results. An agency should strive for balance and look at more than one way of attaining a particular objective.

Goal Setting

Goal setting is the quantification of objectives. The purpose is to determine how much assistance is going to be provided and how many beneficiaries will be recipients. (It is at this point that the quantification of the disaster assessment is helpful.)

Some examples of goals from the CRS program:

To reach 25 percent of the low-income people within the project area;
To provide 1000 loans, 5000 subsidies, 1000 grants in the project area;
To increase the margin of safety in the housing affected by this program by
     50 percent.

Goal setting in itself is not a difficult process, but establishing realistic goals requires much forethought and discussion. It is at this point that the agency must balance its desire to help against the realistic assessment of its own capabilities.

The Determination of Strategies and Approaches

The determination of strategies and approaches is the final step in conceptualizing a relief or reconstruction program.

To differentiate between the two terms, a strategy is the *plan* for attaining the goal, while an approach is the *method* used. The following example should clarify the differences further. In order to provide replacement housing after a disaster, the strategies open to an agency are:

1. To provide indirect assistance by stimulating the housing industry;
2. To provide direct assistance by giving loans and grants;
3. To provide direct assistance by establishing a housing program.

Assuming that the strategy chosen by the agency is to establish a housing program, some approaches that might be available include:

1. To provide the needed construction materials and tools;
2. To provide materials and technical assistance in an aided self-help construction program;
3. To establish a construction team and build frames and roofs of houses, but leave the remainder of the construction and finishing details to the homeowner;
4. To establish a construction team and rebuild complete replacement houses for a designated number of people in the project area.

The selection of one strategy or approach should not preclude the adoption of others if the resources of the agency allow. It is especially important that approaches be balanced and complementary.

SETTING UP THE PROGRAM

Once an organization has conceptualized its program, the process of putting it into operation begins. This entails allocating resources, developing program management, and monitoring the projects.

Resource Allocation

The allocation of resources, especially money, is one of the most difficult choices that an agency will face. It is important to balance the program and to try to develop an appropriate mix of responses. It is impossible to describe all the choices that exist for programs in each of the different sectors, but there are some concepts that are helpful to know for programs in general. The first set describes ways in which funds can be stretched; thus they are known as funding concepts.

1. *Linking to other programs.* This is the simplest and most effective way to expand the capabilities of an organization. The methods usually considered are cost sharing, pooling of resources, or contributing matching funds.

2. *Recoverable funding.* In recoverable funding, all or a portion of the funds distributed are returned to the program (usually for reinvestment). The most common examples are revolving loans and sales or subsidy schemes. Recoverable funding increases the number of people who can be served and extends the "service" of the cash originally committed.

3. *Maximization of buying power.* This refers to the practice of selectively spending money so that the financial power of either the programs or the beneficiaries is extended. For example, if loans are determined to be a viable option, an agency can use its money to guarantee loans from normal financial institutions to clients who normally would not be eligible, instead of using its own resources to make the loans. In this manner an amount of, for example, $100,000 could be used to guarantee up to $1,000,000 or more in loans, thus increasing ten-fold the buying power of the money the agency has on hand. At the individual level, an example of maximizing expenditures is the use of coupons or redeemable certificates (such as food stamps) to increase the buying power of the people. In this way, the resources of the agency can be "piggybacked" with the resources of the victims.

4. *Multiple objective planning.* Here expenditures are targeted so that more than one objective is reached with each disbursement. At its most sophisticated, it is the placement of money in the community in such a way that most will stay in the community or at least pass through several hands before leaving. A sample scenario: a work project is established to repair a road damaged by the disaster, people are paid in cash and coupons redeemable in local markets only, the workers spend the money and help stimulate recovery of the market, which in turn buys goods from the farmers affected by the disaster. The objectives reached: a road is repaired, capital is provided to the victims, the victims' buying power is extended, the market is stimulated, an economic unit (the market) is assisted, and finally, the farmers (victims themselves) are assisted. The number of contacts handling the money: three.

The second set of concepts describes some guiding principles for balancing a program.

1. *Concentration of resources.* In order to have the maximum effect on a community, a program should concentrate its resources in a specific geographic area. The size should be such that funding activities are

complementary and expenditures in one sector can have an effect on other sectors in the same community. If an agency is funding a housing program in one community and an agricultural recovery program in another, the result will be less effective than if they were in the same community and the overall cost will be higher.

2. *Balance between family and community assistance.* Most international relief agencies, especially the volags, tend to respond to disasters with programs to assist families. Community assistance is left to the government and its donors. In certain situations it is impossible for intervenors to coordinate so that both families and communities receive assistance concurrently and a degree of balance is attained. Yet, because full recovery is not complete until all sectors are restored to normalcy, it may be necessary for volags also to provide assistance to community projects, especially following large disasters where the agency is operating in remote rural areas. As a rule, one-fourth to one-third of the project funds should be used for labor-intensive community projects in these situations.

3. *Loan to grants ratio.* When direct assistance is provided to families, the financial capabilities of the average family to be served should be considered before deciding on the financial approach. The proper balance for loans and grants is approximately 80-20. It should be remembered that grants or donations are nonrecoverable and an assistance program will soon be out of business if this course is pursued. For Integrated Recovery Programs (see chapter 9), a suggested balance is 40 percent subsidies, 30 percent loans, 20 percent community assistance projects, and 10 percent grants.

Program Management

The next step in setting up a program is to establish the management apparatus. Activities include establishing a table of organization (or organigram, as it is often called), developing a budget, and hiring the staff and consultants. The more professional agencies have organized project management systems that provide a sequenced guide for the staff to follow.

Whatever method an organization chooses for managing its program, several aspects of each activity should be considered.

ESTABLISHING A TABLE OF ORGANIZATION

As pointed out earlier, tables of organization can have a subtle effect on the way in which programs are executed. In theory, a table of organization is the instrument for organizing the staff and for establishing lines of authority, a hierarchy of responsibility, and lines of communication. Setting up an organigram is in itself an art, and care must be taken to ensure that decision making is not inadvertently restricted and that the flow of information is not inhibited.

1. *Form should follow function.* The structure of an organization should be built around the activities that it is going to conduct. To do this, the planner classifies all the activities that are related by either function or by the skills or compatibility of skills necessary to carry out a set of tasks. Administrative tasks, for example, should be assigned to administrative staff. Operational tasks should be assigned to operational units or personnel with operational skills, tools, or other capabilities.

2. *The organigram should encourage participatory management.* While decision making and clear lines of authority are required, there must be appropriate mechanisms that give people access to decision makers and encourage participation at the highest levels. This can often be accomplished by establishing citizens' advisory councils or boards at the upper levels of the program and project area committees at the lower levels. By developing mechanisms for participation by the victims, an agency facilitates the flow of information from the community to the program.

3. *Retain a reasonable span of control.* A common weakness of many tables of organization is that key people are assigned too many responsibilities. In management, this is known as "exceeding the span-of-control limits." Span-of-control describes the number of subordinates or activities that any one person can control or supervise effectively. Individuals have a limit as to how many different activities they can juggle at any one time. The maximum is seven. For most people, the span-of-control limit is between three and five. Thus, when setting up an organigram, care should be taken that the number of subordinates or activities that an individual is required to supervise does not exceed this limit.

4. *Establish shortcuts.* In establishing an organigram, the planner should ensure that there are channels that allow those at the lower echelons of a program to have access to those at the upper echelons and persons in authority. In industry, this is handled by establishing workers' committees, unions, or trade guilds. The larger a program, the more important it is for the people who are doing the work to have a voice in the program and a representative or advocate at the highest levels. Because of the nature of relief programs, the higher turnover of staff, and the mix of expatriates and local people, staff problems are greater than in most other organizations. If mechanisms are placed into the organigram that can provide an "escape valve" to relieve the pressures, a program will run much more smoothly in the long run.

STAFFING

Staffing of a relief program also requires careful consideration. In the initial aftermath of a disaster, there is an abundance of volunteers for emergency programs. The majority of these are victims and they can be hastily organized to carry out the relief activities. (The more sophisticated activities, such as epidemiological surveillance, initial damage assessment, and restoration of lifelines are normally carried out by pre-designated agencies or officials according to a disaster response plan.)

In the later phases of a disaster, a different type of staff is normally needed to carry out recovery and reconstruction programs. Additional skills will be required in administration, as well as certain technical fields, and a greater degree of sophistication in overall program planning and management will be necessary. The bulk of the actual fieldwork, of course, will still be carried out by the victims themselves and persons recruited from the project area or the surrounding area.

At the end of the emergency, a change in staffing will be necessary. Most emergency activities can be carried out by volunteers, whereas in longer-term reconstruction and recovery activities, workers will require payment. The failure to prepare for this transition can delay a relief program when persons in key positions quit to return to their normal work. Unless this transition is anticipated, time and money can be lost while waiting for replacements. Many agencies are disappointed that people do not seem to want to volunteer for the longer-term activities, but people should not be expected to work without pay. Agencies that are committed to using volunteers or schemes that pay in kind, such as food-for-work, often find it difficult to operate beyond the transition period.

Another staffing question is what to do with expatriate volunteers. Under most circumstances, the majority of the relief work should be carried out by local personnel. In certain positions, trained professionals may be needed, and often they cannot be found within the stricken community. Thus the hiring of expatriates may be required; however, organizations should attempt to rely as much as possible on local personnel.

Here are several suggestions on staffing for intervenors:

1. Do not hire an expatriate when a local person with the same skills is available.
2. A proper balance between local and expatriate staff should be achieved. Local personnel must be included at all levels, not just the lower ranks.
3. Only expatriates with technical skills should be placed in positions as advisors. Expatriates in advisory positions should be assigned local

counterparts and see their tasks in terms of training, demonstrating, and organizing.

4. Equitable and equal salaries should be paid to both expatriates and local personnel (Intertect 1974).

A final question that arises in relation to staffing is the use of technical personnel and consultants. In recent years there has been an increase in the use of consultants at all levels of the relief system. Until ten years ago, most consultants advised governments and international organizations. Since the 1970s, local governments and voluntary agencies have increased their use of consultants, especially for specific technical services. The choice of whether or not to use a consultant is always difficult, and experience and results are varied. For the most part, the performance of consultants has depended on their previous experience, and at present, there are very few consultants who have had extensive field experience in the actual preparation and execution of post-disaster programs. Without this base of experience, it is difficult for them to be effective. The use of academics and technicians from non-disaster-oriented firms, for example, has generally met with poor results.

The problem is that there are few consultants who can be chosen at random and assigned to a disaster. Thus agencies should assess what type of services may be required and develop linkages with consultants before a disaster strikes. Consultants should receive orientation and training about disasters and the *modus operandi* of the organization. If this is done, both the program and the consultant will be more effective.

BUDGETING AND MONETARY CONTROL

Money is the oil that keeps the relief machine running smoothly; thus simple, accurate systems that facilitate budgeting and cost control are important considerations. Budgeting for post-disaster programs is usually a trial and error process. Because of the nature of the appeals system, relief agencies rarely know precisely how much money they have to operate with, and this, coupled with the uncertainties until the disaster assessment is completed, makes it difficult to allocate financial resources.

The popular image is that budgets are overestimated in the early stages when financial resources are plentiful, or that an agency expands its activities beyond the resources available. In practice, this is usually not the case. Most disasters attract an outpouring of aid, and if the major donor nations become involved, substantial resources will be available. Trying to allocate resources wisely or to establish programs that match the capabilities of an organization are more often the problem than not having enough resources.

Anticipating later funding difficulties, many agencies tend to develop their budgets early in a program. In agencies where rigid financial policies exist, a quickly prepared budget may inadvertently become an instrument that controls the program, rather than vice versa.

The most realistic way to overcome budgeting problems is for an agency to establish a policy on how and when it will commit its funds in each phase of the disaster. For example, some agencies place a significant portion (up to 75 percent) of all funds received from initial appeals into a contingency fund for use in longer-term programs during reconstruction. This allows the field staff to develop more realistic budgets in the later stages of recovery.

Whatever approach is used, a budget must be flexible and especially allow for inflation. If it is formulated during the initial stages of a disaster, a large portion of the total budget should be left in uncommitted contingency reserve so that the field staff can adapt to the changing situation and respond to unmet needs.

Many agencies experience difficulty with monetary control and have trouble accounting for funds. Usually this is because they do not use accounting systems that are adapted to a disaster situation. Good field accounting requires a simple field-accounting system that is easy to use, easy to carry, and places the emphasis of trust on the user; and training in how to use the system before disaster strikes. Field representatives, especially in the emergency, must have an accounting system that recognizes the need for flexibility as well as simplicity. Several agencies have recently begun to use simplified field-account books that have built-in impression pads, so that duplicate or triplicate records can be prepared and maintained.

PROJECT MANAGEMENT SYSTEMS

For agencies that are involved in large-scale or complex projects, a method for managing, sequencing, and monitoring activities and progress is needed. Most programs consist of a number of separate activities or operations that are related to each other in varying degrees. Some activities cannot be started until certain other activities are completed, while some are not directly dependent upon any others. A management tool that can be used to show the sequence of and relationship between various operations is the flowchart. Business and industry have long used methods such as bar charts, CPM (Critical Path Method), and PERT (Project Evaluation and Review Techniques) for planning and managing projects, and these techniques can be adapted for disaster programs.

A flowchart is a network diagram that graphically depicts the project activities and puts them in a logical order. Flowcharts highlight the critical path[1] and activities that must be administered to help keep a project on schedule. Program managers, using flowcharts, can monitor progress and determine when it is necessary to speed up certain activities or operations to complete the project on time. Using a flowchart, it is possible to understand how the parts of a project should fit together. A program coordinator and staff can visualize how the different parts of the project relate to each other and test the logic of proposed actions. Furthermore, the network diagram is an excellent method for showing workers the plan of the project and their role in relation to that of others.

There are many flowcharting techniques that can be adapted to disaster usage, and several agencies have developed their own approach or technique. Flowcharts are used in two ways: (1) to illustrate a plan for responding to a situation that has not yet developed, and (2) to plan a program where the resources and events and objectives are known in advance.

The greatest benefit of using a flowchart is that a plan must be formulated for the entire project. This planning process is itself worthwhile. If properly developed, a flowchart can become the instrument for project management and control.

Monitoring and Evaluation

Throughout the course of a program, it is important to analyze actions and events. Two activities are required: monitoring and evaluation. Monitoring is the process of watching the program to ensure that it is operating smoothly. Incoming information is used to determine the performance of the program by measuring it against objectives. Items monitored are: whether or not the program is proceeding according to schedule, cash flow, overall performance of staff, and overall performance of the program. Monitoring is used to identify bottlenecks and obstacles that cause delays or that require a reassessment. It is a continuous process and is the basis for making adjustments while the program is in progress.

Evaluation, on the other hand, is a detailed review of the program upon completion of an important milestone or at the end of a specified period. Evaluations should be carried out both during and after the program. The purpose of evaluation is much broader than that of monitoring. It determines whether or not the program approach is valid and assesses the

---

1. The critical path is that sequence of dependent operations from the beginning to the end of a project that requires the greatest amount of time.

impact of the program on the community. It also helps agencies to develop a base of information and to derive lessons learned that will help agencies in their future activities.

Thorough evaluations of post-disaster programs are rare. Usually intervenors prepare detailed post-disaster reports listing the assistance provided and prepare a cost analysis or audit of how the money or aid is accounted for. True analysis is relatively rare, however. Few reports state what the initial objectives of a program were and whether the program met these objectives. Performance data about programs are sketchy, and virtually none of the reports examine the impact of activities on the victims or the community.

There are several reasons why agencies do not conduct evaluations. First, most agencies do not plan in advance for evaluation, or they may cancel evaluation plans in an attempt to reduce overhead costs. Second, there is usually a high turnover of field staff, making it difficult to determine the basis of decisions or actions.

Some critics claim that for some agencies, evaluations may be threatening. No one likes to admit that they have made mistakes, and for agencies dependent upon the public's perception of their efficiency, an evaluation may be too threatening. And, some agencies simply fail to see how any assistance that is provided for humanitarian reasons can have an adverse effect. A more pragmatic reason is that many agencies do not know *what* to evaluate or how to go about it.

Evaluations require three steps. The first is to determine what will be evaluated. The second is to choose the criteria against which events or decisions will be assessed. The third is to select the method that will be used to obtain the information.

An evaluation must be more than an audit. Among the things useful to evaluate are:

1. *Issues that arose during the course of the program.* The term *issues* refers to the broader questions that were encountered throughout the program. An example of an issue that always seems to arise is whether or not aid should be free, subsidized, or sold at full price. By identifying issues and examining how the program responded to each, it is possible for agencies to extract policy lessons that will help them to frame future programs.

2. *Policy lessons.* Specifically, how workable were the policies that were in effect and what was their impact on the program? Were they helpful in decision making, restrictive to the program, or simply not appropriate to the situation?

3. *The structure of the program.* How did the structure of the organization (the organigram) affect decision making? What organizational models were

used and how did these facilitate or inhibit information from reaching those who should have had it?

4. *The allocation of resources.* Did the program represent the best possible use of the resources available?

5. *The sequence of events.* Were activities carried out in a coherent manner and was this sequence the best that could have taken place? Could shortcuts have been developed? If shortcuts were used, how did they work out in the end?

6. *The impact of the program.* Evaluting the impact of a program is the most important aspect of program evaluation. Especially important to determine are the effects of the program on the coping mechanisms of the community. What effect did the program have on local processes and the way in which people interact, and what future problems may have been resolved or created?

Once an agency has determined what it is going to assess, it must develop the criteria for the assessment. Typically, organizations tend to examine programs in terms of their own needs and capabilities rather than the needs or interests of the victims. Care should be taken to ensure that the criteria reflect the viewpoint of the persons who are being assisted.

The next step is to determine how the evaluation will be conducted. There are three general methods for carrying out an evaluation. The first is to hire someone from outside to conduct the study, the second is to carry out a self-evaluation, and the third is a combination of the two known as an aided self-evaluation. There are advantages and disadvantages to each, but in the opinion of the author, the most effective method is the aided self-evaluation, for it brings together the people who have carried out the program so that *they* learn the lessons. By using an outside facilitator to assist in the process, people hear a different point of view, and if all the key decision makers participate, the evaluation can have positive results.

No matter what methods are chosen, evaluating a program is very important. Without evaluations and documentation of experience, agencies will repeat mistakes that have been made countless times before, and not take advantage of lessons learned in previous disasters. Thus each time a disaster strikes, someone will have to begin from scratch and relearn all the lessons.

7. *Winding down or knowing when to quit.* Terminating program activities can be more difficult for agencies than would be expected. Most programs end when the stated goals, usually in terms of numbers of beneficiaries, have been achieved. Ideally, the time frame of a certain activity should be coterminous with each phase of a disaster in which it occurs. Thus, when a particular phase ends, activities in that period should be phased out. Because of the funding procedures for most agencies, however, funds may

be just arriving when a phase ends, and if they are earmarked or already committed for activities in that phase, a program may just be starting when events dictate that it should be ending.

As a general rule, relief (charity) programs should end with the emergency. Transition programs should end shortly after people have returned home or have gone back to their regular work. Reconstruction programs should be phased out either when all activities are back to normal, or when it is obvious that processes initiated by the program can continue without further support from the agency.

By timing relief programs to events, agencies can exert some influence over recovery time. If, however, programs continue that are inappropriate to the particular phase, the recovery time will be increased.

14
Trends and Future Directions

Disasters and disaster response can be expected to receive growing attention from both the international community and the Third World countries. Here we will examine some of the current trends in disaster response and present some of the challenges that will be faced in the next decade.

TRENDS

Many of the trends begun in the 1970s will continue. An increased interest in the topic of disasters, coupled with an awareness of the impact of disasters on development, should lead more organizations (especially development agencies) to become involved in disaster-related problems.

A number of articles in the 1970s proposed that a central World Disaster Coordinating Center be established (in Geneva) as a way of achieving control over disaster response worldwide. These papers, some of which were commissioned by the United Nations Association, pointed out that instantaneous international communications are now technically feasible and proposed that the means of coordinating disaster response be centralized and automated to the greatest extent possible.

Yet the moral and practical reasons why such a center should not be established are overwhelming. The tendency would be to perceive the center as the place where "the action is" instead of at the level of the affected country. Decision making must be locally based, not transferred tò Geneva, New York, or Nairobi.

In the mid-1970s, a new issue was put forth for discussion by humanitarian organizations. Intervention in disasters was redefined as a human rights issue (Green 1977). Proponents came to see disaster aid as the right of poor people in the Third World, an extension of their right to survive and the basic rights guaranteed under the UN Declaration of the Rights of Man. Advocates pointed out that many Third World governments either lacked the capabilities for an adequate response or, for political reasons, refused to allow international aid to disaster victims. Of special concern were famines (many of the proponents had been active in the Sahel and Ethiopian famine relief programs). The advocates believed it was the obligation of the industrialized countries to provide aid to disaster victims regardless of the wishes of the affected country and urged that international conventions be established to facilitate intervention.

An alternate view, sometimes called "accountability," was also proposed. Advocates argued that intervention is far from perfect and that since international aid can have only limited effect, the responsibility for disaster response and mitigation must remain with the host government. Efforts should be taken to strengthen disaster preparedness and response capabilities of local government and NGOs. Intervention was not seen as a totally positive influence, and it was argued that forced intervention was neither politically feasible nor desirable from a development viewpoint. Advocates argued that intervention is already overemphasized, and that it obscures the fact that most response actions are carried out by local groups and the host government. If increased emphasis is to be placed on disasters, the focus should not be on intervention but on pre-disaster planning and helping local institutions cope with the problems.

With rising nationalism, however, it is questionable whether Third World governments would tolerate unilateral intervention by donors. If, however, most governments in the Third World continue to be totalitarian, and the internal politics continue to be laced with fraternal squabbles resulting in "minidisasters," the humanitarian organizations will likely take a more activist posture (as some have done in certain refugee situations), and develop modes of operation whereby they can supply relief materials without regard to international borders. The consequences of this type of relief activity remain to be seen.

The interest and expertise in disasters is still concentrated in the donor community. In Europe there has been increased awareness of the influence of disasters on development in the Third World. New relief organizations are formed each year, and governments and the EEC are increasing both their bilateral disaster aid and their assistance to NGOs. The new volags have tended to follow the traditional patterns set by the existing NGOs, and most are active in social services and the medical and nutritional sectors.

The European governments have been searching for new organizational structures and innovative ways to provide disaster assistance. Two organizations are indicative of this search. In Sweden the government has formed the Swedish Standby Force for Disasters. It is included within the defense ministry and is a civilian branch of the Swedish defense forces. It is composed of military personnel temporarily released from active duty to perform duties in disaster relief without loss of rank or pay, and a cadre of civilians who sign up on a voluntary basis for a period of twelve months. The standby force is organized along military lines and draws the majority of its equipment from military material. The role of the team is to provide emergency services of a relief nature (Bruzelius 1978).

The Swedish Standby Force reflects a common perception mentioned earlier; namely, that disasters are essentially logistics problems, similar in nature to military operations. Thus it is considered both reasonable and proper that groups organized along military lines be assigned a major role. The Standby Force is an attempt to develop an organization with military-like capabilities, but without direct military involvement and its connotations. (The neutral Swedes also see this as a way in which they can give their senior military officers some exposure to the Third World).

The Swiss Disaster Relief Team reflects another train of thought. The Swiss have formed a specialized civilian unit to conduct research and prepare technical teams for service in the Third World. A small core staff is responsible for management and research, and a team of technicians headed by a permanent member of the staff conducts the fieldwork. Most assignments to date have been carried out under the banner of one of the international organizations with headquarters in Switzerland, especially the United Nations High Commissioner for Refugees. The Swiss team has taken a much wider view of disasters and is concentrating its efforts not only on the emergency period, but also on the later phases.

Of the two organizations, the Swiss example is considered by most observers to be more flexible and responsive to the needs of natural disasters. Most of the personnel supplied by the Swiss have been engineers, architects, or other technicians, who in most cases have provided skills that were not available locally. The makeup of the Swedish Standby Force and its military orientation have prevented the group from being effective. When it has been "sent into action," the results have been disappointing. With large numbers of untrained, inexperienced personnel groping to find an appropriate role, the force has been characterized as an "overresponse." In part, this is due to the lack of adequate orientation (at present, less than two weeks) and also to the nature of their organization, which is heavily, and unnecessarily, oriented toward total self-sufficiency in communications, logistics, and transport. But more basic is the role they have defined for themselves and their perception of disasters as a tactical problem.

The Swiss team, on the other hand, has maintained a low profile and because their senior staff are full-time disaster specialists with field experience, the organization is evolving into a much more flexible structure with a more meaningful role.

Disasters are also becoming of more interest to the European university community. Until only a few years ago, disaster research in Europe was mainly found in the British universities. Now active research centers exist in Belgium, France, Germany, the Netherlands, and Sweden.

Except in the fields of health and nutrition, where pioneering work has been carried out at the London School of Hygiene and Tropical Medicine, and at the Catholic University of Louvain (Belgium), European institutions trail their North American counterparts in research and applications. Most of the emphasis is on the medical aspects of disaster, and the few newcomers who are branching into other areas of disaster research are trodding along well-worn roads, seemingly oblivious of the work already done and the lessons painstakingly learned.

The appropriate technology (AT) movement has had an impact on some European organizations, though most of the work in AT is still carried out by small groups that receive only limited support from the major aid organizations. The Intermediate Technology Development Group (ITDG) of London and its counterparts are making progress, and specific disaster-related needs are receiving more emphasis. There have been new efforts to link AT and mitigation measures. A promising development is the establishment of the Panel on Vulnerability Reduction in the U.K., with ITDG one of the core groups.

In the U.S., interest in disasters is more diverse, and the country leads in both research and development. The disciplines of sociology, anthropology, history, economics, engineering, architecture, and meteorology all have their specialized interests in disasters.

Research in the U.S. received a major boost after 1976 when, as a result of devastating earthquakes in Guatemala, Indonesia, Italy, China, and Turkey, major funds were appropriated for disaster research. Most is for earthquake research and disaster problems within the U.S., though many findings and spinoff technologies have been developed that are applicable to Third World situations.

In a move opposite to that of their European counterparts, many U.S. relief agencies are shifting their emphasis from disaster relief to concern with the development aspects. Their approach overall is generally more sophisticated and flexible than that of the European agencies.

World hunger was the major concern of the American volags in the 1970s. Many of the newer organizations were in fact founded to address the hunger problem. Thus food aid in both normal and disaster situations was of prime interest to the American volag community. This interest should broaden and many of these organizations will become more heavily involved in disasters.

Because food aid and agricultural development are so closely related, and hunger, especially famine, is considered a "disaster topic," many organizations that began as food donors quickly moved to provide a broader range of services. This has brought about an increased understanding of development issues, which in turn has played a part in increasing the organizations' awareness of the interrelationship between development and disaster issues. This increased understanding is expected to pay off in more meaningful disaster assistance programs.

The U.S. government has continued to be a leader in disaster response and research. Its emphasis and directions have not been consistent, however, due to the number of administration changes in the 1970s. Continuous emphasis has been placed on the application of technology, and OFDA has been under constant pressure to modernize disaster assistance and apply new technologies. As a result, AID and the National Science Foundation have stimulated much of the high-tech research. The High Wind Study conducted by the National Bureau of Standards (1974), much of the recent earthquake research, and pioneering efforts in the use of satellite technology and remote sensing for monitoring disasters (Robinove 1975) are examples of the work carried out in the last decade. The emphasis on technology will continue, though emphasis will also be placed on intermediate-level technology.

In the American university community, many disciplines are involved in disaster research. In the 1970s, most of this effort was concentrated on emergency operations and reconstruction. Today, more emphasis is being placed on mitigation and prevention. In the early 1970s, the social sciences received the bulk of the research funds; today engineering and "hard" science predominates.

Appropriate technology (AT) has also had an impact in the U.S. Most of the disaster-related AT work has concentrated on the development of simple and low-cost ways of modifying housing to resist high winds and earthquakes. In 1978, the U.S. Government made a major commitment to support AT and created a special foundation called Appropriate Technology International (ATI) to support and encourage such activities in the U.S. and the Third World. ATI has already provided funds to support work in disaster-resistant housing and to establish a network of researchers exploring the problems of earthen buildings in seismic areas. ATI, VITA, and other AT groups should have a major impact on small-scale disaster technology.

Despite some promising efforts, the Third World has still not placed much emphasis on developing disaster response capabilities or on research. In the literature from the less developed countries (LDCs), there has been almost no interest in the development-disaster link. At the government level, this is partly a result of funding patterns and the assistance available to governments without excess resources to devote to disaster research and preparedness activities. Few volags in the LDCs have the resources to invest in disaster preparedness activities. As one representative said in a recent conference on preparedness, "We are too concerned with day-to-day survival activities to worry about disaster problems that may not occur during our lifetime." Until more Third World volags are established, most of the emphasis in preparedness and mitigation will still be placed on the government and the international voluntary agencies. (The Red Cross is an exception, as mentioned earlier, having been the leader among Third World NGOs in its concern with disasters.)

Until now, Third World universities have neglected disasters, both from the point of research and from that of preparing graduates to deal with disaster-related problems or even to address the issues of development and poverty. There are few architects or engineers who can deal with the problems of reinforcing traditional housing to withstand earthquakes or high winds, and few social scientists who can advise civil defense or other governmental ministries in planning an appropriate disaster response to meet local needs.

There are some notable exceptions. In Turkey, where earthquakes are recognized as a major threat, the government, universities, volags, and some corporations have combined resources to address the problem. Emphasis has been placed not only on response, but also on preparedness and mitigation activities. To date, most of the approaches taken are along traditional lines, but the degree of sophistication and experience developed in Turkey makes it a leader in earthquake research and application in the Third World.

Mexico has also made great strides in this field. Early work was conducted in the universities, and recently the government has created a special office at the presidential level to coordinate research and response activities. Mexico's efforts have focused not only on earthquakes, but also on floods and hurricanes, and interest spans all phases of a disaster.

Peru has tried to develop a coordinated approach to addressing the problem of earthquakes. Most research has concentrated on the improvement of traditional buildings, but efforts have also been made to improve disaster preparedness and response capabilities throughout the earthquake zone. In recent years, however, runaway inflation has caused severe cutbacks in these activities, and preparedness measures have suffered as a consequence of austerity moves.

In the Caribbean, Jamaica is a promising newcomer to disaster preparedness. Activities were initiated by a consortium of volags under the leadership of Christian Action for Development in the Caribbean (CADEC), which encouraged the government to increase its preparedness measures. Following heavy flooding there in 1979, and a close brush with Hurricanes David and Frederick, the government established an interim emergency preparedness plan and shortly thereafter, set up a formal emergency coordination office. The staff there has begun to develop many innovative approaches for disaster preparedness and mitigation, such as a simplified storm surge warning and evacuation plan, and it is integrating comprehensive housing vulnerability reduction activities into the national housing program.

Other countries whose preparedness or disaster response activities bear mention are Sri Lanka (cyclones), India (housing research), the Philippines (typhoons, floods, earthquakes, and tsunamis), and Guatemala (preservation of historic structures in earthquakes).

THE ROLE OF VOLAGS

Throughout the relief system, in both the donor countries and the Third World, the voluntary agencies have played a key role in disasters. In the last decade, the volags have developed most of the practical approaches and technologies for disaster response. In the near future, their disaster role will expand. Because of their flexibility and diverse capabilities, volags will continue to be the working laboratories for different approaches and techniques for dealing with disasters. Because volags have exceptional capabilities at the village level (as well as flexibility), governmental and intergovernmental agencies have relied on the volags to implement their programs, and it can be expected that this trend will continue.

The increasing emphasis on use of volags by their governments has meant that expanded sources of funds are available, and many agencies not previously involved in disasters have expanded their services to include relief and rehabilitation work. But the increased availability of governmental support has also created a dilemma for some agencies: how to increase services while maintaining independence as a nongovernmental agency. As the 1970s drew to a close, many agencies were seeking new formulas for receiving government support and developing new relationships.

The growing awareness by volags of the connection between disaster response and development is the single most important trend in disaster programs today. More agencies are taking a hard look at their performance and the relationship between their post-disaster programs and longer-term development activities.

With this increased awareness of the disaster-development link, agencies have begun to expand their disaster preparedness capabilities. Many agencies originally viewed preparedness in terms of limited steps (such as stockpiling) that would speed material aid. A more sophisticated approach is now being taken. Overall, the opportunities for improving the whole range of response in all phases of a disaster and at all levels of the relief system are beginning to be exploited. As preparedness pays off in better-executed and more effective programs, agencies will place increased emphasis on this activity.

While the number of agencies becoming involved in disasters has grown, so has the scope of the problem. The increasing number of major disasters and the growing number of people who are adversely affected by disasters each year have severely taxed the capabilities of all relief agencies. To meet expanded needs, many agencies are pooling their resources and working together. This cooperation has taken many forms. Sometimes it is simply designation of a "lead-agency" with experience in an affected region to serve as a conduit for funds and materials. In other cases, a more expanded multiagency effort has been undertaken. The pooling of money, expertise, and staff, and concentration of these resources at field level, has proven beneficial in most cases, and the continued establishment of consortia and task forces as an approach to disaster relief is a growing trend that can be expected to continue.

CHALLENGES

In the future, not only will the scope of the disaster problem increase, but so will the diversity of the challenge. As both our technological capabilities and our understanding of the social and economic aspects expand, we will be called upon to participate in a wider range of activities than ever before. The technological aspects will bring, perhaps, the most visible changes. Earthquake prediction, for example, is only a matter of years away, and agencies can expect to be called on to provide support in a variety of new roles resulting from this capability. Many activities, such as aid and comfort to evacuees, will be an extension of present roles. Others will require new approaches and skills. For example, if an earthquake is predicted not days, but months ahead, tasks that might be required could include assistance in temporary relocation, rapid modification of houses, warning dissemination, family preparedness counseling, and provision of temporary work for evacuees, just to name a few. Thus a major challenge for agencies is not only to keep abreast of the technical developments, but to begin now to explore new opportunities for service and modes of involvement.

As disaster technologies and capabilities are improved, volags will be faced with a parallel challenge—how to keep technology at an appropriate level. There is already a tendency, especially for governments, to seek high-tech solutions to many disaster-related problems. Simply because a technological capacity exists does not mean that it is appropriate, and volags, by virtue of their work at the community level, will be asked to determine the technological parameters of disaster relief.

Our growing understanding of the social and economic aspects of disasters will present other new challenges to volags. The current trend toward increased preparedness activities will naturally lead to more interest in opportunities for disaster mitigation. Many agencies, especially those involved in both relief and development, will complete the circle, realizing that the connections between disasters and development also run in the other direction (that is, development to disasters). The challenge will be to formulate development programs that include disaster mitigation as an integral part. As more and more poor communities are built in vulnerable environments, development agencies will be called upon to initiate programs to reduce this vulnerability or to stimulate alternatives. Thus the most important challenge will be to develop a broader understanding of the development-disaster-development continuum and the opportunities for mitigation. If this is done, we will surely begin to take the "natural" out of disasters.

Abbreviations

AID: Agency for International Development
AT: Appropriate technology
ATI: Appropriate Technology International
CADEC: Christian Action for Development in the Caribbean
CARE: Cooperative of Americans for Relief Everywhere
CRS: Catholic Relief Services
CWS: Church World Service
DAST: Disaster Assessment Teams
DEC: Disaster Emergency Committee
EEC: European Economic Community
FAO: Food and Agriculture Organization
ICRC: International Committee of the Red Cross
ICVA: International Council of Voluntary Agencies
IDI: International Disaster Institute

IRP: Integrated Recovery Program
IRDP: Integrated Rural Development Program
ITDG: Intermediate Technology Development Group
LDCs: Less developed countries
LICROSS: League of Red Cross Societies
NGO: Nongovernmental organization
OAS: Organization of American States
OFDA: Office of U.S. Foreign Disaster Assistance
OXFAM: Formerly Oxford Committee for Famine Relief
UNDP: United Nations Development Programme
UNDRO: United Nations Disaster Relief Office
UNHCR: United Nations High Commissioner for Refugees
UNICEF: United Nations Children's Fund
WCC: World Council of Churches

Glossary

Access survey: The identification of disaster-caused bottlenecks that will prevent or hamper search and rescue operations or delay other response activities. The survey would include the identification of landslides closing roads and the inspection of bridges to ensure that they can be crossed following an earthquake or a flood. See **Disaster assessment**.

Accountability: The structuring of programs to increase control and participation by persons in the affected community.

Aftershock: Continued shaking after a sizable earthquake, which may be as powerful as ordinary shocks. A large aftershock may originate closer to a center of population and cause more damage than the main earthquake.

AID: Agency for International Development, an agency of the U.S. State Department.

Aid (and assistance): Can be one or all of the following:

a. A provision made by individuals, agencies, or governments with the objective of alleviating suffering and injustice in the developing world;

b. A mechanism for maintaining trade balances;

c. A tool of foreign policy by donor countries in their dealings with developing countries;

d. A method of maintaining the status quo of poor countries, thus ensuring preferential trading positions for donor countries.

"Circle of Fire": The circum-Pacific belt of active volcano activity. Small-scale maps showing active volcanoes and epicenters of large earthquakes illustrate a similar distribution.

Coping mechanisms: Those means by which societies, unassisted from the outside, meet relief and recovery needs, and adjust to future disaster risk.

Critical facilities: Those structures critical to the operation of a community and the key installations of the economic sector. Examples are hospitals, fuel storage depots, government administrative buildings, central data processing centers, central banks, and police stations.

Damage assessment: The determination of the extent of physical damage to buildings and manmade structures. Two types of damage assessment are normally carried out. The first is to determine the gross damage to a

261

community so that reconstruction planning can determine the aid level required. The second is a detailed structural analysis of typical buildings to determine the causes of failure and methods for modifying the structures so that during reconstruction, suitable steps can be taken to make the building safer. See **Disaster assessment**.

DAST: An acronym for Disaster Assessment Teams. DAST units are provided by the United States Army to assist in the initial disaster assessment.

DEC: An acronym for Disasters Emergency Committee. DEC is the main coordinating body for the largest British charities. Members include the British Red Cross, CAFOD (Catholic Fund for Overseas Development), Christian Aid, OXFAM, Save the Children Fund, and War on Want.

Development: The modernization of a society.

Disaster assessment: Surveys carried out to determine the effects of a disaster on a community and a society. Disaster assessment has three subactivities: **needs assessment**, **damage assessment**, and **access survey**.

Disaster "Continuum": A conceptual framework for depicting disasters and showing how one phase leads into the next.

Disaster-resistant construction: Used to denote the degree to which a structure can be made more resistant (or safe) to certain natural phenomena. The term recognizes that no building can be made totally safe, but that certain steps can be taken to improve performance or survivability.

Disaster response: Refers to those activities that occur in the aftermath of a disaster to assist disaster victims and to rehabilitate or reconstruct the physical structures of the society.

Disaster Spectrum: A means of visualizing disasters, showing how pre-disaster and post-disaster activities relate to each other.

Donor: Individuals and organizations that collect or give aid for disasters or development. Donors are distinguished from intervenors in that the former do not participate in the actual field operations.

Earthquake focus: The point of first release of the energy that causes an earthquake.

Epicenter: The point on the earth's surface that lies directly above the focus of an earthquake.

Fault: A fracture along which the opposite sides have been displaced relative to each other.

Fault zones: A zone thousands of meters wide, consisting of numerous interlacing small faults. Earthquakes tend to occur near fault zones.

Hazard: A threatening event in nature such as an earthquake. Hazards are of two types, primary and secondary. A primary hazard disrupts human settlements. A secondary hazard occurs in the aftermath of a primary hazard and contributes to further suffering or loss.

Hazard mapping: The process of establishing geographically where certain phenomena are likely to pose a threat to human settlements. Hazard maps identify areas that are subject to natural phenomena, such as earthquakes, hurricanes, and tornadoes, and areas that could be threatened by manmade disasters, for example, areas surrounding nuclear power plants, chemical disposal sites, or areas (such as refineries) subject to threat from explosion or fire.

Housing education programs: A program offering vocational training to home-owners or builders in how to build a house that is safer or more disaster-resistant.

Housing modification: The process of altering the design of a structure before it is built to make it more disaster-resistant.

Intensity: A subjective measure of the force of an earthquake at a particular place as determined by its effects on persons, structures, and earth materials. Intensity is a measure of effects as contrasted with magnitude, which is a measure of energy. The principal scale used in the U.S. today is the Modified Mercalli, 1956 version.

Intergovernmental agency: Organizations that are made up of two or more governments, for example, the United Nations or Organization of American States, and their divisions (for the UN, for example, UNDRO and UNICEF).

Intervenor: Any organization from outside the disaster-stricken community that provides disaster relief or reconstruction assistance.

Isoseismals: Map contours drawn to define limits of estimated intensity of shaking for a given earthquake.

Landslides: Mass movement or sliding of hillsides caused by the ground shaking of earthquakes.

Lifelines: Those facilities that are crucial to life support and that should receive high priority for protection or restoration following disasters. Lifelines include water systems, electrical systems, gas systems, and transportation networks.

Liquefaction: Transformation of a granular material (soil) from a solid state into a liquefied state as a consequence of increased pore-water pressure induced by earthquakes.

Magnitude: A measure of earthquake size that describes the amount of energy released.

Mercalli Scale: A rating scale for classifying the degree of ground shaking at a specific location. The scale is graded by roman numerals from I to XII.

Microzonation: Risk mapping at a very small scale. Within any particular area, there are numerous geological variations that make certain areas safer or more hazardous than others. Microzonation delineates each of these areas so that communities can select the safest possible sites for development or the location of critical facilities.

Mitigation: The taking of actions that reduce the harmful effects of a disaster. Mitigation accepts the occurrence of extreme natural phenomena, but attempts to limit both human and property loss.

Monitoring: Surveys of on-going activities to determine their progress and effectiveness.

Needs assessment: The determination of the needs of the victims. These are usually divided into immediate and long-term needs.

NGOs: Nongovernmental organizations in the private sector, both nonprofit and profit-making, that provide services in development and disasters.

Pre-disaster normal: The conditions, life-style, and standard of living that exist prior to disaster impact. An understanding of the pre-disaster normal is essential in the formulation of emergency programs.

Pre-disaster planning: The process of planning actions that will prevent, mitigate, or prepare for a disaster. Pre-disaster planning includes the tasks of disaster prevention, disaster mitigation, and disaster preparedness.

Preparedness: The attempt to limit the impact of a disaster by structuring the response and affecting a quick and orderly reaction to the disaster. Preparedness is unique among all pre-disaster planning activities in that it addresses actions in both the pre-disaster phase, for example, warning and evacuation, as well as the post-disaster phases.

Prevention: Activities to prevent a natural phenomenon or a potential hazard from having harmful effects on either persons or property. Disaster prevention includes such activities as cloud seeding to control meteorological patterns, the construction of dams or dikes to prevent flooding, and attempts to reduce tectonic tension by such measures as pumping water into earthquake faults.

PVOs: Private voluntary organizations, nonprofit organizations in the private sector that receive a portion of their funds through voluntary contributions from the public in order to provide services in development and disasters.

Quick and dirty programs: Programs designed to provide a quick response with massive material aid. The objective of this approach is to saturate an area with relief items in order to create a high impact with as little "entanglement" as possible. The prime criterion of this type of program is speed of delivery. Quick and dirty programs usually have very little long-term effect on recovery.

Remote sensing: The acquisition of information or measurement of some property of an object by a recording device that is not in physical or intimate contact with the objects under study.

Return period: The time period (years) in which there is a good statistical probability that an earthquake of a certain magnitude or a hurricane will recur.

Richter Magnitude Scale: A measure of earthquake size that describes the amount of energy released. The measure is determined by taking the common logarithm (base 10) of the largest ground motion observed during the arrival of a P-wave or seismic surface wave and applying a standard correction for distance to the epicenter.

Risk: The relative degree of probability that a hazardous event will occur. An active fault zone, for example, would be an area of high risk.

Risk mapping: The process of identifying high-risk areas. This is done by correlating a hazard, such as an earthquake, to the terrain and to the probability that such an event will occur. The results of these analyses are usually presented in the form of *risk maps*, which show the type and degree of hazard represented by a particular natural phenomenon at a given geographic location. Risk mapping is usually the first step in vulnerability reduction.

Search and rescue (SAR): The first activities normally conducted following a disaster, the intent being to locate disaster victims and to ensure their physical safety. SAR activities can include locating victims trapped in collapsed structures, removing victims from perilous locations surrounded or threatened by flood waters, or evacuating families or even whole communities from areas subjected to secondary effects of disasters.

Seismic: Pertaining to earthquake activities.

Seismicity: The worldwide or local distribution of earthquakes in space and time; a general term for the number of earthquakes in a unit of time, or for relative earthquake activity.

Surveillance: An epidemiological survey or the health monitoring of the affected community.

Tectonics: The study of earth's broad structural features.

Tsunami: A seawave produced by large-area displacements of the ocean bottom, the result of earthquake or volcanic activity.

Volag: See **PVOs**.

Vulnerability: A condition wherein human settlements or buildings are threatened by virtue of their proximity to a hazard, the quality of their construction, or both.

METRIC SYSTEM

1 mile = 1.609 kilometers

1 kilometer = 0.6214 mile

1 foot = 0.3048 meter

1 meter = 39.37 inches = 3.281 feet

Bibliography

Agnew and Patterson, "Performance Specification for Emergency Shelter," Report 188.1, Dept. of Design Research, Royal College of Art, London, 1976.

Allen, Mark E., Zakaria Sibahi, and Earl D. Sohm, *Evaluation of the Office of the United Nations Disaster Relief Co-ordinator*, Joint Inspection Unit, United Nations, Geneva, Oct. 1980.

Appropriate Reconstruction Training & Information Centre (ARTIC), *Seminar Report: Problems & Lessons from the Andhra Pradesh Cyclone*, Vijayawada, A.P., India, 1978 (available from INTERTECT, Dallas, Texas).

Bates, Frederick L. (ed.), *Recovery, Change and Development: A Longitudinal Study of the 1976 Guatemalan Earthquake*, Guatemalan Earthquake Study, University of Georgia, 1982.

Bates, F.L., et al., *The Social and Psychological Consequences of a Natural Disaster*, National Research Council Disaster Study #18, National Academy of Sciences, Washington, D.C., 1963.

Bates, Frederick L., W. Timothy Farrell, and JoAnn K. Glittenberg, *Changes in Housing Characteristics in Seventeen Guatemalan Communities Following the Earthquake of 1976* (Substantive Report #2, Guatemalan Earthquake Study), prepared for the National Science Foundation, Washington, D. C., Feb. 1979.

Brown, Barbara, *Disaster Preparedness: The Role of the United Nations in Advance Planning for Disaster Relief*, United Nations Institute for Training & Research (UNITAR), New York, 1979.

Bruzelius, Magnus, "Disaster Relief within the Scope of the Swedish Stand-By Force in the Service of the United Nations," *Disasters*, Vol. 2, No. 1, 1978, pp. 32–36.

Center for Building Technology, *Building to Resist the Effect of Wind* (NBS Building Science Series 100), National Bureau of Standards, U.S. Dept. of Commerce, Washington, D.C., 1977.

Committee on International Disaster Assistance, *The U.S. Government Foreign Disaster Assistance Program*, National Academy of Sciences, Washington, D.C., 1978.

Cuny, Frederick C., Ian Davis, and Frederick Krimgold, Unpublished study on the provision of emergency shelter and housing following natural disasters, undertaken for the U.N. Disaster Relief Office (UNDRO), 1977.

Cuny, Frederick C., and Eduardo A. Perez, *Improvement of Low-Cost Housing in Fiji to Withstand Hurricanes and High Winds*, Office of U.S. Foreign Disaster Assistance, Agency for International Development, Washington, D.C., 1982.

Davis, Ian, *Emergency Shelter and Natural Disasters*, INTERTECT, Dallas, Texas, 1975.

DeNevi, Donald P., *Earthquakes*, Celestial Arts, Millbrae, Calif., 1977.

Dynes, Russell, R., *Organized Behavior in Disasters*, D.C. Heath & Co., Lexington, Mass., 1970.

"Foreign Aid—The Facts," *New Internationalist*, No. 82, Dec. 1979, pp. 8–9.

Form, William H., and Sigmund Nosow, *Community in Disaster*, Harper & Brothers, New York, 1958.

Fritz, Charles E., "Disaster," in *Contemporary Social Problems,* Robert K. Merton and Robert A. Nisbet (eds.), Harcourt, Brace & World, 1961, pp. 651–694.

Fritz, Charles E., *Report on 1970 AID National Disaster Preparedness Planning Seminar*, Institute for Defense Analyses, Arlington, Va., 1971.

Froman, Jo, Robert Gersony, and Tony Jackson, "A Contrastive Analysis of Alternative Reconstruction Models After the February 1976 Guatemalan Earthquake," *Guatemala: AID Disaster Relief Program Reports on Post-Earthquake Distribution of Building Materials*, Agency for International Development, Washington, D.C., 1977.

Goulet, Denis, *The Uncertain Promise*, IDOC/North America, Inc., New York, 1977.

Green, Stephen, *International Disaster Relief: Toward A Responsive System*, Council on Foreign Relations, Inc., McGraw-Hill, New York, 1977.

Hindley, Keith, "Beware the Big Wave," *New Scientist*, 9 Feb. 1978, pp. 346–47.

Inter-American Foundation, *They Know How . . . An Experiment in Development Assistance*, U.S. Government Printing Office, Washington, D.C., 1977.

INTERTECT, *Administration & Resource Management (Vol. I): Relief Operations Guidebook*, Dallas, Texas, 1974.

Kieffer, Margaret, *Disasters and Coping Mechanisms in Cakchiquel Guatemala: The Cultural Context*, INTERTECT, Dallas, Texas, 1977.

Krimgold, Frederick, *The Role of International Aid for Pre-Disaster Planning in Developing Countries*, Avdelningen för Arkitektur, KTH Stockholm, 1974.

Linden, Eugene, *The Alms Race: The Impact of American Voluntary Aid Abroad*, Random House, New York, 1976.

McKay, Mary, "The OXFAM/World Neighbors Housing Education Programme in Guatemala," *Disasters*, Vol. 2, No. 2/3, 1978, pp. 152–57.

Office of Emergency Preparedness, *Disaster Preparedness*, U.S. Government Printing Office, Washington, D.C., 1972.

Office of the United Nations Disaster Relief Coordinator, *Shelter After Disaster: Guidelines for Assistance*, United Nations, New York, 1982.

Proceedings of the International Workshop on Earthen Buildings in Seismic Areas, University of New Mexico and INTERTECT, Dallas, Texas, 1981.

Quarantelli, E.L., and Russell R. Dynes, "When Disaster Strikes (It Isn't Much Like What You've Heard and Read About)," *Psychology Today* 5, Feb. 1972, pp. 66–70.

Ressler, Everett M., *Accountability as a Program Philosophy*, INTERTECT, Dallas, Texas, 1978.

Ressler, Everett M., *Post-Disaster Technical Information Flow for the Reconstruction of Housing*, INTERTECT, Dallas, Texas, 1977.

Robinove, Charles J., "Worldwide Disaster Warning and Assessment with Earth Resources Technology Satellites," *Procedures of the Tenth International Symposium on Remote Sensing of Environment*, Center for Remote Sensing Information & Analysis, Environmental Research Institute of Michigan, Ann Arbor, 1975, pp. 811–20.

Rosene, Chris M., *San Andres Itzapa, Guatemala: The Impact of a High-Aid Housing Program*, INTERTECT, Dallas, Texas, 1976.

Rosene, Chris M., *San Antonio Cornejo, Guatemala: A Study of Limited Housing Assistance to a Community*, INTERTECT, Dallas, Texas, 1977.

Save the Children Alliance, *Second Report for Joyabaj Reconstruction Program*, Guatemala, Sept. 15, 1976.

Sommer, John G., *Beyond Charity: U.S. Voluntary Aid for a Changing Third World*, Overseas Development Council, Washington, D.C., 1977.

Taylor, Alan J., *Assessment of Victim Needs*, INTERTECT, Dallas, Texas, 1978.

Taylor, Alan J., *Coordination for Disasters*, INTERTECT, Dallas, Texas, 1978.

Taylor, Alan J., *Relief, Development and the Foreign Voluntary Aid Organization*, INTERTECT, Dallas, Texas, 1978.

Taylor, Alan J., *The INTERTECT Disaster Management Training Package (Number 1)*, INTERTECT, Dallas, Texas, 1977.

Taylor, Alan J., "The USAID/Guatemala Lamina and Housing Materials Distribution Program: Ex-Post Evaluation Report," *Guatemala: AID Disaster Relief Program Reports on Post-Earthquake Distribution of Building Materials*, Agency for International Development, Washington, D.C., 1977.

Thompson, Charlotte, and Paul Thompson, *Post-Disaster Reconstruction of Housing in Latin America*, INTERTECT, Dallas, Texas, 1977.

Thompson, Charlotte, and Paul Thompson, *Reconstruction of Housing in Guatemala*, INTERTECT, Dallas, Texas, 1976.

Western, Karl A., *The Epidemiology of Natural and Man-made Disasters: The Present State of the Art*, Dissertation for the London School of Hygiene & Tropical Medicine, University of London, 1972.

Index

Page numbers in *italics* indicate illustrations.
Page numbers followed by *t* indicate tables.

Forte of agency for establishing
    post-disaster programs, 151
Foundations in relief system, motivation of,
    111
Funding process, disaster response and,
    144–45
Funds
    development, competition for, 100
    earmarked, for establishing post-disaster
        programs, 151

Gifts, donor constraints on, 126–27
Goal setting in program planning, 238
Goals, reappraisal of in disasters, 12
Government(s)
    influence on disaster response, 141–43
    local, motivation of, in relief system, 114
    outside U.S. in relief system, 116–17
    in relief system, motivation of, 111–13
    role of, in disasters, 12
    smaller, aid programs of, in relief system,
        117
    U.S., in relief system, 115–16
Grief, coping with, relief programs and, 86
Guatemala
    earthquake in, reconstruction program
        after, 164–93. *See also* Programa
        Kuchuba'l
    housing in, before earthquake, 168–69

Hazards, disaster, 21–39. *See also* Disaster
        hazards
Headquarters level, problems with decision
        making in relief system, 125–27
Helplessness of victims, myth of, 85–86
Human rights issue, intervention as, 250–51
Humanitarian concerns as motivation
    of donors, 110, 111
    of organizations receiving contributions,
        111
    of volags, 113
Hunger as American volag concern, 253–54
Hurricane(s)
    Borracho (fictitious)
        emergency phase of, 66–75
        pre-disaster period of, 63–66
        reconstruction phase of, 75–79
    causes and characteristics of, 29–36

Implementing instrument in disaster
        preparedness, 221–22
Inflation, recovery time and, 200
Information sources, influence of, on
        disaster response, 139–40
Initiative, expectation of aid as disincentive
        to, 100
Institutions, religious, in community
        reaction to disaster, 81

Insurance
    in economic disaster mitigation, 217
    in preparedness, 234–35
Integrated Recovery Program (IRP), 161–62
Intergovernmental agencies in relief system,
        118–20
    motivation of, 113–14
International Disaster Institute (IDI) in
        relief system, 124
International political context of disaster
        response, 15–20
International relief system, 107–37. *See also*
        Relief system
Intervention, 87–193
    effects of, on coping mechanisms, 89–93
    general aspects of, lessons about, from
        past, 103–4
    as human rights issue, 250–51
    needs assessment for, 236–37
    outside, myth of need for, 86
    positive aspects of, 105–6
    set back problem from, 99–100
    use of term, 7–8

Land
    impact of disasters on, 13, 50–51*t*, 52–54
    ownership of, disaster relief and, 53–54
    values of, disasters and, 52
Land tenure, problems of recovery time
        and, 200–201
Landslides from earthquakes, 26
Leadership
    community
        effects of disasters on, 13, 55
        intervention and, 90
    recovery time and, 198
League of Red Cross Societies in disaster
        preparedness, 230
Lifelines, critical damage to in disasters, 56
Limited authority approach to decision
        making in relief organizations, 126
Liquefaction from earthquakes, 23
Local organizations, problems with
        overloading in relief system,
        129–30

Market, recovery time and instability of,
        200
Materials
    delayed, recovery time and, 199–200
    salvaged, recovery time and, 199
Medical effects of disasters, 44, 46–49
Memory, collective, lack of as obstacle to
        change, 132–33
Microzonation in risk mapping, 209
Military, use of in disaster preparedness,
        227–29
Missionaries in relief system, motivation of,
        114, 115